NEITHER USE NOR ORNAMENT

Bill Naughton (standing, far right) with friends, Bolton, 1928.

NEITHER USE
NOR ORNAMENT

A Memoir of Bolton: 1920s

Bill Naughton

*For dear Alfra Silfe:
in memory of Bill Naughton
with love from
Erna Naughton
24. 6. 95*

BLOODAXE BOOKS

ISBN: 1 85224 303 1 hardback edition
       1 85224 304 X paperback edition

First published 1995 by
Bloodaxe Books Ltd,
P.O. Box 1SN,
Newcastle upon Tyne NE99 1SN.

Bloodaxe Books Ltd acknowledges
the financial assistance of Northern Arts.

Cover printing by J. Thomson Colour Printers Ltd, Glasgow.

Printed in Great Britain by
Bell & Bain Limited, Glasgow, Scotland.

In memory of my mother Maria
1875-1949
and my father Thomas Naughton
1873-1957
Ballyhaunis, Co. Mayo, Ireland

CONTENTS

CHAPTER 1

Birthday Morning

I remember most clearly my fourteenth birthday, Thursday the twelfth of June 1924. The night before I had gone to sleep with the thought fixed in mind: When I wake up I'll be fourteen! I was woken in the morning by a sudden movement, realised that it was brother Edward lifting up the mattress to take out his trousers after their nightly pressing, and to make things easier for him I got out of bed, decided it was not worth getting back in, and knelt in my shirt against the old rocking-chair to say my morning prayers. Then I stood up, pulled on my black, ribbed stockings, took my breeches off the brass knob on the bedpost and put them on, slipping my braces loosely over my shoulders, but for the time being left the buttons open at the knee – knickerbocker style breeches had given way to short trousers, but I had always worn them and felt too old to start showing my bare knees. I took my boots from under the bed, slipped them on, tied the laces loosely, then went down the bare wooden stairs. I spoke a quick word to our May, who was hurrying in the back door to go off to Kershaw's factory where she was a weaver, then I went out the open back door to our privy closet in the backyard.

The weather was warm and the air still, and as I closed the door, and sat down on the wide wooden seat, I began wondering what job I might be doing in a month's time, when I would have finished my last fortnight of school, and June holidays would be over. Next I went into the backyard and began my Swedish drill, followed by a bout of pressing up two duck-stones. I was at the age when a lad takes life and himself seriously – or at least I did. I caught sight of Alice Wood next door hurrying out of their closet, but went on exercising. Although your every move would be watched in the street, there was an understanding that backyards were private – you were not supposed to see or hear anything that went on in the next-door backyard, for to do that would be regarded as 'tooting'. There was a chorus of the quarter-to-eight mill buzzers wailing away; the last buzzer always went on much longer than the earlier ones, then cut off with a sharp warning note: *Get a move on or we'll shut the mill gates on you!*

I went into the back kitchen and saw Edward stooped over the slopstone gazing at himself in the looking-glass that was hung from a nail. He always ate breakfast first, gulped it down so that he could give the final touches to his toilet before going out. In the front kitchen Mother was at the side of the window, peeking through the lace curtain toward the corner round which my father always came after his night shift at the pit, and she turned to me, 'Are you up, agraw?' she said. 'Yes, Mam,' I said. 'Poor Dad isn't home from pit yet,' she said, 'I wonder what could be keeping him.' She was always anxious any time he was late, and I had sensed the different atmosphere in the home, relaxed in his absence. She's forgotten my birthday, I thought, but I'm not going to tell her.

Mother went to the door and opened it a little more, in case she might miss the sound of his heavy clogs across the cobbled street, then turned and came smiling to me, 'The Lord save us, isn't it a great thing altogether – your birthday an' you're fourteen years of age!' and she gave me a kiss. 'Yes, Mam,' I said, 'an' no job to go to when I leave school.' 'Wouldn't it be a grand thing,' she said 'if someone was to give you a job in an office or the like. Musha I'd hate to see you go into some dirty job in a factory.' 'I reckon I'll be lucky to get one,' I said. 'Ah sure isn't it all in God's hands,' she said. 'I've a nice barmcake put at one side for you,' she went on, 'an' a taste of bacon. Oh, an' wouldn't you take off that ould shirt that's so soiled on you, an' after your wash put on the one I have all ironed an' fresh.'

'Is it worth it, Mam,' I said, '– on a Thursday? I mean what'll I do for a clean 'un for the weekend?' 'Oh sure I'll have that one washed an' ironed for you – somehow or other.' I had just the two shirts, the same as most boys, a fresh one that I put on every Sunday morning for Mass, then wore the week at school, but sensing she meant it as a little birthday treat, I said, 'All right, Mam, nowt I'd like better.' Edward came in from the kitchen, ready for going to work, and taking a final look at himself in the big mirror which formed the overmantel of the dresser: 'It's Bill's birthday today,' said Mother. He turned to me, 'Congrats, Bill,' he said, '– many happy...!' 'Ta,' I said. I admired the slick way he had of saying things, and when he said something I felt that he really meant, it was so unexpected that I was touched by it. 'I must go an' call young Jim,' said Mother. 'God bless and go careful,' she said to Edward, and she went into the kitchen. He took another look at himself in the mirror, then opened the door 'So long, Bill,' he said, and with that he put on his smiling street manner which he liked to display to the world. You would hardly know it was the same Edward.

Jim came downstairs, 'It's your birthday, isn't it, Bill?' he said. 'Good luck an' all the best!' I turned from washing, 'Ta, Jim,' I said. Jim was a good-natured boy, but as he was only ten it seemed that his interests were not mine – no more than mine were Edward's. I had something secret on my mind, and I quickly dried myself so that I could have a check on my savings, hidden away in the drawer that Mother had promised would be for me alone; we each had one, and there was an understanding that you never pried into the drawer of another. My drawer, in the wide, old chest of drawers in the back kitchen, the big awkward bottom drawer, close to the mangle and not easy to get at, just suited me. I had a way of opening it quietly, and after doing so I delved down into the far corner on the right, where there was a pile of old magazines, under which was a stiff-backed text book on mathematics, which I had saved from being burnt when two students who lived opposite were flitting and burning old books in the backstreet. I lifted the end cover, and without taking the book out, just made sure the coins were secreted between certain pages. I saw the half-crowns and other coins, pressed tight against the binding, and felt my heart warm at the sight of all that money, around thirty shillings, all mine. Then I quietly closed the drawer and went into the front kitchen to enjoy my breakfast with the home still free of my father.

I was seated at the table, feeling full of myself in the clean shirt, and enjoying the dipped barmcake when Mother made a sudden move to the door. Her quick ear had caught the sound of my father's clogs coming across the cobbled street, and she had the door open for him. His face was begrimed with coal dust as he stood on the mat, all black except for his eyes. He looked weary as he handed his cap and his big tea-can to my mother. 'You're home safe, thanks be to God,' she said softly. He stayed on the mat, silent, and then stooped slowly to unfasten his pit clogs before stepping on to the linoleum. Jim and I greeted him, 'Hello, Dad', but so quietly that he didn't need to answer. Mother helped him off with the clogs, and something prompted me to step forward, 'I'll take them, Mother,' I said. She seemed glad of that, as I reached out and took the clogs. She had her usual quiet manner to suit my father's mood, sympathetic and ready, but not fussy, avoiding any word that might set him off cursing the coal-mine and all to do with it. 'I have the pans of hot water ready,' she said, 'an' I'll have tea wet for you –' 'I'll not wash yet, woman,' he said quietly, 'but maybe rest a minute or two in the chair.' 'Sure won't you feel better for it,' she said, giving a turn to his rocking-chair, 'an' I'll wet the tea at once – the kettle is boiling.'

As I walked into the back kitchen and out into the backyard with my father's pit clogs, I found it hard to imagine how he could have worn two such heavy and clumsy clogs all night long. And when I emptied out the particles of coal I wondered how any man could walk with all that grit under the soles of his feet, especially so my father, since he was normally so careful about all he wore. What he would have enjoyed more than anything at the moment, I knew, would have been a bottle of Magee's Crown Ale, but Mother had had no shilling on a Wednesday evening, yet I was now aware of having my own money hidden away. What a humbug and hypocrite I was not to have given Mother some money last evening – say a half-crown, which I would hardly have missed. Oh but yes I should! – for I had become very fond of money. It seemed that once the intense sexual feelings of early puberty had subsided, in their place had come a keen interest in money – how to get hold of it, and keep it, and increase it, and not part with it. I should have put it in the post office and forgotten it, I thought, but somehow I liked to look at it and feel it now and again. It seemed that if you escaped one longing that plagued you, another would take its place.

It was odd to see my father sitting in his rocking-chair in his pit dirt when I went back in the front kitchen. He was a man of scrupulous habits, usually insisting on washing as soon as he came in, changing into a flannel shirt and clean trousers, so that he could sit quietly reading the *Daily Herald*, waiting until we had gone to school before eating his breakfast of porridge, that had been cooking overnight in the big iron saucepan. Mother was quick with the tea, and handed my father his mug, from which he took two or three drinks before speaking: 'My hand is shakin', I can hardly hold the flamin' mug,' he said, 'after all the work we had to do – it would kill a horse, let alone a man. There was a big fall of dirt in the Plodder mine,' he went on, 'just as we had our night's work done – an' didn't the three of us have to clear it for the day shift – tons and tons of it.' He caught my eye and I stood still to give him the full attention he liked to get. 'That was what we contracted to do – an' that was what we had to do, after the rest of the night shift went off home.' He drank more tea, 'May the divil roast Lord Ellesmere,' he said, 'the bloody mine-owner – makin' his millions out of the sweat of the poor old miners.' I saw Mother bless herself quietly, to take the sting out of the curse.

CHAPTER 2

Jackie Seddon

The time was approaching noon, the sun high enough to slant through the tall windows of our first-floor classroom, as our teacher, Mr John Seddon, was pacing to and fro before the class of thirty-seven boys. The lesson was the occasional one referred to as 'hygiene', and as nothing had to be remembered the atmosphere was free of that tense feeling associated with learning; moreover, Jackie, as we boys called him among ourselves, never displayed signs of temper, used the cane sparingly, and with an almost apologetic air. He was a man of medium height, square of build, with a wide forehead, greying hair parted across from the left side, blue eyes, and a mole on his right cheek. Every face I saw made a lasting impression, set there in my memory for life, and to hear the voice that went with it, created for me the most interesting thing to be met in life – another human being. Jackie had what I took to be an English face, nothing underhand or shifty, with a calm expression, and what I particularly liked about it was the 'Great War' look. At the big corner where men and youths gathered in the evening, and boys like myself could stand on the outside listening, I could always spot the face of the man who had been in the War. It was as though life in the trenches had stripped away the civilian face, revealing some deeper nature of the man; by 1924 such faces were seen less often, and soon they would hardly be seen at all, except on the framed photographs on the mantelpiece or dresser of many homes – of a husband or son that never came back.

Jackie had returned from the War to take up teaching in the same school, and from the occasional remarks he made of having been among men from different walks of life I gathered that they had not been officers, and I imagined him as Corporal Seddon. He was married but childless, and could be seen coming to school with that same steady walk, never hurrying, never dawdling, wearing a neat suit of dark grey, stiff collar, plain tie, black boots with a broad plain top, and a faded trilby hat. It was the custom of the day for the respectable man to be habitual in dress and behaviour, and Jackie was of this turn of mind, as though any deviation was an affront to others. Even on our annual Walking Day procession he always wore a Sunday suit of the same grey, the same kind of boots and a better trilby hat.

The hygiene lesson, inculcating the need of taking regular baths, may have struck Jackie as being of little purpose, considering that only two or three boys before him had ever seen a bathroom, let alone enjoyed the luxury of getting into a bath, and now he surprised us by venturing into biology, with talk about Darwin and the Origin of the Species: 'Man is said by Darwin to have descended from the monkey,' said Jackie, adding quickly, '– which of course the Church denies. Nor has anyone yet discovered the "missing link". What is perfectly obvious, however, is that parents pass on characteristics to their children, such as, for instance, ginger hair, brown eyes or big feet, or other distinctive features,' and he grinned as he eyed certain boys. His manner became more serious as he stood still and faced us: 'Let us take the case of dogs – two dogs of the same breed, greyhounds for instance, a male and a female. Let us suppose one is very fast, the other not so fast but has staying power; the aim of the owner will be to breed a fast dog with stamina.' I couldn't quite follow what Jackie was getting at, for now he started pacing about again before going on: 'The same is true of breeding racehorses, Derby winners and the like.' He stopped once more and faced us, 'What happens,' he went on, 'is that the two dogs, or the two racehorses, a stallion and a mare, are brought together at the appropriate time – when in season…' he hesitated, 'what occurs is known as *mating* –'

As he uttered the final word Jackie's poise deserted him, and a flush suddenly suffused his face, the soldier-like bearing giving way to embarrassment. We were all silent as he turned from our gaze, and with his back to us picked up the duster, and began to wipe the blackboard. I looked at the back of his neck, red above his white collar, and I realised that Jackie was not the cool man I had imagined him to be. Certain words made a marked impression on me, and evoked a memory of when I first heard them – and *mating* was one.

CHAPTER 3

Street Scene: 1917

On a Monday dinnertime in 1917 I was on my way home from school, and had turned the corner of our street when I heard voices raised, saw neighbours at their doors, a few men and boys standing around watching something in the middle of the street, and realised there must be something unusual going on. Monday, the regular weekly washing day, was not an occasion to hurry home to, unlike Wednesday, baking day, so I was glad enough of any bit of excitement to delay me. Ernie Fairclough, an older boy but a good mate of mine, was standing near the corner, and I went to him, 'What's up Ernie?' I asked. 'It's only two dogs stuck,' said Ernie, '– that bitch, Lady, fro' Greenhalgh's next door to us, an' Jack Nightingale from the outdoor licence.' With that we moved closer to what was going on, and I saw the two dogs, Jack, a fat Airedale, belonging to old Mrs Nightingale, and so taking the surname, the other, Lady, a black-and-brown spaniel. The dogs, facing in opposite directions on the cobbled roadways, looked as though attached tail-to-tail. Lady had her head hung down in shame, and the usual jaunty Jack looked guilty, and this made me feel sorry for them. 'They musta been stuck for a good ten minutes,' said Ernie.

Mrs Challoner, a posh widow with gold-rimmed spectacles, came to her front door, broom in hand, and called out in her refined voice, 'I say, will someone clout them with this – the filthy things!' and she offered the broom to a man called Herbert Haddock. 'Nay, Missis,' said Herbert, refusing the offered broom, 'I'm not goin' to touch 'um! after all, they're only matin'.' 'Mating!' she shrilled, 'I'd give them *mating*! It's a disgrace it is – to look through the front window an' see that sort of thing going on in the street.'

Herbert muttered something about she'd sooner see that than be blind, and the next thing Mr Greenhalgh was seen standing on the doorstep at number 9, looking across at us on the lower level. I had seen him arrive on leave on Saturday evening, an impressive sight he had made, as he strode boldly along in the colourful uniform of a Highland regiment, kitbag on his left shoulder, the splendid Tartan kilt swinging in rhythm with his step. Although he was wearing the kilt he was not stepping it out, and in place of the tunic he had a crumpled jersey on, and as he was bareheaded and rather bald he was not quite the same striking figure, but was out-standing enough as he called out, 'Don't lay a hand on our Lady!'

For a moment I was shocked to hear, 'Our Lady!' but then I realised that it was the Lancashire 'our', and that he was referring to their dog and not the Blessed Virgin. Ernie beckoned at him and gave a sniff, 'Him an' his bloomin' kilt!' he said. 'He's not a proper fighting soldier – he's not been across the water to France, or to Mesopotamia like mi dad. Mi mam reckons he's never had his big nose out of the country – he's only one of these camp swaddies, trainin' the recruits.' Herbert Haddock called out, 'Don't you worry, Mister Greenhalgh – I won't touch either of 'em. I were just sayin' to Missis Challoner as they were only matin'.' 'She's only been out five minutes,' said Mr Greenhalgh as he came striding up, '– she's in season and got out without me seein' her – an' that dirty thing from the outdoor licence got at her –' and he glared at Jack Nightingale.

' "There was a Scotch Highlander," ' Ernie began to hum out of the corner of his mouth, ' "Who fought at Waterloo – The wind blew up his petticoat – an' showed his dolly blue." ' I couldn't resist humming also, as it was an Irish tune, 'The Wearing of the Green'. 'It's not our Lady to blame,' went on Mr Greenhalgh – there he goes again, I thought, these poor Protestants, blaspheming away and don't even know it – lucky for them, since it's not a sin if you don't know. Lady looked up at her master, her brown eyes pleading to be forgiven for the lapse. Ernie went on with the ditty, ' "His dolly blue was dirty – He showed it to the Queen –" ' I was just about to join in again, when I spotted Mr Greenhalgh looking at us, but Ernie continued, ' "The Queen was so delighted – That she licked it very clean". '

At that moment there was a loud shout as out of number 7 came Ernie's eldest brother, Tommy, a big lad who came clattering along in his pit clogs, carrying a bucket of cold water, 'Hy out, everybody!' he yelled, 'hy out the way! I'll douse 'em wi' this lot. That'll bloody part 'um.' 'Don't you dare wet our Lady!' called Mr Greenhalgh, and I made the sign of the cross over my heart, '– fling it all on that filthy thing.' Tommy swung the bucket, and aimed at Jack, who seemed to be towing Lady around, but Jack partly dodged it, so that the cold water came down on the rear parts of the two dogs, at which they both began to shiver. 'I'll fotch another bucket,' said Tommy, who clearly enjoyed flinging water about. 'I doubt tha'll ha' need,' said Herbert Haddock, as the two dogs somehow got free of each other, and Jack, who was shamefully exposing himself, quickly made off. 'The horrible thing!' exclaimed Mrs Challoner. Lady went crawling on her stomach to her master, and as he stooped to stroke her Lady's tail began to wag pleadingly. 'Hy, Mister Greenhalgh,' called Herbert, as the scene was breaking up, 'I wonder if owt comes of yon affair – d'you think you'd keep me in mind for a pup?' Mr Greenhalgh looked at him but seemed to feel it was below his dignity to answer, and with Lady at his heels he made his way back to number 9, his kilt now swirling lightly.

Ernie's mother, a big woman with the sleeves of her blouse rolled up showing her plump arms, now appeared at their front door and called out, 'Our Ernie! Come in!' 'Oh Mam!' protested Ernie. 'I said, "Come in!"' said his mother. 'You've no right to be standin' there watchin' that sort of carry-on!' Ernie knew better than refuse a second time, gave me a look and off he went. I went to our house at number 8, and found myself humming 'The Scotch Highlander'. I was eager to talk of the incident – I nearly always went in home with something special to tell my mother – but I had a feeling that this sort of thing was best kept to myself, and reminding myself not to let my tongue blab it out I went in home – which may have been one reason why it was to remain so vividly in my memory.

CHAPTER 4

The Facts of Life

The second time I hear the word *mating* is in our own home –
possibly it was that same Monday evening in 1917. The front
kitchen is heavy with the silence which always settles on it
when my father comes down from his daytime sleep to prepare
himself for going on the night-shift to pit. He is seated in his
big rocking-chair reading the *Bolton Evening News*, wearing
the heavy union shirt in which he has slept during the day,
shiny old trousers of blue serge, laceless old boots that serve
as slippers, and has a pair of wire-rimmed spectacles perched
on his nose, and looking like a man of sixty but in fact is only
forty.

'The Lord in heaven save us,' he sighs, picking up his pipe,
'but aren't they destroyin' one another out in France!' Next
he starts the business of filling his pipe, first knocking the top
of the bowl against the palm of his hand to clear it, cutting
up his thick twist tobacco, rubbing it, pressing it into the pipe,
between taking sips of tea from the fresh mug that my mother
has put there for him. I watch the performance out of the
corner of my eye, as he begins to tear strip after strip from an
old newspaper in attempts to light the pipe. If only he would
take one decent piece, I think, fold it carefully and light it, it
would stay in long enough to take hold on the tobacco. He
mutters a curse or two, and I hold my head down – but hurray,
he's managed to get it going, and he puffs away! Peace in the
home for five minutes!

Next he turns to the inside pages, and with a more eager
air he looks for news of Ireland and Eamon de Valera. My
father is not a man of mettle, except in his own home; he will
shrink from encounter with anyone in uniform – indeed we
are all habituated to observing the social form and rule of law
in our adopted country, and over the sixty years ahead not
one of us will have been found guilty of the least infringement
– and he remains awestruck at the boldness of the Easter
Rising in Dublin in 1916. That a rebel force should proclaim

an Irish Republic, against the might of British rulers, struck my father as an act of unbelievable bravery, making de Valera his great hero for the rest of his life – as Lloyd George was to become the biggest villain.

The bright gas mantle overhead makes a low throbbing drone, with the odd hiss in between, the alarm clock over the fireplace ticks urgently and loud, yet to me the fingers appear scarcely to be moving, so slowly does each minute pass when my father is present. The strain of sitting mute and unstirring – the behaviour which he expects from us – seems to be too much for Eddie and May, and Eddie has gone off to play in the home of a pal called Arthur, and May is next door in the Wood home, talking to Alice; even the baby, James, still in his cradle, though getting big for it at the age of two, senses he had better keep quiet, and there isn't a budge out of him.

I am at the table with a book, but aware that for some reason nothing irritates my father more than the sight of my reading. Yet so addicted am I to the printed word that I'll risk even his displeasure, although I would not have the cheek to read comics in front of him. The book is *Kitchener's Army*, a big one with pictures, given out free by the grocer, Edward Heyes Ltd, in Derby Street, to help recruit soldiers for the war. With extreme care I turn each page, so as not to disturb my father; Mother is moving gently around, humming softly to herself, putting his pit clothes to warm in the recess over the oven, preparing his snap for him to take to pit, and giving me the odd wink. I always sit as far from my father as is possible, yet must face in his direction, and I find the left side of my face is hot from the heat thrown out by the big coal fire – miners being allowed a load of coal at cut price, we always keep a good fire – but even so the right side feels cold, and my legs under the table are chilled from the icy draughts that come in through the badly-fitting door of the front kitchen, which opens directly on to the street.

My father gives a nervous jump at the sudden sound of singing voices passing outside our door: 'Why don't you 'list!/ Why don't you 'list!/Why don't you 'list in Kitchener's Army!' I hear the hearty voices of a gang of boys going by, their clog-irons clacking the pavement in time with the tune of 'Alexander's Ragtime Band'. 'Ten bob a week and nothing to eat,/Damn' big shoes an' blisters on your feet!/Why don't you 'list! – Why don't you 'list!/Why don't you 'list in Kitchener's Army!'

That's the odd thing about Lancashire people, I find, and it takes some getting used to – the way they can make fun of everything, nothing is excepted. The Irish are supposed to be comics, but I never heard an Irishman that could compare with a witty Boltonian, and certainly none that would make a skit of de Valera. 'The divil shoot them,' says my father, '– they have an awful start knocked out of me!' Yet there is a mild note in his voice, from which I gather he is not as upset as he would make out, and perhaps like myself and Mother, he may be glad to hear the cheerful voices breaking in on the stifled atmosphere of the home.

I move from the table as Mother lays my father's place with two slices of cold bacon and buttered bread. He sits at the table, blesses himself before touching the food, eats in his usual manner, never making a noise, or putting the cup to his mouth until he has swallowed every particle of food, a model of a dainty eater. Then he rises slowly, and Mother takes the pit clothes and hurries into the back kitchen to lay them out for him on a chair. At last it seems that the long strain of the evening is coming to an end, and soon I shall be able to let myself relax. My father comes out of the back kitchen, ready for going off to his night's work at the mine, and just then, our May, aged nine, hurries in from next door, so as to give him the nightly kiss goodbye, but Eddie is not home yet. Now comes the awkward moment when he must make the decisive move of picking up the large metal can of tea, and then stand while Mother puts the two small packs of sandwiches – one in each side pocket of his jacket. For a time he had had the usual miner's tin in which he took the sandwiches, the tin being carried awkwardly inside the shirt at the chest, supported by a belt, leaving his right hand free to grasp the upright rail of the tramcar to get on. But it may have proved too bulky, or his appearance could have embarrassed him, the sensitive man that he is, and he now prefers the simpler but less protective way of using his pockets.

May kisses him first, and as I kiss him and get the smell of the coalmine from his old pitclothes, feel his stubbly chin, I think, Poor Old Dad – although I am aware I don't really mean it. He and Mother never kiss or make any endearing gesture in front of us, but the helpless way he looks at her, as he stands there, a lonely figure in his old pit clothes, and the quiet and tender look she gives him, touches me, despite my boyish concern with self, and I am struck with a fear: Will Father reach home safely in the morning from the dangerous pit? I have heard it whispered how on the night of the fearful Pretoria Pit disaster in 1910, in which hundreds of miners were killed, my Uncle William was caught in the cage, held suspended for some hours, and so convinced that he would not come out alive that he scraped out a will on his big tea-can with a pen-knife. Later it was said that he never recovered from that ordeal.

The kisses and farewells are over, and my father moves away from the doorstep around which we are grouped, and walks with his usual hesitancy across the slippery cobbles of the street – his footsteps quite unlike the swift step of other miners. His figure cannot be seen in the pitch darkness of the unlit wartime street, but the pause tells us he is at the corner, and Mother calls out, 'Godspeed!' and we call the same softly, and he is gone. We remain at the door for a few moments, all silent, then we turn in home, close the door, and at once Mother goes down on her knees by the sofa: 'Jesus, Mary an' Joseph –' I hear the whispered prayer, 'I give you my heart an' my soul…' and on she goes with prayers to the Holy Family to safeguard my father down the mine.

'Now I wonder,' she says, on rising from her knees, 'would it be safe for ye two children, if I went off to join Mrs Lafferty? The draw is on tonight, an' I've a feelin' maybe I'd be lucky. Would ye watch young James, an' on no account go near the fire? An' Edward should be home any minute now.' May and I are not fond of our elder brother, and we assure Mother we shall look after everything. Mother puts on her shawl – her coat is worn only for Sunday Mass – gives us both a hug and kiss, and a penny each, and next she goes off into the night. Well there you are, Dad, not a word was said whilst you were here – and weren't we all at the door, so anxious at your going, so full of pity and worry, and now a couple of minutes later aren't you almost forgotten – out of sight, out of mind, as they say, and surely nothing truer. Already I am humming away, 'Oh the moon shines bright on Charlie Chaplin, / His boots are crackin', / For want of blackin', / And his old baggy britches, they want mendin', / Before they send him, / To the Dardanelles.' I am well up to the simple deceptions carried on by Mother, when she has need to do something which my father would disapprove of, and I have learned to keep a discreet tongue, and although she is not one to lie, she would where the truth didn't fit or would cause pain.

The draw she was going to was at a house in Shaw Street, a ten-minute walk from our home. On the first visit to this 'dicing club' or 'shilling club' as it was variously called – to which she had been introduced by Mrs Lafferty – Mother had taken me to show her the way as she got lost among the maze of narrow streets. Even in the dark we found the house easily enough, from the sound of women's voices, and when we entered the little front kitchen I could hardly get my breath, the coal-fire was that hot, the room so crowded. There must have been a score of women, all wearing shawls across the shoulder, the heads bobbing and turning, their faces lively and eager, as they talked incessantly, some grouped round the table, where they were taking turns at throwing dice from a small mug, in which they shook them, covering the pair of dice with the palm of a hand, then flinging them out on the table top. The cries and calls accompanying this, some happy, others less so, according to the numbers that came up, and all the talk and commotion that went on, made a din that seemed to deafen me, and I couldn't make out a word they were saying.

I turned to my mother for the usual comforting word or look, and was disconcerted to see that she seemed to have forgotten all about me. In no time, it seemed, she was caught up in the mood of the women together, talking, laughing and gesticulating like the rest of them, her blue eyes shining, the colour high on her cheeks, and an elated look on her face – so different was it from the Mother seen around our home that I should hardly have known her. It came as a shock to me to learn that under that family Mother was another woman, ready to spring to life once given the chance by such female company. This was one of the rare glimpses I was to get of the way a woman can change when feeling free of husband and children, and it was to make its keen impression on me. I also got a feeling that, among all those women, even I, a boy and as small as I was, may have been something of an intruder, and that my sister May, being one of them would have been more welcome in that company. Dicing clubs flourished in most of the poorer working-class areas of Bolton at the time, each one with its own local flavour. Such a club would be set up by a woman who had some money, and had a nose for making a bit more, and who often did money-lending on the side. The Shaw Street club, near our own church of SS

Peter and Paul, was made up mainly of Catholic women, many of Irish extraction, who lived within an area of a half-mile or so. The reason for the club – apart from the prime one of making money for the woman who ran it – was to answer the yearly money worries that beset mothers of Catholic families when Walking Day came round, and new suits and dresses had to be bought for the children.

Each member could take up as many single shilling shares as she felt she could pay for weekly, each share to be part of the kitty of a twenty-week period – although an extra shilling was added to pay for the trouble and expenses of the woman running the club. On the opening night for each club there was a hat full of slips numbered 1 to 20, from which each member drew a slip, the payment of the twenty shillings corresponding to the week ahead of the number; and there was also the shaking of the dice. My mother took out shares in four of the multifold clubs that ran concurrently, for I used to take two florins to the house on the following Mondays. There was an arrangement, however, by which any woman drawing a late number yet urgently in need of money, could be paid out at once. The interest on money advanced, seven shillings in the pound, was deducted at source, so that for each twenty shillings due, the woman received thirteen shillings in cash. It was a rate of interest equalling a hundred percent per annum, but women were glad of any help that 'saw them over', as the saying went. However, to women already living on credit – and my poor mother was becoming such – it was one more obligation added to the load of debt, all to be paid in weekly instalments.

May and I enjoyed having the home to ourselves, and as I was making myself a piece of toast – a trying task holding a slice of bread on a short fork before the glowing bars – somehow we never went to the trouble of getting a long toasting fork – May began to tell me some secret she had in mind: 'Our Bill,' she began, 'You'll never guess what Alice Wood told me tonight!' 'What did she tell you?' I asked. 'She said –' May stopped, '– you won't tell Mother, will you?' ' 'Course I won't,' I said. 'Well, she said to me that nurses don't bring babies in them bags they carry –' 'Oh,' I said. I had never quite believed they did, but had once broached the question with Mother, and from the deft way she changed the subject I got the hint that it was not a line to be pursued. 'Missis Wood has just had one,' May went on, 'an' Alice told me what happens – I mean how a baby starts –' 'Starts!' I said, 'how does it start?' I had the notion that the baby itself marked the start. May hesitated before going on, 'Well what Alice says, is that the man has to put his – his y'know – y'know what boys have got – inside the woman – an' it's that starts off the baby.' My interest was caught up at once, and I even felt myself go a bit tight in the throat – for it was something I spotted as likely to be true. Then May went on about Alice telling her that it was something men and women always did in bed on Sunday afternoons – that was why children were sent to the cemetery to put flowers on graves on Sundays. That's strange, I thought, and I began to feel more uneasy, for although we had no one at the cemetery as yet, Eddie was always made to take May and me for a walk after Sunday dinner, when we were given a penny each, but even so we went off reluctantly, as Mother and Father went off to bed. I shut my ears to her voice as May went on about Alice saying it was the same as animals *mating* – and for once I was glad to see the door open and Eddie walk in with the usual, 'Where's Mother?' to put an end to the disturbing subject.

CHAPTER 5

The Groups at School

Jackie turned from the blackboard and faced the class, 'Grace before meals,' he said, motioning us to stand for prayers. His gaze was averted as he waited for us all to rise to our feet, and hearing about me the noisy shuffling of clog-irons on the wooden floor I stood up: 'In the name of the Father, and of the Son, and of the Holy Ghost, Amen.' As I heard the boyish voices chanting away, my own husky voice out of key with the rest, 'Bless us, O Lord, and these Thy gifts, which we are about to receive from Thy bounty, through Christ Our Lord, Amen,' the thought went through my mind that 'Bless us, O Lord, and these Thy gifts –' conjured up some image of hot meat pies or at least pasties, something that a lad could get his teeth into, with the nice peppery gravy slavering round his chops, yet I knew for certain that on a Thursday some boys who were up on their feet uttering the prayer would be lucky to get a brawn butty for dinner, or bread-and-dripping and a mug of weak tea, or even a sauce butty – that being a sprinkle of HP Sauce between a folded slice of bread. There in front of me was Jimmy Enty praying away fit to stir any heart, and at playtime I had seen Jimmy spending his twopence dinner money – his mother worked in the mill and Jimmy stayed in for his dinner – at the school sweet stall that had been set up to help pay for the gear for our newly formed school football team. The school did provide cold water for such boys, which could only be enjoyed in the cloakroom, but the enamel mug had long gone and boys had to drink it from cupped hands, because the mouth could not be got under the tap. 'Wut did you 'ave for your dinner, Jimmy luv'?' – 'A sup of cowd watter, Mam, an' a walk round t'schoolyard.' Jimmy would also recite his thanks in the Grace after meals when school began again after the break.

'And now,' said Jackie, who was slowly recovering his composure, 'let us say an Our Father, Hail Mary, and Glory be, for the soul of James Golding.' James, a quiet boy, and fairly good scholar, had died that week from some mysterious fever; he had seemed all right on the Friday afternoon he went home, never to return. We all prayed, in voices much louder than usual, as though making a definite appeal to the Creator – and although I prayed with some fervour I was aware of my main feeling being one of gratitude that it was James who was being prayed for and not myself.

Now there could be heard a factory buzzer as the classroom door was opened. Noon had been announced, and in fifteen minutes there would be scores of those buzzers trumpeting the dinnertime break for mill workers. Boys made an eager move to the door, but I hung back, as I didn't care for the horseplay on the steps leading down to the schoolyard, or for any showing off. I liked to take things easy, stroll along on my own, enjoy a good think, or better still meet some crony of mine, or even two or three congenial pals. I was the last one to leave the classroom – apart from the few staying in to dinner – and as I went down the flight of stone steps leading to the schoolyard I glanced toward the corner below, where the rails and wall met, and there came to me a memory of my first day in the big school.

I was seven at the time, and found myself in a schoolyard which was packed with boys, yelling and running madly around, chasing each other wildly, and, shrinking from the tumult and the din, I had eased myself into a quiet corner spot by the railings. After a time I became aware of three half-timers beside me – boys of twelve who spent a half-day at school and the other half working as little-piecers, always recognisable as such by the greasy pallor of the skin. One was crouched down lighting a cigarette-end, the other two hiding him from sight of the teacher on playtime duty, and I watched as they furtively passed the damp butt from one to the other, each putting it to his lips in the style of the habitual smoker, then 'doing the swallows'. The docker was brought to the lips, there was a sharp intake of breath through nose and mouth, a swelling of the chest with the nostrils widening, the cheeks sucking in to increase the pull of the draw, the lips shutting tightly, the expression on the face becoming transfixed for a moment, then slowly relaxing as the smoke was blown out – except for one boy who brought it down his nose.

It was the manner of little-piecers as they hurried out of the mill at dinnertime, they would take a fag-end from a pocket, often out of a small Oxo tin, cadge a light from a mate, and then inhale deeply, as though they could not have survived another minute without a smoke. I was up beside the smokers, but so insignificant that my presence wasn't worth noticing, and never had I seen schoolboy faces so sly and shifty; and how I longed to possess a mite of their indifference towards the scene around, for they had only to glare or growl at any young lad who came up too close in his play to send him scurrying away in fear. The next thing I saw our Eddie come edging up – he had rather neglected me, as later I was inclined to overlook my young brother James – and he tugged me away by the sleeve of my jersey, 'Are you out of your mind, Willyeen?' he whispered, as we got away. 'What's up?' I said in alarm. 'Don't you know who you was standin' up agin,' he said, '– Kelly, the Cock of the School!'

Many a Cock of the School had come and gone since those days, some doughty fighters they had seemed to me after 1918, when the school-leaving age was raised to fourteen. And when I thought back of my seven-year-old self, with the queasy stomach and flutey Irish voice, it was odd to think that now, to no one's surprise perhaps more than my own, here was I, the so-called Cock of the School. At least there was no other cock around. Moreover, I could even pass for a born Boltonian, although the broad dialect did not come naturally to my tongue. The boy from the top class, who came out highest in the yearly exams was said to be top boy, but among the mass of boys in the schoolyard he was a nobody – the Cock of the School was the admired and respected one.

The social mix of boys that attended our Catholic elementary school of SS Peter and Paul in Bolton in the early 1920s, before there was a Catholic secondary school, could be said to come from three distinctly contrasting kinds of homes and families. To start at the bottom, there were the boys that came from the most wretched homes, situated in the poorest districts. There would be three or four of these in each class, up to Standard Four, but they seldom got any higher. Almost everything about such unfortunate boys made them recognisable for what they were – their old and ragged clothes, mostly unpatched, sweat-grimed jerseys with holes in the elbows, down-at-heel clogs or cheap galoshes, their peculiar smell from a bug-infested home, and often their furtive manner. They had no Sunday clothes, and were chastised for missing Mass; they were absent from all sports day celebrations, never appeared in any play, and seemed denied the simple comforts of even the poorest good home. There was little hope for such boys, they seemed doomed to delinquency, menial work and often ill health. I became friendly with different ones, three whom I knew well were sent to reformatory schools for petty pilfering, two spent long periods in prison, and one, Francis Mundy, became a notorious cat-burglar.

The middle group were all from working-class homes, varying from boys whose fathers were miners, spinners and fitters. I judged myself as being just within the upper range of this group, for I now went to school in boots instead of clogs, was of a tidy appearance, and what my family may have lacked in social standing I made up for by scholarly attainment and manner generally. In one sense this was the most difficult group of all to belong to, since it involved so much striving to keep up appearances, selling raffle tickets, going to Mass every Sunday, a new suit for every Trinity Sunday procession, and much else.

The comfortably-off top layer consisted mainly of boys from St William's School, from where there had been an influx when the senior school closed down two years earlier. This school had been in an area that was edged away from the dense clusters of streets, and most of these boys came from better-class homes, were more confident of manner, and although their intrusion was mildly resented by us, their presence caused a softening of the rather harsh regime of the school. These were the boys with influential parents, and they became identified with the established tone of the school, their homes were visited by Fr Leighton. He had succeeded the well-loved Canon Holmes, a parish priest of distinction, who came into the classroom wearing a long morning coat, carrying a tall top-hat, smoking a large cigar, a warm smile for all of us, a deft way of making mistaken catechism answers appear to be the correct ones, a true priest in that he was kindness itself to the poor.

CHAPTER 6

The Mother the Guiding Influence

I walked across the schoolyard, conducting myself in what I took to be a modest manner, as though engaged in deep thought, 'Hy, Bill,' called a familiar voice, Jackie Doherty, a plump and lively lad, lived at 44 South Street – I knew the address of every boy in the class – 'what d'you think struck old Jackie?' I resisted an impulse to gossip about the incident – it seemed it wouldn't be fair to Jackie. 'I dunno,' I said, my eye scanning the schoolyard as the swift rush of the juniors from the ground exit mingled with the older boys, watching for a likely mate who would be going my way. I was hungry for talk at dinnertime, and enjoyed a good chat with the right sort of mate – but neither of these was that one.

'Howgo, Bill!' I turned as I felt someone come up on me and nudge me with his elbow. Desmond Emmet, just the lad, a mate of mine, yet not a crony; Desmond was the sort that had no cronies, but joined with any likely listener. There was just he and his mother, and boys who lived alone with their mothers tended to be different, rather one-sided and didn't make a good mix of boyish chat, but usually had something fresh to say. Desmond had dark blue eyes, high cheekbones on which shone a few light hairs, the first dark growth of hair on his upper lip, and an operation scar on the throat. 'Desmond –' I began – how I envied him that great Irish name, smacking of the 'bold Robert Emmet', and I never abbreviated the first name to 'Des' – but already he was away with his quick sentences: 'Did tha see old Jackie's physog' – when he went beetroot bloomin' red? I wonder what came over him – poor old sod – it were when he came to talk about mating. I'd a feelin' he were goin' to give us a talk on the facts of life, bein' as we'll be leavin' school. I were sorry the bloody bell rang – I'd have liked to hear more, eh?' That 'eh?' was as far as Desmond would let you get in a chat: 'Hy,' he broke off to yell at some youngsters in our way, '– get from under the feet!' They turned, saw who we were, and at once moved aside to clear a way for us through the narrow passage leading to the gate. I liked to fancy myself as something of a talker, but I was in the ha'penny place beside Desmond, for the various inter-jections that sprang to my lips never got uttered, so swiftly did his flow stifle any interruption.

'Jimmy Golding –' he began 'Aye, poor old Jimmy,' I said. 'Tha knows what he died of – doesn't ta?' went on Desmond. 'Some said it was fever,' I said. 'Nah,' said Desmond, '– *shock*! That's what killed Jimmy. He went home from school that Friday afternoon – went in the back way – they had to keep the front door locked against the bum bailiffs. The first thing he saw – almost walked into, was his uncle's body hangin' from the ceiling – he'd fixed a rope round the top of the clothes-line fitting. Shock – that was what killed him. They say fever – but poor Jimmy took sick after seeing that – took sick an' died.'

I felt a swift and almost sickening stab of memory there in the sunny street at Desmond's words, for there was one memory of mine so striking, so secret that I knew it would be with me the rest of my life. It had occurred one such June day in 1921, when I had been aroused from sleep by a commotion within our home. And as I was being led from the bedroom by our neighbour Mrs Walsh, I got a sight of my Uncle William propped up against the bed, with my father and Tom Walsh trying to cover a wound across his throat, when he tugged the towel away. He was to die in the ambulance. 'Hy, just listen to this – tha'll never believe it – tha knows Willie Morris…?' ''Course I do,' I said, '– he used to be in our class – got an older brother Cyril – left school a couple of year back.' That's him – the same old Willie,' went on Desmond, 'lives up Morris Green. His Mam sent him to some secondary school where they pay – Bolton School or summat – oh no, Saints Peter an' Paul's not good enough for our Willie!'

The mention of Willie struck another private chord in my memory. Although he and I had not been close mates – he was a year older, and we were different types in every way – there had been an understanding of sorts between us, of a matter we kept wholly to ourselves, yet behind the tacit front looks and nods were exchanged, but only once had I broached the subject, which remark of mine Willie pretended not to hear. I had been sorry about his departure from school, for such loud and lively personalities as Willie's were few, and they added zest and variety to the atmosphere of the schoolyard at playtime; if Willie had not been particularly missed his absence had certainly been felt by myself. He was fair-haired, inclining to sandy, with a big round face and a broad head – almost brachycephalic – and could at once be recognised as coming from a good home, with the glowing skin of a boy well washed, well fed, and well cared for; he wore the usual Eton-style celluloid collar, a tweed jacket and short trousers, hand-knitted wool stockings, and stout boots that had been well polished before leaving home. Willie had no trace of the mardy look that so often went with such care, but had a lofty manner, and seemed to exude that air of assurance of a boy from a good Catholic home.

'Well, mi Mam were up at their house yesterday,' went on Desmond in lively spurts, 'Missis Morris had sent her a card sayin' she had some clothes to sell – mi Mam does a bit in that sellin' an' buyin' line, see, Bill an' Morris's have this family, all sons, gone up in the world they have, so she's plenty of old clothes to get rid of. She won't give 'em away for jumble no, sales, oh no, not Missis Morris, not bloody likely! She wants money for 'um. An' the way she bargained over every little thing with mi Mam, old suits, shoes, she'd even argue for an extra penny for a pair of bloody old socks, mi poor Mam arrived home exhausted!'

As Desmond was talking I was reminded of the last time I saw Willie, how we had stood side-by-side peeing together on the waste ground in front of Magee's brewery. It was customary for schoolboys to withdraw just inside any backstreet and urinate with people passing by – although it was something I always felt uneasy about and avoided. It was also considered a mark of camaraderie among boys to 'water their horses' together – something one did only with intimate pals. On that occasion there had been myself and two mates, Jim McGuinness and Frank Barrow, on the way home at dinnertime, when we had been joined by Willie Morris. I had a keen eye for the mood of other boys – an Irish way, one of observing much but saying nothing – and I spotted at once that Willie was not quite himself; he looked flushed, rather unwell, which I felt may have been the reason why he had fallen in with us, who were not quite up to his standard, feeling he might not be able to hold his own among the older boys he mixed with.

The presence of Frank Barrow, whose family kept a prosperous public-house, The Ram's Head, and who was equally as well-dressed as Willie, and wore expensive spectacles, may have raised the tone of our company somewhat. Willie, in spite of not being in the best form, was easily the leading figure in our bunch, did most of the talking, and when we reached the spare ground he called out: 'I say, I'm goin' to have a pee – who's joinin' me?' I was surprised that Willie would do such a thing on an open stretch of ground, and also that he should ask us to join in, and I suspected that he may have been giving way to some weakness of the bladder, to do with his not being well. Willie stood without looking round – he was not one to care much about others – opened his trouser flap, looked at me, and began peeing. I could seldom pass water unless I was alone – unlike most boys I would visit the schoolyard urinal scarcely once a year – but feeling a response was needed I joined in, and so did Jim, but not Frank Barrow, who felt himself above that sort of thing. Willie even led in this by showing how high he could send a jet, but from the look Frank Barrow gave him I could see he did not approve of this display.

'Know what – mi Mam reckons she'll have a job to get back what she paid for the bloody old clothes,' I heard Desmond reeling off. When walking along a street chatting to a mate I also enjoyed taking in some of the passing scene, but with Desmond this was not possible, for he insisted on full attention, grabbed you by the lapels of the mind, as it were, as the flow of words left his tongue. 'Folk with money – mi Mam reckons, they're the worst of the bloody lot – an' I don't know whether tha knows it or not, Bill, but Missis Morris is Irish – Aye, Irish the same as me an' thee – an' the Irish, mi Mam reckons, are usually only too glad to give old clothes away, St Vincent de Paul an' all the rest of it – that is if they have any, which is bloody seldom – but not Missis bloody Morris!'

I knew Willie's mother was Irish – although I should never have thought so judging from Willie and his brother Cyril, who had no trace of Irish. Moreover, I knew that her people came from a village beside that of my mother in Mayo, as did those of the father. What surprised me most when I heard of it was that my father first lodged with the Morris family when he came to England in 1914. And it had been a mention of this that Willie had not responded to.

My father hardly ever spoke of those early months in England, and it seemed odd to think what was now a comfortably-off family like the Morrises should have taken in Irish lodgers, and I simply could not imagine my father living under their roof. He was a shy man, and it was said he would never eat a bite of food except at our own table. At times I had thought of the ordeal it must have been for him, to leave his wife, home and children, an easygoing life in a village outside Ballyhaunis, and find himself living in a strange home, eating strange food, and going off to the arduous work in the coalmine six nights a week, returning grimed in coal dirt, and washing and changing in a strange place. No wonder that six months later when we followed him to Bolton, and I saw him waiting to greet us on the platform with my Uncle William I could not recognise him.

The final Irish impression I had retained of him was of his standing outside the door of our little village shop, sleeves rolled up after opening a barrel of apples, head held erect and thick black hair stirring in the breeze, his plump face glowing, and the powerful voice calling, 'Willyeen! come here now willya – an' take a good smell at them apples. The Lord save us, but you never smelled anything like them!' And as I put my nose over the barrel and took a smell, the rich tang made my senses spin. And the next sight of him, standing there on the platform of the Bolton Station, in place of my loud and lusty father, I saw a lean man with a nervous look, without any colour in his face, and strangest of all, when he lifted his cap to greet us hadn't his hair gone grey and was lying lifeless on his head!

'Mi Mam reckons,' I heard Desmond going on, 'that it's Missis Morris wears the trousers in that house – old Joe, her husband, just stands there an' says nowt, hasn't a word for the bloody cat. He was a bricklayer or summat, an' one time she kept a butcher's shop – but just fancy, I mean who would believe it, an Irishwoman arguing to a bloody penny over old clothes.' We had walked along Pilkington Street to where our ways would part – Desmond to cross Derby Street along which ran the trams, and myself to turn left, and now by luck I spotted the figure of a short lad, with a big head and ears that stuck out: 'Desmond, there's Joe Harrison! I said, 'I'll dash an' catch him – I'll see you – so's you can finish your story.' 'I've bloody finished!' Desmond called back.

This simple incident happened to come up vividly in mind as I was writing – and I have told of it in detail because the subsequent career of Willie Morris illustrates a certain fact about working-class life, and possibly life in general, that the mother is always the one that promotes the ultimate good of the children (the converse may also be true, the one who may fail to, but that need not concern us here). The father can be the most outstanding man, but seldom indeed does he exercise real influence; among the working-class the family appears to rise or fall solely by the character and will of the mother. It appeared that all the Morris sons – by this time, I imagine, they will all have gone to their reward – were fairly successful, each in his own field. There was Joe Morris who had a first-class butcher shop in Derby Street near Swan Lane – not a chap to give one extra weight, and I'll never forget the loud and mock repetition he made of my order when I once went with fourpence for a quarter of steak; Frank and Tom became successful stockbrokers, Cyril a well-known lawyer, and Willie at the bar and beyond. Although worldly success does not impress me, I cannot but wonder at the determination, intelligence and foresight of the mother, who came from a poor village in the County Mayo, and achieved what she did for her family.

Willie Morris I was to see but once again, during my unemployed period in 1933. I was out on the pavement in Folds Road, shovelling a load of coke down the open manhole of Whewell's printers, thinking what would be the best food, bacon and bread perhaps, I would buy with the eighteen pence the job would earn me, to take home to my wife and two children, when I chanced to hear raised voices, with accents unusual for a Bolton street. I looked up and saw two young bowler-hatted gents with briefcases approaching, striding it out in their black jackets and striped trousers. Their dress, urbane manner, and above all their loud speech and accent, set them apart from all that was happening around. The load of coke on the pavement impeded their way for a moment, and in the pause of their going round it I looked up and met the bold gaze of Willie Morris. I recognised him instantly, but had a feeling that myself, dusty of face, wearing old patched clothes and clogs, did not evoke the schoolboy who had once stood peeing beside him. If it did, Willie gave no sign of recognition, and off they went, laughing loudly over some joke, and the thought crossed my mind that my life was as good as over, the best I could hope for, if I was lucky, was a series of labouring jobs to the end of my days, whilst Willie's was just beginning.

At the time I was shovelling coke Willie had graduated from Cambridge – the Irish have always had great respect for education – and was making a name as a barrister. He was to get married – the only Morris son to do so, I believe the mother was difficult to please regarding brides for her sons – and had a family – 'the most be-uncled children of any I know', a friend told me – and was to become a Squadron Leader in the RAF Volunteer Service during the War. Returning to civilian life he was appointed a judge of the Crown Court at Manchester – one who had the reputation of showing scant mercy to the wrongdoer. His career was fulfilled by his becoming the Honorary Recorder of Manchester, Sir William Morris. The Lord have mercy on you, Willie!

CHAPTER 7

Up for the Cup

At the end of every school term came the departure of a number of boys who had reached fourteen during the period. The tradition had been for a boy to be allowed to leave school early on his actual birthday – some boys would slope off at playtime, knowing they couldn't be hauled back – so that he could make a dash to the Education Office in town with his birth certificate, get his school-leaving papers, having already arranged with a spinner to start work in the mill next morning, but now a new ruling insisted that all boys stay on at school until the end of the term. The school term which ended at Easter always had the highest number of school-leavers, the apparent reason for this being that Easter – invariably between March 22nd and April 25th – fell within some nine months of Bolton's annual holiday, and in consequence the birth rate was always higher around that period. At Easter of 1924 a number of lads left school among whom I should never have even approached being the Cock – 'I'm the cock over thee, – If tha touches me – I'll touch thee,' was the recognised challenge, ending with, '…I've touched thee!' followed by a number of touches, which became pushes for the fight to start. The Cock of the School might be seen strutting about the schoolyard with a few mates in tow, the younger boys giving them a clear way, especially in the urinal, and the older ones avoiding them.

Although I ranked among the bigger boys, there were a number taller than myself, but none, and I secretly prided myself on the fact, with the same depth of chest, achieved by my daily work-out in the bedroom and backyard. I was also fascinated by that mysterious power known as 'strength', for it was from a boy's or youth's known achievements in the frequent trials of strength that he gained a certain distinction, one that would usually put him above challenges to fight. Muscle and strength were much admired, and as I enjoyed some quiet admiration I was constantly exercising to increase my own, and always ready for a contest. Tussles and mock fighting bouts I greatly enjoyed at playtime, and having learned a few good wrestling holds I became unbeatable. There was one known as 'the squeeze', in which two boys faced up, got a hold around each other, hands clasped behind the back of the opponent, and pulled hard stomach-to-stomach, until one or other could no longer breathe; because of my abdominal exercises I never came across another boy with such a hard stomach, and was always the winner. I was often called upon to demonstrate the breaking in two of the tough mill banding with my bare hands, which was considered an extraordinary feat, as surely it would have been as a test of strength, but I did it by a trick of winding one piece of the string across the other, so that they cut through one another – a knack I kept to myself. For some time the school had been without any recognised cock, but as the term went on it seemed that I became known as Cock of the School.

A less pugnacious cock than myself would have been hard to find – for it was only the friendly fight I enjoyed. There were three or four boys, all smaller than myself, from poor homes and rough districts, but with that aggressive streak essential to the real fighter. Any one of these, had they only known it, could have beaten me by their very pugnacity and the swift blows from their hard fists; but by displays of strength and the occasional mock wrestle, I had scared them off. Moreover, I had discovered an innate weakness – one that was to remain with me the rest of my life. In various fights forced upon me away from school life – I would never duck a challenge – when on occasion I had not been able to overcome an opponent by a quick grip, and some unfair tactic such as a kick had aroused my anger, immediately there was a sudden draining away of strength. It seemed that the moment I became excited and angry – unlike most boys who seemed to be galvanised by anger – power deserted me, the muscles became weak, and I became feeble. I had to strive to mask this disquieting weakness, and would cause some interruption, until I calmed down and recovered. But unable to feel any hostility toward my opponent, I couldn't bring myself to throw a punch of any kind, and always depended on a grip to disable him. However, by tact and cunning I was able to survive as the Cock of the School.

It was during that final year at school that Jackie was inspired to organise a school football team – something previously unknown at SS Peter and Paul. This it was that brought about a welcome change, for it turned out that the boys from the better-off homes were no good at football – something of a streetcorner game. The best footballers always came from the poorer areas in which there was a lively streetcorner life, and a ball – if not a ball then a pig's bladder for heading, or a tin can was frequently kicked about, or dribbled for fun. If there happened to be a nearby park where boys could practise, this added much to the skills that could be acquired; in the same way the best swimmers always came from streets near a public swim baths, for lads did not care to move from familiar areas. And so our football team was drawn largely from boys who lived in streets around Heywood's Park, where there was a cinder-covered football pitch. Suddenly, it seemed, lads who had been of little account now became popular figures, since there was a schoolboys' league, and games were reported in the local newspaper. Jackie became manager and trainer of the team, and he spent evenings with the boys at the park, took them all to the swim baths, and generally mixed with them until a sort of camaraderie was created between him and the footballers, of a kind that had never before existed in the school, which made a radical difference to the spirit of our school.

The event that inspired this sudden interest in football was none other than the first FA Cup Final to be played at the new Wembley stadium in 1923, between Bolton Wanderers and West Ham United. No one who has not lived in a town with some twenty-five thousand regular football supporters can imagine the enthusiasm pervading the entire populace from their football fervour when the town team is in the Cup Final. In the general euphoria many thousands set off from Bolton for Wembley, in train, charabanc, some in cars, many on motor-bikes or push bikes, and others walking.

As for that first memorable Cup Final, the crowd proved to be enormous, far more than had been expected; there was con-fusion at the turnstiles so that thousands too many were let in, hundreds flooded on to the pitch, and the start of the match was held up for half an hour. There was not a newspaper in the land, on the Sunday and Monday that did not make that occasion its front page splash, with the picture of the single policeman on a white horse coaxing the good-tempered crowd to move back so that play could begin. To crown it all, the Wanderers were to win, and return triumphant with the FA Cup.

It seemed a remarkable feat for a town like Bolton – not insignificant by any means, with its 180,000 population, but not to be compared with cities like Liverpool or Manchester, let alone London – to be able in those days of depression to field a team of footballers second to none in Britain, which unquestionably meant at the time in the whole world. No one could escape the surge of enthusiasm around, no other topic would serve for weeks after, and in fact I was to become as familiar with every move in the famous game as though I had been there. On the following week I was in Harry Jackson's barber shop at the bottom of Cannon Street, and had watched Harry during the course of three haircuts and two shaves – he had been one of the spectators edged off the pitch, and said he had been in actual contact with the rump of the white horse – demonstrating with hand-clippers, scissors or razor in hand, certain nifty moves and dribbles, as he gave a dramatic minute-to-minute account of that famous match.

I was so blinkered at the time that it took me another thirty years to catch up with the thrill of this greatest of all sports. Let me add, however, to compensate for my ignorance, that it was not as a spectator I came to enjoy football, but as a player in Hyde Park with scratch teams on three occasions a week, Tuesday, Thursday and Sunday mornings. Although wholly lacking the skills of a natural player, I made up for this by a keen eye-on-the-ball approach, combined with a pig-headed tenacity, in my role as full back. In 1966, in my middle fifties, I was taking my morning jog through Central Park, New York, always the lone jogger – I had two plays being presented on Broadway – when my attention was caught by a bunch of American youths playing soccer. I was longing for a kick at a ball, and seeing one side had six players and the other five, the latter being out-played, I asked might I join in to balance the sides. They looked surprised, and suggested I be goalie, but no, I said, I'd play full back. Whether it was the fact that I hadn't kicked a ball for a month, or simply a visitation of sorts, I struck a phase of remarkable form. When the game was over, some half-hour later and our side from trailing 3-0 had won 4-3, one of the players came up to me. 'Excuse me, sir,' he said, 'but onetime were you a professional footballer?' 'Not exactly...' I said. I reckoned that moment alone was worth all the rest that happened on that trip.

CHAPTER 8

Joe and Gertie

I hurried up Derby Street after Joe Harrison, crept up on him from behind and took a firm hold on his shoulder, ' "O what can ail thee, knight-at-arms,' I intoned into his ear, ' "Alone and palely loitering?" ' Joe half-turned, his mouth opening into a big grin, and responded with, ' "I met a lady in the meads, Full beautiful – a faery child, Her hair was long, Her foot was light, An' her eyes were wild." How arta goin' on, Bill?' 'Not bad, Joe,' I said, '– what about theyself?'

Joe and I often used snatches of poetry for comic effect. We had been the best of school pals from the age of five, sitting next to each other in the infants' school, and over the years this had grown into the close mateyness fairly common among boys. Joe lived some quarter of a mile from our neighbourhood, but in the same direction from school, and this meant that we often walked home together at the end of the day, sharing the usual understanding among boys: 'If tha'll walk a bit of the way with me – I'll walk a bit of the way with thee.' Sometimes our long chats and swapping of tales and experiences led to our taking circuitous routes, when we would find ourselves in danger from lads in other streets on whose territory we were regarded as trespassers. However, I always gave way to Joe when finally we heard the five o'clock buzzer blow, a warning that he had better dash home, let in his younger sister Gertie, light the fire, lay the table, put the kettle on the little gas-ring in the kitchen and do a few jobs around the house before his mother got home from the mill just after half-past five.

We were ideal mates in that our different natures so responded to each other that it seemed we could talk to one another as though talking to ourselves – at least that was how I could talk to Joe, and often enjoy the delight of his seeing some new aspect of the matter. Moreover, Joe was cheerful and glowing with good humour – moody lads could be interesting, but they rather got me down – and above all he had what I thought was a right good sense of humour. He not only twigged every joke I made, and they were many, but even whilst I was telling a joke his piggy eyes, bright and blue, would be fastened on me, glinting with anticipation, his wide mouth twitching at the sides, eager to burst into laughter – all of which put me on better form. And if that wasn't enough in a pal, he hardly ever got me to listen to one of his jokes.

Over the past year or so Joe and I had found ourselves in different standards, so that we got no chats in the classroom, and as we didn't always come out at the same time we often missed each other on the way home. Joe was an intelligent lad, perhaps not as good as myself at sums and composition, but better at geography and history; yet he had stayed down a standard when I moved up into Jackie's class. He was not deliberately kept down, but at certain periods Standard Seven could take no more boys, and there had to be a selection. Had Joe belonged to one of the better-off families from Great Lever, his parents would have visited the school to find out why he hadn't moved up, or visited Fr Leighton, the parish priest, but Joe's mother did not belong to that class of mother who complained about such matters, nor would she have had much opportunity to. And so Joe, and boys like him, who lacked parent power, would go through life always being held back for need of a mother – as I say, it was always the mother – to push him ahead.

I almost never saw Joe without there came up in my memory an episode involving him and myself, and his sister Gertie – of which I feel a need to tell. On this certain holyday of obligation, Ascension Day, when Catholic schools alone had a holiday, Joe and I had fixed up that I would call for him at eleven o'clock and he and I would go for a good walk together for the entire day – a recreation we never had a chance to indulge. I hurried home after the compulsory nine o'clock Mass, and having told my mother of our plan, she added to the spirit of it by making corned-beef sandwiches with barmcakes she had baked the day before – most mothers never concerned themselves with boys on holiday – and she also slipped me threepence. I was eleven at the time, as yet happily free from the troubles of puberty, and after kissing her goodbye I went down our street, waved back to her from the corner, and made off to meet Joe, taking deep breaths of the sunny morning air to prepare myself for a right good walk. I went down Cannon

Street, past Emmanuel Church, into Jackson Street, down the backstreet with one side Cannon's mill, and straight down to number 22 Dover Street, where Joe lived.

I found him standing waiting for me at the front door, and for once a dejected figure he looked: 'What's up, Joe?' I said, rather put off by his unhappy appearance. 'It's our Gertie,' said Joe, nodding toward his ten-year-old sister who was standing some yards away watching us. 'I told mi Mam I were goin' for a walk with thee, an' she said I've not to leave her on her own. An' if I go anywhere I've got to tak' her with me.' It often happened that a boy had to suffer the minding a younger brother, but as Joe knew, it was unthinkable for two lads to go for a walk and be lumbered with a younger sister. I was touched by Joe's look of misery: 'Let's tak' her with us, Joe,' I said, '– what's wrong wi' that!'

'Art tha sure tha doesn't mind?' said Joe, his face breaking into a smile, yet not seeming to believe what may have seemed a change of fortune. ' 'Course I don't,' I said, feeling it was the only way out of the difficulty. 'Come on, let's get going.' Then I called to Gertie, 'Come on, Gertie – we're going for a walk. An' you're comin' with us – if you don't mind.' Gertie, a pert girl, much like Joe in her colouring, but quite pretty, eagerly came up and joined us. 'Let's go up the Middle Brook, Joe,' I said, 'like we agreed.' 'Aye,' said Joe, and turned to Gertie; 'You walk back a bit behind us,' he said, 'me an' Bill have a lot to talk over.'

It made a fair start to our walk, especially as Gertie didn't seem to mind tagging along in the rear. We went down to Deane Road: 'Come 'ere, Gertie,' called Joe, 'while we all cross the road together.' He turned to me, 'It 'ud be a nuisance if she got run o'er or owt like that,' he said, 'mi Mam 'ud most likely blame it on me.' There was a toffee-shop on Deane Road, and after a good look in the window I went in and bought a penn'orth of barley sugar pieces and a penn'orth of acid drops – not the best of sweets, but they were easy to share and lasted for a while – and kept a penny in my pocket. I held out the open bags for Joe and Gertie to take one, in the manner of posh folk, and as long as they lasted – not very long – we shared them. It was a role very much to my taste, that of the rich uncle. We called Gertie to come beside us as we came through a tough district known as The Pocket, where lads were known to hold up our sort and demand coppers, and next we were walking alongside the Middle Brook – a pleasant wide brook on one side, the adjoining path and railway track on the other – here we let Gertie trail once more behind us, seemingly content enough. We came to what was known as the First Bridge, where the overhead road crossed the railway line and Middle Brook, and I stopped: 'This is always a good spot to come fishin' when it's rainin',' I said to Joe, pointing to a patch of water beneath the bridge. 'Oh aye,' said Joe, '– how's that, Bill?' 'All t'fish,' I said, 'they come shelterin' underneath.' Joe was such a good pal that he let out a laugh at that old joke, and Gertie, who had been edging in nicely, laughed also, which rather pleased me. I felt myself to be in charge, and decided the walk wasn't going too badly – much better than I had expected.

'Hy, what about goin' up Deane Clough for a bit of a change?' said Joe as we came to the steps. I agreed at once, for the cinder path did become rather monotonous after a time. So Joe and I raced up the steps on to the open road above, waited for Gertie, made along the path to Deane Clough, and then decided to climb over the wooden rail and rest on the lovely grass of the golf course. I took the sandwiches out of my pocket, and by luck Mother had made three, so we were able to have one each, as we all sat together on the grass in the sunshine. Having Gertie there meant that Joe and I couldn't tell tales, or make dirty jokes, and although it was a bit dull at first, once we'd got used to it I rather appreciated having to curb my tongue, feeling that a bit of discipline gave me a firmer hold on myself.

'By gum,' said Joe, 'thy mam knows how to make flour cakes, Bill!' Gertie also smiled her approval, and I smiled back at her. I always enjoyed a bit of praise. Joe had lain himself back on the grass, arms behind his head, looking up at the sky, then suddenly he sat up and came stealthily over beside me: 'Tha knows what I were thinkin' to ask thee, Bill,' he whispered, 'as between two good mates – would tha like me to get our Gertie to show thee her split lemon?' For a moment I didn't quite catch on, but then I sensed that Joe was intent on repaying me in some way, and it struck me what he meant by split lemon – the expression was used at the streetcorner – but the invitation had come so unexpectedly that I wasn't sure I had heard aright. Then I turned on him – I had spotted that Gertie may have somehow got the drift of his suggestion, for she got up and walked away – and I answered him in a way I felt any upright lad ought: 'Nay, nay, Joe,' I whispered, 'hold on a tick – that sounds a bit much.' But I said it in a way that my words could give no offence to my pal Joe, and although on the surface it might have sounded as though I meant every word I said, yet I knew Joe and I had this understanding between us, by which one could be blunt in such a way as to indicate to the other he might have just the opposite in mind. 'Besides,' I added, 'she's gone off.' That at least would let him know that I could be persuaded.

'Our Gertie won't mind,' went on Joe, '– she never makes a fuss about owt like that. Suppose I go after her?' 'Nar, Joe, nar don't bother,' I said, and this time I somehow meant it. It had seemed an enticing idea when he first broached it, but on thinking it over it seemed there was something not quite right about it. Joe, however, was already on his feet: 'Hasta ever seen one?' he asked me, before going off. 'No,' I answered, 'never!' 'Tha'll never stop laughin' when tha does,' said Joe, going after Gertie.

I had a feeling to call Joe back, but didn't, and I sat there wondering what would happen and how she would go about it, and at the same time I felt the uneasiness that a sense of sin always brought over me. My hunch said no good would come of it, although I resisted the warning, for I was as prying as any boy about sexual things, and one detail I was most curious to know was whether girls had an appendage underneath like boys. Sitting there in the sunshine, with the smell of newly-mown spring grass from the nearby green wafting across, I was also taken up with the novelty of the prospect; in any case, at Confession, I decided, I would not go into detail, but slip it under 'for these and all my other sins which I cannot now remember'.

Joe came back looking puzzled: 'She said, Nar, she wouldn't,' he said. 'That's all right, Joe,' I said quickly. 'She reckons she'd never show thee, Bill,' went on Joe, '– she likes thee too much an' doesn't want thee to think bad of her.' I was rather flattered by that, 'All right, Joe,' I said, 'let's forget all about it.' Then Gertie came back near us, looking shy and mistrustful. I tried hard to banish all memory of what had been suggested, but I couldn't, it seemed to cling in the air, so that all our chat, asking riddles, or even showing how you could play a tune on a blade of grass held between two thumbs, smacked of humbug, and couldn't dispel it.

After a time we got up, but the carefree spirit had gone out of our walk. For some reason Joe persisted in trying to coax Gertie, and as we were walking up Deane Clough I heard him chiding her about all I'd given them, and how she was too stingy just to let me have a look: 'There's nob'dy about,' I heard him say, 'an' you could slip into that cave there – take off your bloomers, an' then sit on that little mound up there with your legs open, as if nothin' were. Me an' Bill'll just walk past, an' Bill will get a sken at it from a distance – an' nob'dy any the wiser.' I felt shamed for myself and for my mate Joe as I heard his urgent plea, 'Go on, Gertie, be a sport – after all he did whack his toshies with us.' But Gertie firmly shook her head against it – which in some way rather pleased me. I felt I shouldn't have even glanced if she had agreed, and decided I never wanted to see that or any other split lemon for the rest of my life.

Joe tried hard to make up for it by a description on the way back: 'There's nowt to 'um,' he said, 'nobbut a little slit. Or better still, tha knows that little hollow there is on one side of a plum, they're summat like that. I can never make out what all the fuss is about over 'um – I mean the way some of the lads at the corner go on about it, they'll walk miles to see one – but I thought I'd never seen owt so funny lookin' in all my life as when I first saw one.'

It was around that period, before real sexual feelings begin to stir in a boy, that I began to identify all such feelings with Satan, or with the word used by the Irish, *badness*. On the way back home, after I had left Joe and Gertie, I kept thinking how happy we three had been before Joe had brought it up, and how miserable we all were after, how the day was spoiled – even the happy part, for we had been unable to shake off the feeling.

CHAPTER 9
Spinners and Others

Joe would be leaving school in a fortnight, at the same time as myself, and as we strolled up Derby Street I asked him, 'Any idea, Joe, what you're goin' to do when you leave?' 'Nar, not for certain,' said Joe, '– except most likely I'll be goin' into the spinnin'.' To go as a little-piecer in the cotton-spinning mill or 'snuffy' as it was called, was the almost inevitable but least enviable of all jobs a school-leaver of our class could take, for almost any job was considered preferable to that of little-piecer. As for the work itself, there was the intensely humid atmosphere of the mill, to which in time most boys got used, and the feeling of being under the eye of the spinner all day, not an easy boss to please; and also the concentration and manual skill required for piecing up broken cotton ends. As well as consequent physical enfeeblement – no spinning room employee could compare with the miner or outdoor worker in physique or strength – there was the mass of un-sightly blackheads known as grubs, which sprouted on the legs of boys from the little-piecer's task of 'wiping under'. Not, it has to be said, that the boys themselves appeared to mind, accepting such tribulations as one with life.

The spinner – that is the man known as the 'minder', who had his own mules or 'wheels', paid the sidepiecer and little-piecer out of his piece-work earnings for the weekly amount of cotton that had been spun – was a figure of some social standing in Bolton, as well he might be, since the entire cotton industry depended largely upon him. No spinner needed the reassurance of Carlyle's platitude, 'All work, even cotton-spinning, is noble' – not that the work conduced to nobility of character. Spinners could be said to be the smuggest not to say canniest, of the Bolton artisan working-class, and it would seem that the constant care and attention the job of spinning demanded, and the fact that any moment the wheels were still meant that they were not earning money – it was paid entirely on piece work – brought about similar attitudes in their daily lives. Spinners were men of unusual discrimination if not refinement, sharply contrasting with miners and other heavy workers in their way of life, and were set apart from mechanics and skilled workers. The spinner was extremely tight-fisted, known for his frugal diet of lettuce and tomato butties, over which he would drink pint mugs of tea, to replace the extreme fluid loss caused by the work in the humid atmosphere. Little-piecers at the streetcorner liked to tell the latest of the many tales about minders and their meanness; the spinner himself could not only shrug off any ridicule of that kind, but appeared to get a certain satisfaction out of it, coming as it did from those not nearly so well off as himself.

There was not a single spinner that walked the streets of Bolton who could be said to have a hale or even healthy look – only their moderate way of life and avoidance of excess kept them in fair condition – except toward the end of the holiday week at Blackpool, when a sudden redness might mask the usual pallor; returning home many would boast of having gained five or six pounds in a week. At dinnertime no worker walked as fast as the minder going to and fro, but at the end of the day's work he would often stroll home in a languid fashion, released from the stress of keeping the wheels turning and the cotton spinning, on which his wages depended. The spinner had to be accorded respect, even if grudgingly, for he was much envied, in that he had one advantage rare in working-class life – he was independent. Spinners had a strong union, and if a man was a good worker – and all spinners had to be – he could cock a snook at anyone.

The prospect of any little-piecer becoming a spinner, however, was so distant and uncertain that boys never took it into account; their one hope being that they would somehow be able to 'get out of the spinning', as the phrase went, which to me made it sound like a form of prison. The decline in the Lancashire cotton industry had begun in 1920, but so far Bolton spinners were faring better than those in other cotton towns. A spinner rarely left the firm at which he had started work, since promotion was ostensibly by rota, and a side-piecer got his own wheels only when an old spinner retired or died. At the Big Corner there would often be a side-piecer who had been given temporary minding with the spinner off, his wages rising from thirty shillings a week to four or five pounds, and his manner would change accordingly, so that he no longer seemed to fit his old role – at a streetcorner each one had a role of sorts to play – as he became more serious, and cautious about spending. Many a good side-piecer would reach the age of thirty or more before he got his own mules, after having worked for a dozen years as hard as his spinner, yet receiving but a quarter of his earnings – a sum on which he could not possibly hope to marry, unless his young woman had a well-paid job. The spinning-room mentality resisted the rash impulse, and an engagement might drag on for years. For any good side-piecer who was offered a job in another mill, a deciding factor had to be the age and health of the regular spinners, with the side-piecer always keeping an eye on the physical condition of the spinner whose place he hoped to fill, as soon as possible. 'Always look at the back of the neck,' I once heard a man advise, 'an' if tha sees number eleven – two bones stickin' out – it's a fair chance he'll snuff it afore too long.'

I'm afraid that this portent proved only too true, for often the death of a spinner in middle age was from that dread disease, spinner's cancer – resulting from the constant impact over the years of the oily overalls against the body, especially the genitals. (Herbert Turner, a boy in my class, with large eyes of light blue, and rosy cheeks, had given me an account of his own father dying from the disease: 'An' now that he's lyin' dead in the front place, waitin' for the burial on Tuesday, the cancer hasn't stopped,' he told me in his girlish voice. 'As mi mam explained, that goes on eatin' away at him until kingdom come.' It was for me a most frightening image, which I could not get out of my mind for a long time.)

I turned to Joe: 'Somehow, Joe,' I said, 'I don't fancy the spinnin'.' I didn't care to put it stronger than that to my old pal, although my real feeling was that they would never get me inside a spinning mill. I could not forget the occasion I had been sent to Briggs's mill on a Friday with Tommy Walsh's dinner – his mother using it as a means for me to get his wages from him, so that she could do some shopping in the afternoon – and I had only stepped inside the spinning-room when I felt unable to breathe in the airless heat, went dizzy, and before I could turn to get out I swooned over in a faint on the greasy floor.

'Neither do I,' said Joe, 'but I can't see owt else for it – mi mam needs the money to help us out. And although there's no other jobs goin' they're short of little-piecers all over the place – they're even fotchin' 'um in from Salford an' other places.'

'What I fancy, Joe,' I said, 'is a job in the open air, say a bricklayer or summat like that.'

'What a hope,' said Joe. 'They want ten pounds down for takin' on an apprentice – an' my Mam has never seen ten pound in one lump in her life. Besides, what do you get a week – seven an' a tanner, whilst you can earn eighteen bob a week as a little-piecer.' Then Joe told of a mate of his, Sam, who lived in the same street, and worked as a little-piecer; the spinner had told him that if he could bring another lad in to work with him, he'd pay Sam a five shilling bonus on the sly. 'Sam reckons he'll share it with me if I go – an' a half a dollar will seem a lot of money at the end of the holidays.'

My chat with Joe was interrupted by Joe Russell, known as Russy, a tall lad who seemed embarrassed by his height, and had adopted an apologetic stoop. He was standing on the wide doorstep of what had once been a shop, but now served as a cloth warehouse, the plate glass windows having been made opaque by a dark green paint, glossy and giving a vivid reflection; Sandy Fallows, a pal of mine, and young Jackie Profitt were beside him as Russy slowly raised his long left leg up and down, which produced an optical illusion in the glass of both legs being raised simultaneously, with Russy being suspended at the crutch by some invisible power – a trick that had amused me when I was much younger. 'Hy, you two!' called Russy, '– isn't it right what I've been tellin' Sandy here – not to worry if he murders sum'dy up in Scotland, because they don't hang men with red hair?'

Russy, a month or so back, had suddenly become flush, buying toffee on his way to school in the morning, and comics on the day they came out, and getting some lad to slip out at playtime and buy apples from the cornershop – all of which he shared with his cronies, among whom was Joe Harrison who lived nearby Russy. It was always suspect, I had learned, when a boy who has always been hard up becomes open-handed, and what was peculiar about Russy's prodigality was that it was all in silver threepenny bits, which Russy said were a birthday present from his grandmother, with whom he lived. Only by chance did I escape his generosity when he wanted to buy me a meat pie one dinnertime, but the day being Friday, on which Catholics were forbidden to eat meat, I had to decline his offer.

One morning I was asked by an old lady which was the way to the headmaster's room, and I led her there. Soon the word was out that it was Russy's grandmother, and it was whispered that in her cupboard at home she kept a large sealed, thief-proof bottle into which over the years she had put every threepenny piece that came her way – a not uncommon form of saving. But Joe had devised a means of siphoning off a few coins now and again. It was some time before Gran found out what had been going on behind her back – but by then it would seem that her savings were sorely depleted. So upset was the old lady that she felt the proper thing to do was to have Russy taught a lesson he would not forget; he was, of course, too big for her to do it. Mr Smith, apparently, was only too willing to oblige, and Russy was summoned to his study for questioning. In his pockets were found threepenny pieces, and Mr Smith had put Russy across the desk and with his long whippy cane had thrashed him until his howls could be heard all over the school.

It was always painful to see the pitiful state some spirited boy could be reduced to by a severe caning on the buttocks, with the humiliating flow of tears that could not be held in, and I was distressed when I saw Russy at playtime, eyes red, face white, gaze turned to the ground, go hobbling to a quiet corner of the schoolyard, avoided by all except Joe Harrison; nor was anyone to be seen eating an apple in the schoolyard for a long time after. When a boy had recovered from the pain and shock of such a punishment – the shock often seemed to take months to get over – he might gain a certain kudos from his escapade, but not for robbing a grandmother, and getting caught at it, so that poor Russy had remained in disgrace. I had much sympathy for him, feeling that he had shared his ill-gotten pickings with his mates, but retribution had to be endured alone. In an attempt to recover from his loss of face, Russy had taken on the role of comic, and he called out again, 'Isn't it right – they don't hang men with red hair in Scotland?' 'I never knew that,' said Joe. Russy looked at me, 'Eh, Bill – isn'it right?' ''Course it's right,' I said, 'they never hang men with red hair in Scotland – they use rope!'

'Tha bloody knew! tha bloody knew!' Russy screeched out, emphasising his words with a certain rhythm, '– tha bloody knew all the time!' He hopped about in mock fury, his tall thin figure jerking up and down and his clogs making a noisy clatter on the pavement, 'An' coddin' on tha didn't! – tha fawse bugger –' Somehow this outburst seemed to let out any frustration of Russy's, and he became oddly funny, making us all laugh.

Looking back as I write these lines, now in my eightieth year, it seems as though that little scene is one that sticks most vividly in mind. I was becoming more keenly aware of my own particular nature and selfhood – one different from others, and one which set me apart, for it seemed to me that once a boy had known the pull of those deep-seated sexual feelings of puberty, which I had some months earlier, neither he nor life was ever to be the same again. This feeling, and the sexual impulse itself, gave me a sense of being isolated. There are five of us here, yet no two were the least alike – neither in character nor accomplishment, and certainly not in appearance. There was the lanky Russy, two feet taller than young Jackie, a finely featured boy, with a creamy complexion, white forehead on which the black glossy hair fell in a girlish fringe, large eyes of dark blue, a shapely nose, firm lips and a delicate chin. He was a Little Lord Fauntleroy without the velvet, and it seemed odd that a boy of such a tender and pretty appearance, so soft-spoken and mannerly, should be seen around the streets of Bolton. It would surely have gone hard for him had he not had a protector in Sandy – whose side he seldom left, except inside school.

Sandy – I always called him John to his face – was a pal for whom I had a warm affection. He was of broad build, with reddish hair, freckled face, and a slow smile; he had a slight stammer, which among lads who tended to shout one another down made him an agreeable companion; and the sleepy look belied an unusual agility. No boy could spring on to the step of a speeding tramcar like Sandy, and when the conductor approached he would hop off with such perfect balance that left him standing in the roadway, almost like a ballet dancer, arms gracefully raised, body curved, and many a step forward would he need to make to regain his poise. He was an astonishing performer on the various swings in the Heywood's Park, had won what was known as a swimming scholarship, which allowed him to go free to High Street baths where he would do the crawl as though half asleep. Just as no boy was good at everything, so was it with Sandy, for when he was seated at his school desk, with a sum to solve or a composition to write he was lost.

It seems strange, now I think of it, that this was to be the last chat we should have together. In a town like Bolton people tended to keep to their own neighbourhood, and adolescents especially did not trespass, as it seemed, into other districts. Had they been Irish like myself, then after leaving school they would have been accustomed to regard Mass as an essential part of Sunday, and I should have met them there – as I did the boys from better-off families, the Church being part of their social life. But lads from poorer homes whose religious instruction had been marked by canings for failing to memorise the catechism, not one to inspire love of the Church, let alone a spiritual impulse, were relieved to shed all connections with such an irksome affiliation once they got the opportunity.

Sandy I recall seeing only once again; Russy a couple of times when he was home on leave, a six-foot guardsman in his grey top coat. Jackie I was to meet some forty years later, when Princess Margaret was opening the Octagon Theatre, and I had written a play for the occasion. Jackie was a porter at the Pack Horse Hotel; I recognised him at once as he brought the suitcase into my room, and we had a talk. As for my dear pal Joe, who lived only that quarter of a mile away, I never saw him again. He was to go working at Cannon's spinning mill, and somehow our paths never crossed.

CHAPTER 10

Dinnertime Scene

Our Jim, May and Eddie – at times he was our Eddie, but at
others so obviously detached from us all was he that he became
Edward – were seated at the table eating away when I got in.
There was no mention of my being late, for unlike the more
regulated Bolton family we still had the Irish unconcern with
time or punctuality in the home, and each of us needed prod-
ding to be on time for school or work. The same easygoing
attitude could be seen in the variety of the meals being eaten
to fit the different tastes, for Mother tried to please each one,
and seldom forced meals we didn't fancy on any one of us.
Jim had his 'broke-down' – an Irish mixture similar to the
Lancashire 'pobs' but instead of bread and milk it was made
with bread, sprinkled with sugar, hot tea poured over it,
allowed to soak, and milk added; he could eat it at almost
every meal, although of course it did not compare with chip
butties – the ready money for such not being handy on a
Thursday, when the chip shop would be almost empty. May
was having 'banana butties', for after a morning in the mill
she did not feel hungry, and this bland meal with plenty of
tea suited her. Eddie was eating slices of cold bacon, for he
had a good appetite.

I should have preferred a more standard regimen, but I
was a fussy eater myself, and so could not object. At least we
were better organised than an Irish family I knew, by the
name of Wynne, who came from our native town of Ballyhaunis
in 1917, to live in Shaw Street. One mealtime I was in the
home when Mrs Wynne was cutting a fresh loaf, and Paddy
asked for the crust, which she gave him. The younger sister
complained to her mother, and next she cut off the crust at
the other end for the girl, then the two younger children
began to whinge that they had none, and so she turned the
loaf on its side and cut off the top crust, and divided it
between them; at least that was a length my own mother
would hardly go to.

Eddie was seated at his usual place at the table, back to the fire, facing the big mirror on the dresser, into which he gazed as he ate. He took large bites of food, filling his mouth and chewing away, stopping now and again to try out another expression in the mirror, and then taking a gulp of tea. Somehow Eddie never struck me as 'good-looking' but girls certainly went mad on him. By chance I had once met him with a girl called Hilda Fairhurst clinging tightly to his arm: 'Oh Hilda,' he had said, 'you must meet my younger brother Bill...' No 'Our Bill' for Edward. 'He's expecting to continue his education at St Bede's College in Manchester.' Some blooming hopes, I thought. Hilda had insisted on lending me her water wings to help me to learn to swim, but when in the quiet of the bedroom I had blown them up and put them to my chest, I kept thinking of how they must have been up against her plump bosom, and to my Catholic mind it seemed almost sinful to use them

Eddie seldom made more than the odd remark during a meal, preferring to talk only when he had the full attention of everyone, and so forcefully did he elaborate the story he had to tell that even when he had finished he liked a total silence for his words to sink in, and would walk out of the room if anyone brought up a new subject. He was known for his habit of telling whoppers, and as my father used to say of him, 'He's worse than Patsy Finnegan, was thrown out of hell for telling lies.' It needs to be said, however, that so compelling was our Eddie when he got into full flow, that truth itself faded to insignificance.

'Sit down, agraw,' Mother said to me, 'I just have your egg boiled in the saucepan there.' I took my place at the table, and Mother gave me my egg, and poured out a cup of tea for me, then filled Eddie's cup, and remarked casually as she did, 'There must have been a great crowd at Kate's last night.' I saw Eddie look a bit startled, 'At Kate's?' he said. 'Where else!' said Mother. 'Was everyone there?' 'Kate who's!' asked Eddie. 'Kate Meyrick's of course,' said Mother '– I see from the paper she was after openin' a new club in Soho – an' judgin' from the time I heard you comin' in the back door I thought surely you must've been there.' Kate Meyrick, a doctor's wife, with three daughters, was the most famous 'night club queen' of the West End, attracting the aristocracy to her various clubs. Her picture was often seen in the newspapers, a smiling face under a cloche hat. 'Are they out of their minds altogether,' Mother would say, 'to send that decent woman to prison for selling a few drinks after hours!'

Eddie was not one who could stand having a rise taken out of him, and he gulped his tea down, got up from the table, and went into the kitchen to wash before going back to work. May now broke in, 'I was just comin' home, Mam, when Mrs Burton stopped me outside Denton's, "Ee, May love," she said, "you look more like the Duchess of York every day!"' Lady Elizabeth Bowes-Lyon had become a great favourite with the public when she had married the Duke of York the year before, and sixteen-year-old May looked very much like the twenty-three-year-old duchess. 'Except for the smile,' I said. 'Oh you shut up, our Bill!' she said. ' "You could get a job standin' in for her at some of these ceremonies," she said, "folk 'ud never know the difference!"' 'Mam,' I said, 'this egg is as hard as a brick!' 'Sure let me put a taste of butter in,' she said 'that will soften it.'

Jim finished his broke-down and went out to play in the street, Ed came in from the kitchen, looked in the mirror, and went off to work at the Maypole Dairy, and May hurried off to Kershaw's – she always liked a chat with her close friend, Millie Allinson, before starting work. Our cat, Tony, came beside me and began to miaow up at me, and after giving him a few strokes of my hand I got up, and he followed me into the kitchen where I picked up his saucer and poured him some milk from the jug. Tony was actually a female – the frequent caterwauling in our backyard something of a nuisance, and the kittens a problem – but I had named him, since no one else in the family had thought to, and the gender stuck. Next I began attending to certain tasks around the house that I had somehow become responsible for. 'Mam,' I said, 'be sure you have a good cupful of sugar at one side – it's the night for changing the bees.' And I went over to the mantel-piece, on the left side of which stood a large toffee jar, filled to the top with a pale cloudy liquid, which had been clear water when I filled it two weeks before. I watched as the numerous 'bees', looking like large crumbs of white bread, slowly rose from the bottom of the jar to the top, seemingly taking a breath, and then sinking down again.

The bees had been given us by our good friend, Mrs Higgins, who had carefully explained that they were sacred bees, and had come from monks in a monastery. They would work for you, it was said, making wine, providing they were kept warm but not too warm. They must never be sold, always given away – but not on a Sunday, or else they would stop working: nor would they work in a home where there was swearing or too much bickering going on. All they needed was a warm and peaceful home, and a cup of sugar putting in every night on which to feed – and they would toil away to their hearts' content. They had done so for us over the past year, and at the end of every fortnight we poured the wine off into bottles, corked it, and allowed it a few weeks to ferment, filling the jar once more with water that was not too cold. The wine proved to be quite strong, but not exactly to the taste of my father, although Jim and I enjoyed many a drink on the quiet. Indeed I was fascinated by the bees, feeling that they added to the domestic atmosphere, and also that we had much in common, for peace and quiet was something I desired for myself, and I also had a sweet tooth.

One evening our Eddie had brought to the home his friend, 'Our first assistant,' he introduced him to us, 'Lester Kay from Market Harborough!' As May remarked afterwards, 'The way he said it, you'd expect the King of Siam or somebody – not a weedy specimen like he was.' Lester Kay had spotted the bees working away in the jar, and I had explained to him that they were sacred bees from a monastery. Then he put his wire specs on, stared into the jar for a time, then turned and said, 'Yu'know, by rights they're not bees at all – they're only just a fungus as goes up an' down.' Nobody contradicted him, for not only would it have seemed bad manners – much like his own – but none of us quite knew what a fungus was. It rather grated on me, for it seemed like blasphemy, nor did I like to think someone knew more than myself – not that I didn't dismiss it from mind; the funny thing was, the bees didn't like it either, for it seemed that over the next few days they went very sluggish, until May had a good look at them: 'Who does he think he is when he's at home –' she said, 'Lester bloomin' Kay from Market Harborough, the Clever Dick – they're bees as anyone with eyes in their head can see, the way they go up an' down.' And from then on the bees got back on to making wine with vigour.

Next I got up on a chair and took down the fly paper that was hanging beside the gas bracket. 'There's hardly room for another fly on this, Mam,' I said, 'an I'll get the spare one we've got in the kitchen drawer.' I threw the length of sticky flypaper on the fire, and heard the crackle of burning with some satisfaction, for I detested flies and other insects, which in the hot weather, with the many privy closets and middens, had become a plague. After putting up the new flypaper, which attracted a few flies at once, I took up a half-slice of bread, rolled bits of it between my fingers, went over to the fish-bowl, dropping in pellets, which the two gold fish darted at. 'You forgot to feed the fish, Mam,' I said.

Of late I had become rather critical of the way our home was run, and should have preferred it to be on stricter lines, like those of the best Bolton homes I sometimes visited. On the other hand, such homes always had a bossy mother – and most mothers certainly needed to be, for in the domestic climate of the day the kind and tender woman, while she might be loved, had the most difficult time surviving at all; boys with bossy mams were inclined to be softies, the sort before going off fishing or for a walk would say, 'First I'll go an' ask my Mam is it all right.' My own mother was never one to order us about or to chide us, except should we be making fun between ourselves over any peculiarity of another: 'Never say anything against another,' she would say, 'for how do any of us know how we might end up ourselves!' Above all we never had to make a criticism or in any way hurt the feelings of anyone: 'You'd never know,' she would say, 'how easy it is to discourage a person, an' maybe take the heart out of them.' She abhorred the mean act: 'Had you no pride to do a thing like that!' was to me the most cutting remark she ever made. That was why I could not escape my feelings of guilt over my savings safely hidden away in the kitchen drawer.

Mother, I must tell, was standing near the dresser, giving way to a weakness she had, that of eavesdropping on dumpy Mrs Wood next door, berating her husband, Long John: 'You great long streak of piss,' the drone of her deep voice could be heard clearly through the thin walls, 'why don't you go out an' get yourself a proper job like other men, instead of wheelin' a flamin' handcart round the wholesale market every mornin', with a fag stuck in your gob!'

I had seen Long John pass the window a minute or two before, a tall scarecrow figure, with a long nose and a lively

Adam's apple protruding from his scraggy neck, a smouldering cigarette between his lips, his sandy moustache showing dark patches from nicotine and always a smile and greeting for everyone. His wife, Little Annie, as she was called, was as different from him as could be, dark and sullen, and any day when his earnings, which he handed over as soon as he went in, were less than expected, she let him have it. Although I found rows of any kind rather upsetting, these at next door had a nice twist to them.

The Wood family was a fairly happy one, the two eldest girls, Lizzie and Alice, worked in the mill, their one passion was going to the pictures and reading every item they could about film stars, and Jim and young Annie were at school, all highly intelligent, following after their mother; Long John, however, seemed to have acquired a certain prudence beyond that of husbands who may have appeared more clever, in that he never said a word back, never tried to justify himself, making only the occasional apology, 'Aye, I know how you must feel, Annie.' Then, after the long tirade, there would come a lull in Little Annie's outburst, and she would reach a point at which she had discharged all her wrath, and he would break in, 'I know what, Annie – you sit in your rockin'-chair theer, with your feet up, an' I'll make you a nice pot of fresh tea, an' then you'll feel better.' Before Annie had reached that stage, on this particular occasion, our front door was suddenly pushed open, 'Are ye at home?' called a voice, and with it Mrs Thornton looked in.

Mrs Thornton was our one Irish neighbour who lived in nearby Thomas Rostron Street, a Galway woman of forty, tall, good-looking, with blue eyes and blowsy dark hair, who, unlike my mother, had adopted the Bolton clogs and shawl. She had a slow-and-easy gait and a serene air, but whilst most women her age moved with a purposeful air, she always appeared as if out for a stroll, looking one way and another, at anything or anyone that might catch her eye – an attitude which was not approved of in Bolton of the day. She was married to Arthur, a big stump of a man, a horse-carter who was not a town man, and had a broad Lancashire accent, a gentle and kind manner, with an open boyish expression; they had five children, the eldest, John, my own age, being a pal of mine.

My father mildly disapproved of Mrs Thornton, for she took nothing and no one too seriously, especially a man like himself. It was as though she were hinting, I know only too well what you and your kind are, and it's no use coming the big man with me – I've seen your sort before. It was a response he found difficult to counter, combined as it was with her high drawling laughter, and winks and gestures, alive with innuendo. 'Oh hello, Mrs Thornton,' I said. 'Hello, Willie,' she said. 'I've somethin' to tell you,' she said to Mother. 'I'll put the kettle on,' said Mother. 'Look at the size of him,' said Mrs Thornton, 'an' still goin' to school! It's a cryin' shame – our John's the same – that they should be still goin' to school at that age! I thought that with this Labour Government gettin' in they'd drop the leavin' age down to thirteen again – but no sign of it. They're worse than the Conservatives – oh these politicians, once they get in – no thought of the poor mothers needin' that extra few shillings on a Friday.'

'Musha won't he be leavin' school forever in a week or two,' said Mother, 'and isn't it an awful thing to think that he could be workin' away in some place or other for the next fifty years, if God spares him – so what matter a year or two now!' I grinned ashamedly, as well I might, for I was aware of the pest a schoolboy was regarded as being. It was understandable, for a schoolgirl could at least help around the house, and was often good at going errands, but few schoolboys were of much use in the home, and the only way they could help was by getting out. There was almost a stigma about attending school at all – an obligation that denied the family the dozen or so badly needed shillings that could be earned working in the mill. The Bolton schoolboy was like a prisoner in jail – his mind concentrated on the day he would be released and set free to work.

'Aye, but I'll tell you what –' went on Mrs Thornton, her face warming up for a laugh, 'they'll be marryin' their own teachers next! Eh, Willie – what, marryin' Fat Alice! How would you fancy that!' and she let out a cackle and sat down in my father's rocking-chair, displaying an inch or two of knee. Mother put a finger to her lips, and pointed to the ceiling, indicating my father was asleep upstairs, and as she began making tea I slipped into the back kitchen to wash. Young Jim came in from the street, and was satisfied with wiping his face and neck clean with the roller towel before hurrying off to school.

'It was around ten o'clock this mornin', as I was drying myself,' I heard Mrs Thornton talking to Mother in a loud whisper, '– I was all alone, sittin' in front of the fire havin' a mug of tea before I began work, when there was a knock on the door. Now who can that be at this hour, I thought – I mean I wasn't properly washed or dressed, yu'know. I didn't get up at once, but when there was another knock I thought I'd just go an' see – I mean you never know. So I pulled the old coat I wear around the house up at the neck, and went to the door, and opened it an inch or two to peek out, an' there was Father M'Greevy.' 'A nice quiet little man,' said my mother.

'A damn' queer little man, if you ask me,' said Mrs Thornton. 'I wasn't for lettin' him in, d'you know, the way I was, lookin' like an ould slawmeen, an' the house untidy, but didn't he as good as push his way in. An' after one thing an' another, he began askin' me had I made my Easter duties or had I neglected them. I told him that with a husband and a family it wasn't easy to get to Confession, so what does he say but "Kneel down there, ma'am, an' I'll hear your confession now" – an' down he sat on Arthur's rocking-chair, an' pointed to the rug for me to kneel down. I never knew a man so eager to hear sins that hour of the mornin'.' She let out a high wailing giggle, ' "Shure, Father," I said to him, "how could I remember in a minute all the sins I committed this twelvemonth! – I mean this country isn't like Ireland, an' with a husband an' a family to look after, shure I hardly know one commandment from another." '

I could hear the little exclamations of interest from my mother, 'Is that true for you!' and 'The Lord save us!', which seemed to spur on Mrs Thornton, 'As God's my judge,' she went on, 'he said, "Kneel down there an' I'll question you on your sins." An' nothin' else would do him, but for me to kneel on the rug fernenst him, with his little hairy face starin' down at me – I didn't know whether to laugh or cry – an' he wasn't at all interested in missin' Mass or eatin' meat on Friday, but went on about some commandment or other to do with the sins of marriage. An' the questions that man asked, Oh the Lord God, they'd bring blushes to the cheeks of the pictures on that wall! I never in all my life knew a man that would be drawin' answers out of one the way he was! An' all about the one thing – had we this – had we that – for a priest who was never married he knew a great deal about it. An' my one thought was, should a neighbour come in the door what the divil would she imagine was goin' on! An' God forgive me for thinkin' this about a priest of the Church, but with his two little eyes lookin' down on me, there in my ould coat coverin' my nakedness, I was afraid to God what he might say or do next.' And again she gave a laugh.

The next thing I heard a hammering on the bedroom floor above. The knocking followed by a thudding of feet on the bedroom floor, and I swiftly put on my collar and combed my hair. I hurried into the front kitchen: 'Dad's up,' I said to Mother, 'an' comin' down!' 'Then I'm off,' said Mrs Thornton, gulping down her cup of tea, but still half laughing. She was hardly out the door before my father could be heard clomping down the stairs, and in he came to the front kitchen in his trousers and old shirt. 'Yerra what the hell's goin' on here, at all, at all!' he said in a voice thick with anger. Mother said, 'Sure 'twas only Mrs Thornton looked in –' My father burst out, 'Is it that bloody Galway herrin' seller – she has my fine sleep destroyed on me altogether.' I felt it was no time for making farewells, and with a wink to Mother I slipped quietly out of the house, feeling that bit ashamed that Mother would have to endure alone the wrath of my father.

CHAPTER 11

Alice and Rag Bob's Wife

I put all thought of the scene in the home out of mind, as I adjusted to what I took to be my street self – the person I wished people to take me for. I had just got myself in poise when I saw a girl approaching me on the same side of the pavement, and at the sight of her my heart gave a funny shift – for it was dear Alice, my sweetheart of some three years earlier, the love of my young life. How different she walks from other girls, I thought, as I kept my eye on the slim figure in the gingham school frock, a bright spatter of blue-and-white check, moving with that quiet grace and dignity that had so appealed to my young self.

She must have seen me, I felt, as I saw her give a jerk of her lovely head, to throw back a thick plait of her hair that had fallen over her shoulder, then flick it with a touch of her small hand – the hand that I had once lovingly clutched when we went for our walks, away in the country up Dunscar, the other side of the town where nobody knew us. I had had no idea of the wonder it was, having a girl's hand clasped in my own, nor had Alice, it seemed, the way she first put her palm shyly into mine, rather expectantly like a child holding a hand to be grasped. It had been a moment of breathless joy – as though an impulse of love radiated from that girl's palm pressed against mine. It was far beyond what it appeared to be – a mere holding of hands – since countless deep messages seemed to be conveyed to each other in that clasp. It was an intimacy the richness of which I had never before known – not since I left my mother's breast.

Then came the 1921 Coal Strike, and my father, uncle and cousins, all being miners, our family had become one of the three unpopular families in the street, and with loss of wages came loss of face, and Alice's mother and father being right Conservatives, I felt they had put her against me. She had faulted me, if I didn't say, 'I love you –' as often as a boy should, and she did not understand when I tried to tell her that if you really love someone you don't keep saying it, you expect them to feel it. She had been jealous, but that I didn't mind, nor did I mind about our tiffs, or our different religions, but the moment she became cool toward me, measured and critical, it was all over, and I withdrew into my boyish pride. I wanted her love for me to be like mine for her – free of all criticism.

As Alice and I drew closer to each other on the narrow pavement, I felt my heart beating fast, and strived to control the flush I could feel rising to my face. Could we speak? – could we even look at each other after the long years of separation? Did she remember that today was my birthday like I had thought of hers the previous Saturday, the seventh of June? – somehow that she should be five days older than me still irked. I was tense and alert, and should she show the least smile, I decided I would let out on my face all I felt. I might even burst out crying in the street. But no, it was not to be, for she walked past, less than a yard separating our two bodies, not coolly, it seemed, so much as like a girl in a trance, determined to keep her gaze fixed straight ahead. I got a breath of her old fragrance – still lovely, but perhaps not quite so dainty as of old. Hold on! – did I glimpse some sign of breasts on my Alice – two small breasts peeping up beneath her dress! Fancy, my Alice with breasts! – just imagine going out with a girl with breasts! The very thought made me go faintly husky in the throat.

Ah well, one thing for sure, she'd made the biggest mistake of her life – she'd be lucky if the next lad she met would recite poems for her, let alone compose them, and on top of that buy her Mackintosh's toffee, slip the odd sixpence into her hand when arranging secret tram rides to the country. Judging from the attitude most lads had towards girls she wouldn't get a ha'porth of dolly mixtures. One thing I should like her to know – and I hoped it came across in my manner – I wasn't short of money, for I could lay my hands on a few bob with the best of them.

'Ee, but you're a rum lad, Willie, takin' it easy –' called Mr Denton, who was standing at the shop door on Birkdale Street corner, 't'other Cahth'lic scholars 'ave gone runnin' by some time back.' Old Denton, the luckiest thing that ever happened to him, it was said, was when he lost the forefinger of his right hand in the mill. It meant his job as a spinner was over, since he couldn't piece up, and with the compensation he got himself into that corner-shop and had never looked back.

I grinned at him – I didn't have to run. I had been given the only monitor's task I fancied, that of calling to pick up any letters for Mr Smith, the headmaster, which had by mistake been delivered to the presbytery or infants' school. This meant that I could now make my way to school in a relaxed fashion, freed as I was from the anxiety of being late. This transformed my way of life, so that I could view the world as I went along. Just the same, at times I didn't seem to be myself in this monitor's role. I had never been used to privilege – indeed I had become accustomed to its opposite, a sense of handicap – and I didn't adjust to it naturally, and felt there was something missing. I had become so used to the constant tension between Miss Newsham and myself, and the troubles that had beset it, that the year in Jackie Seddon's class seemed to have dulled me in some way, made me less acute, not so aware of life's upsets and troubles.

I was going up Thomas Street, beside the big mill and the row of small houses, when I heard a woman's voice call out to me, 'Hy, love – have you a tick?' I had any number of ticks, and I turned and saw Rag Bob's wife, a woman who had what I took to be a Romany look, with her dark colouring and distinctive manner. In fact I knew her well, for over the years there had grown up an intimacy between us from an incident that had occurred when I was ten. Rag Bob, who had a club-foot, and made ends meet by being a rag-and-bone man at mornings, then opening his front kitchen as a barber shop in the late afternoons, had got me up in the barber chair, the sheet around me, cutting my hair one Friday evening, when a row had broken out between Liza Jane – they weren't actually married, it was said, but living tally – and a customer she was lathering ready for his shave.

I always envied the men who just sat there and had their lower faces lathered by her, the way her woman's fingers would stroke and pat their chins, trying to soften the beards for Bob's razor. This man she was lathering must have worked at a brick kiln, as was plain to see from all the brick dust on his clothes, hair and skin, and even colouring the heap of soapy lather on his chin; and Liza Jane, who may have had a job getting through it to get at his beard, had said something about she wished some folk would wash their faces before coming for a shave, and he said what bloody chance did he get of doing that, and went on about she wasn't watching what she was doing: 'Do you blame me,' she said, 'with a flamin' mug like you've got! Then Rag Bob, a rather serious man, spoke sharply to her, saying something about his customers didn't come to be insulted – he charged fourpence for a hair-cut and twopence for a shave, but new and more fancy shops were opening, and I imagine he didn't want to lose one of his regular customers – and this prompted the man to say something I didn't quite catch, but it couldn't have been very nice, for I saw Liza Jane get angry, and she stuck the soapy shaving brush full of lather right up his nose, making him splutter, at which she burst out laughing. Next there was some shouting and Rag Bob turned from cutting hair and made to hit her, but she dodged him, and ran out just as she was, and Bob went hobbling after her, swearing what he would do if he caught her.

The other customers slowly left, one by one, as the time passed, but somehow I was too benumbed by the situation to move. I felt that if Rag Bob had put me in a chair to cut my hair he would naturally expect me to be there when he got back; I liked to observe what I took to be the social courtesies of life, and felt that a disagreement of that kind should be quietly overlooked. The gaslight went out – it was a penny meter, but I simply could not get myself to take off the big sheet and get myself out of the chair – I was that sort of boy. It must have been around ten o'clock when the front door was suddenly shoved open, and Rag Bob and Liza Jane came clattering in on the stone floor, talking and laughing away, and smelling of beer. The coal fire had burned to a low glow, but I could see clearly, and I kept silent as Bob gave Liza Jane a penny to put into the gasmeter, and then he struck a match and lit the gaslight.

She let out a great cry of surprise when she saw me, and although Rag Bob had not wanted to cut my hair she had made him. He had taken special care over it, and instead of just shearing it all off as he usually did with boys, he gave me a bit of a quiff in front, and dowsed my hair with brilliantine. I felt stiff getting out of the chair, and if Liza Jane hadn't grabbed me I should have fallen onto the floor. She helped me back into the chair, 'Ee, hasta pins an' needles, love,' she said. 'I mun' rub thy legs for thee.' And although I felt shy about it, I must say her hands soon got the blood moving. She even gave me a jam butty, and she didn't charge me, but gave me sixpence for myself. She saw me off, and kissed me, and told me to go careful, and although her breath smelled of drink, it was warm and womanly, and I liked that. My mother was glad to see me back home, and the first thing I did was to wash my hair, for I couldn't bear a sticky or oily feeling, and always longed for cleanliness. Liza Jane was to remain one of the three or four women, mostly plump, warm and easy-going, with whom I was to enjoy bouts of sexual dalliance in my imagination.

I went across to where she was standing beside the rag-and-bone cart: 'Willya gimme a hand, cock,' she said, 'wi' this bedstead? I'm on mi own – yon chap's in the *British Oak* – God knows when he'll turn up. I want to get the handcart outa the way afore we open shop.' I watched across the handcart as she leant over to grip the old bedstead, and saw that she had no corsets on. Take your gaze off that woman's bosom! hissed my Catholic conscience. 'Lord, save me or I perish!' squeaked my soul. With all my will I commanded my eyes to turn from that cavern of white breasts, but they wouldn't budge. If the devil were to take me I had to take in the full stare, so it seemed, yet there was Rag Bob, who could have wallowed there in that breast, felt and smelt to his heart's delight, preferring to stand at the bar in the *British Oak*, supping beer, among a bunch of men as ugly as himself!

'Heave ho!' she called, and together we lifted the bedstead off the cart, carried it through the poky front kitchen, and into the back kitchen, where we put it down. 'Ta love,' she said, 'ta very much.' I turned and stepped into the front kitchen, which served as the barber's saloon. It was a cold and comfortless place in the daytime, the fireplace piled up with ashes, the powdered sandstone on the floor made a gritty sound as we walked on it.

'I've got this damn' place to clean afore we open the barber shop at three o'clock,' she said, seeming glad there was one who would listen to her, 'an' t'floor to mop an' stone, t'fire to light an' everythin'.' She looked at me, and I looked at her. There were some older women, I felt, who could read a lad's thoughts and feelings – girls couldn't read anything – no matter how much a display of innocence he put on, and I almost half-expected her to say, 'Ee, luv, would you like to put your hand down mi blouse – I don't mind if you do – if it 'ud give you any ease –' but she didn't, instead she let out a woman's sigh, long and deep. Then I noticed the dark skin loose below her eyes, and the wrinkles showing up now that she had relaxed, and I thought she looked what they called world-weary, as though she would be happy to depart that very moment were it possible. Poor woman, I thought, making my secret sign of the cross over my heart with a finger, which I nearly always did in moments of sympathy. 'An' yon sod swillin' away,' she added. Then she grinned, got her purse out of her pinafore pocket, opened it to dip in, but I anticipated her, 'No, thanks,' I said, 'but ta very much all the same –' and I was off.

CHAPTER 12

The Come-Uppance

I had walked barely a dozen steps from Rag Bob's, past a few yards of spare ground, beside a low building, when there was a harsh smell of new rope and grease from the rope ware-house, and with it came a memory of how my Uncle William once attempted to carry me to school when I was six years old – but gave up at that very spot. It seemed that every pave-ment flag I walked over and I knew the shape, slope and wear of every single one, had a memory and message for me; every corner, every cobble-stone, every window-sill, so that I couldn't bear for anything to be changed – not that much change took place. Dear Uncle William, his death had been a sorry loss to our home and family life, from which we should never recover.

Suddenly there was a smell that never failed to stir some-thing in me. It was the thick fug that stole out of the open side-door of the Derby picture palace, as the cleaners swept out the fag-ends, orange peel, toffee papers and dirt left from the night before. But to my sharp nose the smell more pungent and pervading than all the leavings was the human smell, left behind from packed bodies after intense excitement. I had paid my first visit to the Derby pictures on a Monday evening in early 1918. The excitement produced in me by being squashed in among masses of little-piecers on hard benches, the heavy pall of smoke, the smells of oranges and mint drops, and the incessant din of voices, was enough in itself without even seeing a film. Then there was the Pathé Gazette short news film about the war, a Charlie Chaplin comedy and an interval before the 'top film'. Mr Booth now stood on the stage, the piano struck up, and he started the singing off. First it was 'Keep the home fires burning / While your hearts are yearning…' and they all knew that, and sang loudly. The most thrilling of all was when they sang the French national anthem, 'The Sons of France shall rise to Glory!' When it came to 'March on! March on!' I suddenly heard my own voice breaking out in song. Then Tutty Booth ended up by calling out, 'Are we downhearted?' to which came loud calls, 'No!...not while Britannia rules the waves...' Then all sang 'Rule Britannia...'

After all this excitement there was the William Farnum film in which Bill Farnum throttled the villain. I came out of the place in an utter daze, and found it hard to believe that there was a queue waiting to go into the second house, women in shawls, wearing men's caps with hatpins, lads calling to those coming out, 'Is it any good?' It gave me a shock; somehow, after all the emotion I had gone through I had expected to see a different world, but to my astonishment everything was just the same. It seemed that when the Great War came to an end in November 1918, the Derby picture palace was never the same again without the singing – not that there was much to sing about, what with the terrible 'flu epidemic that followed, and the big slump of 1920, and the Miners' Strike of 1921.

I walked up Pilkington Street toward our school feeling relaxed, went by the big church door and rang the bell of the presbytery house, attached to the church. The door was opened by Father Hill, who was wiping his lips with a napkin. 'I'm sorry to trouble you, Father,' I said, 'but are there any letters left here for Mr Smith?' He smiled at me – he was a smiling priest, different from other priests in that he had been a Protestant minister before converting to Catholicism; he was free and simple of manner, and did not take on that priestly aura adopted by most priests. 'No trouble at all,' he said, and went to look. 'There are no letters,' he said, with a smile. His warmth of manner added to my sense of well-being, as I went round to the Infants' School. The playground was deserted, apart from a small girl dragging her tearful younger brother by the hand into school. I was touched by the sight, feeling that I knew what was going on inside each of them – the concern of the girl and the dread of the boy. Although I had never to be dragged to school by our May, there was always a sinking at my heart when I entered the infants' playground, as a memory of the apprehension I always felt every morning when I had attended the school. I went inside, turned left along the broad corridor between the classrooms, hearing the voices of the children calling responses to the teachers' marking the attendance registers. I saw Sister Edwardine at the other end, standing outside her office, talking to a woman visitor, and although some eight years had passed by since I was under her authority, and I now saw her twice a day, I had not been able to escape a qualm or two at the sight of that tall and strangely forbidding figure. I slowed my pace at once and approached to what I considered a respectable distance, a dozen feet away, and turned sideways, so as not to impinge in any way on their conversation.

Sister Edwardine was Irish, said to be from Cork, although she had shed all but a trace of the accent; she was about fifty years of age, with rather small eyes of no true colour, and a pale, narrow face, the severe lines of which were sharpened by the tight wimple she wore. As I took the odd glance at her – she need only give me a nod or beckon and I could be off – with her nun's habit, dark and heavy, the stiff breastplate, the large rosary beads and crucifix hanging beside her lower body – where one part of that body ended and another began no hint was given – it struck me how vigilant the Church had been to decree such a garment for a nun. She was so enveloped in black that almost all female life seemed perished, yet since she had no male look, it was as though she had taken on some strange alien sex, one that would stir no breath of temptation in any man – or indeed, woman. I thought I could read most faces, but hers was something of a mystery to me. What a difference between her and Rag Bob's wife! Could it be true I wondered, what was whispered of their having all their hair shorn off – some said shaven to the very scalp – once they took their vows; if so they must present a fearsome sight going to bed at night. Yet Sister Hyacinth in the Girls' School, with her rosy cheeks and happy face, looked most attractive in her nun's apparel, as though the sombre black and the circle of white round the face enhanced her liveliness. As I stood there waiting it seemed I could feel the austere authority of Sister Edwardine radiating down the corridor, and it struck me that over the years she must have instilled fear in many hundreds, even thousands, of small children – her presence intimidating the teachers, let alone the infants. Some teachers had been caners, and although the cane could be frightening, it did give one a chance to summon up a bit of reserve; Sister Edwardine was known as a slapper and ear-tweaker – she couldn't wait to get out the cane. I remembered that it was she gave me the first slap on the face I had ever known – for singing out of tune. She had stooped down to listen to my voice, her stiff white thing had scraped my nose, and the next thing I felt something hit me. It wasn't the pain but the shock, I found myself trembling, and then I had burst out crying. What made it worse – and knowing that this was true made it no better, was that she had called me a softie.

Time was going on, and still they talked, with no sign of stopping, and once or twice I half-turned just to remind her I was there. I didn't mind waiting – I seemed to have spent much of my time doing that – but I was getting a little uneasy about being so late back in the classroom. Finally, I plucked up courage, walked up closer, and standing two yards away I broke in with, 'Please, Sister, are there any letters?' It was rare there was a letter, and I expected her to dismiss me with a nod or wave. She turned and gave me a baleful glare, 'You stay there,' she said, 'I'll attend to you later.' I stood even further away. At least I've an excuse, I thought, if old Smithy should make any remark about my being late. Sister Edwardine kept talking to the woman for a few more minutes, and then the woman went off and I approached her once more. 'Sister Edwardine –' I began, but I got no further. 'How dare you speak to me back there –' she said, 'when you could see I was talking to someone!' So she had been storing it up, I thought, and was alarmed by the tone of her voice, the colour that came to her thin cheeks, and the glint of temper in her eyes. But I was wholly unprepared for what happened next – when she drew her arm back and swung an open-handed slap that struck me on the side of my head and face. It had such force and swiftness that I found myself thrown off balance, staggering a little, aware of a spinning sensation, and a dense, stinging around my temple and ear. I couldn't think what to say or do. I stood there – duty and obedience being natural in a Catholic upbringing – awaiting a reply. Her own expression had changed entirely, in such a way that I felt she might say she was sorry. To slap a boy of fourteen, a monitor, for simply asking for letters, may have even struck her as not quite the thing. 'There are no letters,' she said in a very quiet voice. 'Thank you, Sister,' I said. I looked around and as I walked away along the deserted corridor, trying to keep erect and unstumbling, of one thing I was keenly thankful – that no one had seen the incident.

CHAPTER 13

Tennyson and Street Scenes

I stood outside the headmaster's room, trying to make myself look normal. I had held the left side of my head under the cold tap in the cloakroom, to cool it down, then wiped it with my handkerchief, so that what I felt must be a red splotch would fade down. I knocked lightly on the door, waited, and heard his voice, 'Come in!' I opened the door and looked in, hoping to get away without entering; Mr Smith, a man of fifty with a large dark moustache and a fatherly sort of look, was behind his desk. 'There are no letters, sir,' I said.

He looked up: 'Very well,' he said. 'Oh, I'd like a word with you, Naughton,' he added. I went inside and he looked at me, 'Are you feeling all right?' he asked. 'Yes, sir,' I quickly said. He paused, before going on, 'Have your parents given further thought to your staying on for another term or two, and taking the examination for St Bedes College?' 'Yes, sir,' I said, 'but I think they have other plans for me.' It was such a whacking fib that I had a job to get it out.

'Mr Seddon and I both believe that you would stand an excellent chance of getting a scholarship,' said Mr Smith. Suddenly as I was looking at old Smithy I saw him in quite a new light, a way I had never before thought of. I had judged him to be an uncaring man, the way he could line up latecomers in the schoolyard on cold mornings and cane them, and put others over the desk and tan them, but I realised that he was really concerned about me. The English, Smithy and Fr Hill, were decent and understanding, but that bloody Irish rapp', as my father would say, had to vent her temper on me. I felt I had better get away or else I might just let my feelings out. 'Thank you very much, sir,' I said, and went off.

Back in Jackie's class I managed to slip quietly into my place, avoiding all eyes until I could settle myself down. It was the English lesson, and I picked up the poetry book on my desk, for Jackie was reading Tennyson, 'The Idylls of the King'. He had a good but rather monotonous voice, and he went droning on about old King Arthur, mortally wounded, telling Sir Bedivere, to take the sword, Excalibur, 'And fling him far into the mere:/Watch what thou see'st, and lightly bring me word –' Suddenly he stopped, looked round the class, his eye settling on me: 'Naughton,' he called out, 'take on from there?' 'Yes, sir,' I said, standing up, and fumbling for the place in the book. My first words came out croaky, but helped to clear my throat, and as I read the picture of Sir Bedivere, hesitant about leaving his King, but promising, ' "…Yet I thy hest will all perform at full, and lightly bring thee word," ' created a clear picture in my mind, one into which I could put voice.

Tennyson was not one of my favourite poets, but I read on, felt carried along and sorry for the knight after he had twice lied to the king; ' "Ah, miserable and unkind, untrue,/Un-knightly, traitor-hearted! Woe is me!" ' old Arthur reproaches him, ' "…Authority forgets a dying king,/Laid widowed of the power in his eye/That bow'd the will…" ' and he even threatens Sir Bedivere to ' "slay thee with my hands." ' I could feel the excitement building up: ' "Then quickly rose Sir Bedivere, and ran,/And, leaping down the ridges lightly, plunged/Among the bulrush beds, and clutched the sword,/And strongly wheel'd and threw it".' I had all the class tense now, as I came to what they had been waiting for, ' "So flash'd and fell the brand Excalibur:/But ere he dipt the surface, rose an arm/Clothed in white samite – mystic, wonderful/And caught him by the hilt, and brandish'd him." '

Then as I read on I realised for the first time in my life what a great poem it was, and on I read, of Sir Bedivere making broad his shoulders to receive the weight of the dying King. And of how 'there hove a dusky barge,' and of the decks 'dense with stately forms,/Black-stoled, black-hooded…' then away moved the barge, 'like some full-breasted swan/That, fluting a wild carol ere her death,/Ruffles her cold plume, and takes the flood/With swarthy webs. Long stood Sir Bedivere…' Why had I never glimpsed the power and beauty of this poem before, I thought, and suddenly, as I sat down the strange answer broke through, *It needed that whack from Sister Edwardine!*

Jackie called me aside as the class was going out for the fifteen minute's playtime: 'Naughton,' he said, 'there's a message here I should like you to take to my wife at Number 67 Higher

Swan Lane. You know where it is?' 'Yes, sir,' I said, taking the envelope from him and putting it into my inside jacket pocket. It was considered a privilege to be sent on such an errand, and I was curious what his wife would look like. 'After play-time,' he said, 'we shall be out for walking practice for Sunday's procession. I don't suppose you'll mind skipping that?' 'No, sir,' I said. 'Here's sixpence for your tramfare,' he said, handing me a sixpence. 'I shan't need it, sir,' I said, 'I shall walk.' He hesitated, grinned and put it back in his pocket. 'You can slip out at once,' he said. 'Very good sir,' I said.

I was glad to get away from the school and the sharp eyes of my classmates. I decided to take the familiar Derby Street road there, and as I walked along, feeling the side of my head now and again, regretting I could not tell my mates, for I enjoyed making lads laugh, but somehow that would be a bit too humiliating, something I should have to keep to myself. Near Thomas Street passers-by were stopping to watch some scene in the middle of the road, and I heard a man say, 'It's only Daft Jimmy on point-duty.' In the middle of the roadway I saw the diminutive figure of Jimmy Stewart waving his arms about and calling out as he controlled the traffic. Jimmy often came to the Big Corner, a shrunken little man of forty, with a white, hairless face; he was always clean and spruce, wearing a natty suit too big for him, his highly-polished dancing clogs, with brass rivets and pointed toes – 'Jimmy Clean Clogs' was another name given to him. A tram came swinging along down from High Street, the driver clanging the bell, but Jimmy had his hand in the air, and waved to a horse-and-cart to cross the road. The tram-driver kept on coming clanging louder, shuddering right up to Jimmy's behind. Jimmy piped out to the horse-carter, 'Come on, mate – we haven't all day!' and there were smiles and laughs all round. That's the way it was in Bolton – they'd stop anything for a laugh.

As I was standing there watching, a boy on a bicycle drew to a halt just beside me – Charlie Scarlett, a lucky lad! Charlie was my age, taller than myself, but on the thin side, said to be 'outgrowing his strength'. In fact, he had not had need to attend Emmanuel School for some months – another thing I envied. He lived at the bank; his father was said to be the bank manager, and the authority with which he opened the bank promptly at ten o'clock each morning, wearing his smart uniform, added to the mistaken impression, for he was the caretaker and commissionaire. Charlie was wearing a fairly new brown suit, tan boots with the new pointed toe to go with it, a soft Luvisla collar and a bright tie; except for the collar, the thought struck me that such an outfit would be ideal for me to parade through town in three days' time in the Trinity Sunday procession; instead Mother would have to make my old navy-blue suit look new with a good sponging and ironing. But what caught my sight even more than the rig-out was something most rare in our part of Bolton – a brand new bicycle, and a Rudge Whitworth at that, with the special pointed mudguards

'Howgo, Charlie,' I said.

'Howgo,' said Charlie. His mouth was full of toffee, and he put his hand in one of the large pockets of the jacket and pulled out four or five Nuttall's mintoes, handed me a couple, then took the paper off the others, threw it away, and put them in his mouth, but instead of sucking for a bit, the way lads made toffee last longer, he started chewing away at once. 'Ta, Charlie,' I said, 'ta very much.' Charlie didn't say anything – he wasn't a talkative lad. 'That's a right brawmin' bike you've got, Charlie,' I went on.

'It's not too bad,' said Charlie, ringing the bell. His legs were so long that with one foot on the pavement he could rest himself on the seat as we stood there. Somehow he didn't seem that interested in it, or indeed in anything except chewing toffee, which he did in a manner unlike any other lad I ever knew, chewing away absent-mindedly, which meant you weren't concentrating on your pleasure and so missing the best part. In fact for all his posh clothes and new bike there was something missing about Charlie Scarlett, and the saying, 'He's not wearin' that suit, t'bloody suit's wearin' him,' seemed to fit him.

'I'm just going up Higher Swan Lane,' I said, feeling in my inside pocket to make sure I'd got the letter for Jackie's wife, and at the same time making a bit of a move. 'Wilta be at the Big Corner tonight?' asked Charlie. 'I will for sure, Chey,' I said. It was the first time I'd called him 'Chey', as we weren't that close. 'I'll see yu'there then,' he said. 'I'll just tak' t'bike in t'back way,' and with that he pedalled slowly off and turned at the corner, the bike spindles glittering in the sunshine. The drawback of living at the bank – despite it being said that Charlie could have as much money as he wanted – was that he had no streetcorner to go to, and so was glad of someone to talk to when he came to ours. The idea of living in a place where all your mates did not gather of an evening was unthinkable to me – it must be like living in a desert. In fact I had three streetcorners into which I could fit, but my favourite was the Big Corner, among the men and youths.

As I went on up Derby Street I began to wonder what Jackie's wife would be like. I had some vague daydream of her and Jackie adopting me, and saw myself as the only son in an English home where there would be peace and quiet, everything running smoothly, which was what I fancied. There'd never be holes in my stockings, the heels of my boots wouldn't be worn down, no uneasiness around my breeches backside in case I stooped there was a sudden tear, always a clean handkerchief, and I'd be able to have a good bath at least once a week – what a treat, a bath to oneself! – and quiet evenings reading in the front parlour and drinking a cup of Rowntree's cocoa before going to bed. Of course at times I might miss the excitement of the Big Corner, but then one couldn't have everything. I was interested to see how much she would offer me for delivering Jackie's note, for although I had decided to refuse outright, graciously of course so as not to offend, but firmly, for after all I was no pauper, with money tucked away and also in my pocket, I had found generosity to be a fairly reliable guide of other womanly qualities. I reckoned that considering the long walk it was worth at least a tanner, coppers were for kids, and a silver threepenny-bit had a skimpy look.

I decided to look into Skinny Nancy's window as I was going up Derby Street, and have another peek at Sandow and his lovely muscles, for it seemed as though the very secret of strength and muscle was there inside the dusty box, waiting to be revealed to you, once you handed over your money and took it home with you. I had an idea I might one day even splash out on a Sandow's Developer. Also, going into Skinny Nancy's was something of an adventure in itself. Nancy and Mark Davenport were brother and sister, in their early sixties, a pair wellknown among boys for being misers. I felt for the shilling I had in one pocket, for the first thing you had to do when you went into the shop was to display a coin in your palm, for Nancy was not interested in answering questions about the price of this and that to lads with empty pockets. Once she had seen your money you had her, and she also had you, for although she would answer any question, she was also a cunning temptress. Her eyes would never leave you – no matter how many boys came in she seemed able to keep in eye contact with each one.

The shop was crammed with sports goods of every imaginable kind, footballs, cricket bats and balls, fishing rods and lines, all manner of boxed games from draughts to ludo; also Indian clubs, chest developers, fireworks, false faces, and various practical joke items, and sooner or later Nancy would find a boy's weakness and play on it. Even the dust added to the enticement, as though each article were pleading neglect, asking to be taken to a nice home, wiped clean, loved and cared for, in the way only a boy could treasure his most valued possessions. For any lad to escape Skinny Nancy's with his money intact was almost unheard of, and as cute as I thought I was, she had never failed to trap me, one way or another. If guile failed she would summon authority, so that I found I simply dare not leave without buying something. Once the transaction was over, Nancy's manner changed abruptly, and she could not get you out of the shop quickly enough.

Mark, the elder and milder of the two, was an asthmatic man with a pale, pockmarked face, unwashed and grimed over with shop dust; his bristly moustache hung over his loose, half-open mouth, through which he breathed with difficulty, and sometimes seemed in half a mind about stopping altogether. He wore an old shirt open at the throat, and a dark and faded old suit, but for all that Mark was nice to talk to, and listened patiently to the lads telling him what they wanted. Nancy, the dominant one, was small, petite, with a peculiar dignity, for despite the old dark garments, and film of dust on her grey hair, gold-rimmed spectacles and face, she had a voice of ringing clarity, an educated accent of a kind rarely heard, and so authoritative was her bearing that she could usually quell the most unruly boys.

Just as I got near the shop I heard a sudden yell of boy's laughter, wild and gleeful and at once I knew who it was, and feeling an uneasy spasm I dodged out of sight beside Blackwell's florist's, and peeped round the corner. The next moment I saw the stubby figure of a boy come bounding out of Skinny Nancy's shop door, followed by Nancy and Mark who stood on the shop doorstep. 'Go away, you wicked boy!' cried Nancy. 'Aye, clear off,' cried Mark in his hoarse voice, 'an' leave us a bit of peace. You'll be settin' the shop on fire next! ' 'I can soon put it out, ' replied the boy, who was fresh-faced with curly hair, and wore short flannel trousers, grey socks, good boots and a red jersey, and taking a water pistol out of his pocket he shot a squirt of water at Mark.

Then he began dancing about on the pavement, delighted at their discomfiture, taunting the pair as he took a bag of paper pellets from his pocket, and flung them one by one at the shop window, each one exploding with the sound of smashing glass. Next he took some small objects from his pockets and smashed them on the ground, and at that I saw Mr Blackwell run from his own doorstep, 'Stink Bombs!' he yelled out, '– what bloody game, eh, letting stink bombs off beside my shop – an' me tryin' to sell flowers!' The boy, seemingly pleased to have upset someone else, ran away up the street, laughing loudly. I knew him fairly well, having once been in the shop with him when Skinny Nancy had sold him stink bombs and pellets, which he then flung around to torment the pair of them.

CHAPTER 14

Music and Torture

The boy, Ernie Hilton, had come fresh to SS Peter and Paul from a private school, and being a year younger than myself, there was little that would be likely to create a friendship between us; however, we did go the same way home, and sometimes he joined me and others, and on one occasion his mother had met us. Mrs Hilton was a milliner and hat-maker, a short woman, prim and plain, with rimless spectacles, who kept a rather fashionable shop in Derby Street. A few days later I was with a school pal, Jim McGuinness, when suddenly she hurried out and called me into her shop, which was not the sort of place I felt comfortable in.

'Oh William,' she said, 'I wonder would you do me a great favour –' I was only too pleased to be asked to do someone a favour, especially a woman with a shop. 'I wonder would you befriend Ernest. He's new to your school, and he's never been able to make friends, or to find another boy to play games with him. And he admires you so much!' Some intuition warned me that there must be a good reason why a boy could never get another boy to play with him, but of this I thought it best to say nothing. She told me that she and Ernest's father had to go out on the following Wednesday evening, and would I come round at seven o'clock, to keep Ernest company in the home.

I had become a bit wary of mixing with boys of a rather better class than my own, for somehow no good had ever come of it. It seemed that the gulf between the comfortably-off lower middle-class home – no such usage was heard, it was either 'posh' or 'ordinary' – and those from my own neighbourhood was unbridgeable. It was not solely a question of money, but the contrasting attitudes to life between those who were secure and those who were insecure. For a long time I had done my best with a friendship offered by Frank Barrow, but it had never even approached that warm mateyness that existed between Joe Harrison and me. It seemed that well-off lads never quite grew up, for it was not so much that Frank, a nice enough lad, knew so little of the scruffy side of life, and had no tales to tell, but that it would seem he never gave such things a thought. There was a gap of some years between Frank and his two elder sisters, Doris and Joan, and about twelve years between him and John, the eldest son, so that Frank had the petulance of an only child. However, there were special treats in going to the Barrows', such as when he and I occupied the spacious first-floor clubroom, and he would ring the bell and order two shandies. An even more exciting pleasure for me was when he sat down at the piano, took off his spectacles, spent a minute breathing on them and wiping them clean with his handkerchief – he looked so odd and naked without them – and then seemingly without effort filled the room with the most exquisite music. Suddenly he would be transformed for me into an image of his favourite composer, Liszt – of whom he often spoke. I would have had him play every evening, but Frank would play only when he was in the mood. In fact, on one occasion when his father, the choleric Jack Barrow, had called him in to play for a few of his cronies, all Frank would pound out on the piano was, 'The Cat jumped over the Garden Wall to have a look at the hen –' And neither inducement nor threat would alter his mind. My own musical talent, that of playing ricks – two flattish bones from the butcher's, boiled and dried, held between the fingers – as an accompaniment to my whistling, seemed trifling indeed compared with that of Frank.

The most impressive figure in the Barrow home was John, the eldest, who had lost an arm during the War. He was a swarthy, well-groomed man, and I was much engaged by his evening manner, that of someone about to go out enjoying himself. I envied him the way he could rise up after stooping, the long hair, dark and well brilliantined, hanging over his face, and with one swift jerk of his head send it all back in perfect place. I was also fascinated by the artificial arm, and the manner with which he would use it to take out a long silver cigarette-case, and deftly fill it from a packet of Three Castles cigarettes. After which he would select one, tap each end on the case, then light it from what was the most rare object, a cigarette-lighter, take a deep draw, give a sigh, and put the lighter into a vest pocket, and the case in his inside jacket pocket. To me he represented the strong silent man I often read of in my mother's weekly *Girls' Mirror*, and for long after it was my ambition to possess such a silver case, fill it and smoke in the manner of John Barrow; I could not hope, however, to train my own unruly hair to fall into place. Once when I went into the Barrow bathroom I saw a rack with half-a-dozen toothbrushes on it – one for each member of the family. I could hardly believe it, when I pictured our own worn-down toothbrush near the tap in our own home. What put an end to our friendship so far as I was concerned was that one evening when I had been put in the clubroom to wait for Frank, I had one of my urgent needs to relieve my bowels, and found I was unable to get into their bathroom, and I had to speed off home in a frantic state.

To Mrs Hilton's appeal, I agreed at once, knowing I wouldn't be missed at the Big Corner. Later, my pal Jim McGuinness told me something about the Hiltons: 'It's not his real father,' he explained, but his stepfather. You'll have seen him, he's a mill manager or something, goes to work in an overcoat with a fur collar, an' wears a pot. Ernie's proper name is Killalea – his mother's been married twice – an' he can't stand the step-father, who can't stand him either.'

I was always interested in visiting new homes, for it seemed every one had a number of surprise items, and it proved so with the Hiltons'. Ernie saw me through the small window from the sitting-room, came out and led me in, to a carpeted room with a nice fire burning. The surprise was to see a woman in a shawl, sitting at the table and chatting away to Mrs Hilton, in what seemed an intimate manner. In fact I vaguely knew her, a Mrs Chadwick who lived off High Street, and was the mother of a big family. Mrs Hilton gave me a brief smile, and turned at once to talk to Mrs Chadwick, and ask her questions. It was only when I saw the woman holding a teacup in her hand that I realised she was reading the tea-leaves, and telling Mrs Hilton's future. There was talk of a dark man, a journey, a visitor – all of which prompted Ernie's mother, now looking like some romantic girl, to ply her fortune-teller with further questions about it all. The conversation ended by Mrs Hilton giving the woman a shilling and arranging for another visit.

At eight o'clock a taxi called to take Mrs Hilton off to meet her husband in town. I promised her that I would stay with Ernest until they came home later, then after warning us not to touch the fire, she went off in her fur coat, and Ernie and I were left alone. I had resigned myself to an empty evening, for Ernie had no turn of mind that interested me, hopping from one subject to another, lacking in thought. Nor was the room proving to be one in which I could relax – there was a model of the upper part of a woman in one corner, and on a small table was one of a woman's head, and so odd and life-like did they seem to me that I had a nervous feeling of there being a woman-and-a-half around, listening to all that was being said. What did impress me secretly was Ernie's physical live-liness, for he was like a jack-in-the-box, springing up and down unexpectedly. At one time we had a wrestle, and I was astonished at the firmness of his body; his skin was hard and scaly, his short thick fingers were most powerful, as were his arms, and had I not got my familiar grip on him, his head pressed tightly against my hip, I should have had difficulty in beating him. Yet he seemed quite unaware of being strong, and didn't boast in any way. The small brown eyes, dark and gleaming, had some strange look in them at times that made me uneasy,

'I know what we'll do –' said Ernie, in the loud voice that boys of his type used, '– we'll play at robbers. You can be the robber and tie me up – I've got some rope, and you can tie me to this chair and see can I escape.' This seemed to me to be kid's stuff of the most boring kind, but to please the boy and get the evening over I agreed. Ernie brought a long rope and sat in the chair, eager to be tied up. I started on him, but he kept saying, 'Tighter – tighter – it's not hurting me!' and so I began to pull the knots of them tighter, but he was out of them in half a minute. 'Now I'll tie you up,' he said. Feeling strangely nervous I sat in the chair as Ernie got hold of the rope, and I was aston-ished at his speed and skill in tying knots; I tried to keep one hand free, but he caught it in his hard grip, whipped it behind the chair, and the next moment I found myself trussed up, help-less, unable to move. Ernie was clearly pleased at the sight, as he hopped around in front of me, taunting me to get free. It was an eerie experience – the first time in my life I had felt so utterly helpless. But I wasn't going to let a youngster like Ernie Hilton see any sign of my fear.

'Good lad you, Ernie,' I said, 'I give up – I can't get out – you win – so unfasten me please.' 'I will,' said Ernie, 'when I'm ready.' There was a new note in his voice, a threatening one; then I watched as he went to the fire, picked up the fancy tongs, then carefully chose a half-burnt piece of coal, and turning to me said, 'But first I'm going to brand you with this –' and he came toward me gurgling with anticipation it seemed, holding the red and smouldering coal in front of him.

For a moment I thought he might just be trying to scare me, and I didn't care to have him take a rise out of me, 'Don't be so daft, Ernie!' I called, putting on my senior manner, but he seemed deaf to my words. 'I love a bit of torture,' he went on, and as he drew nearer with the live coal, and I saw the expression on his face, the two piggy eyes gleaming at me, I lost all control, and let out a yell of real fear. My feet were on the floor, and I gave a wild fling backwards away from the hot and smoking lump of coal. The chair went right over, the top striking the floor, and the next moment, feeling dazed and chafed, but relieved that a hand was free, I managed partly to disentangle myself.

'You silly chump,' I called out, making light of the incident, and talking like one of the boys from Greyfriars, in my determination to conceal any fear, 'you might have easily set the house on fire – playing a joke like that. Undo this bloomin' knot around my ankle.' Ernie now seemed relieved to settle for a joke, as he put back the coal, and slowly I was able to reassert the authority of age over him. I was relieved to see that I had not actually broken the chair, but I never took my eyes off him for the rest of the evening. I kept alert, listening for the front door opening, and at last I heard it, and Mrs Hilton came hurrying in. 'Is everything all right?' she asked me at once, seemingly surprised that it appeared to be.

'Yes, ma'am,' I said. Then in came Mr Hilton, wearing his dark overcoat with its fur collar, looking rather severe, and Ernie suddenly became very subdued. It seemed bad manners to dash off at once, but I felt I couldn't get away quickly enough. Mrs Hilton saw me to the shop door, and tried to press a shilling on me which I firmly refused. I felt that money could not recompense me for that scare Ernie had given me. Then I hurried up Derby Street and turned down Cannon Street, hoping fervently that there would still be a few mates lingering at the Big Corner, so that I could get the memory of the evening out of my mind. Yet somehow I couldn't help but feel kind of sorry for Ernie, and for his mother too – the scene in that room as I left did not bode for happiness. (The next I was to hear was that his stepfather had sent Ernie to sea – it was said he knew the skipper of a ship, a man that would lick the lad into shape.)

CHAPTER 15

Petty Tyrants

I was passing 'the biggest spinning mill in the world under one roof', Swan Lane, an impressive building with its hundreds of windows, which on dark and wintry days, when suddenly all the lights began to be switched on, and the silhouettes of side-piecers and little-piecers could be seen moving about, looked rather picturesque – from the outside of course. Going up Higher Swan Lane, considered a fairly select district – it seemed the higher the altitude the more posh the people – I wiped my face and hands with my handkerchief, and generally tidied myself up, not that with clean boots and white collar I wasn't respectable. What may have marked me as being different was that I always went around bare-headed, at a time when every other boy wore a cap. The only occasion I wore one was on the annual Trinity Sunday procession, and even then I had difficulty keeping it on, for I had a large head of black hair, thick and glossy, and I liked to keep it cool and free.

My heart began to beat faster as I neared Jackie's home, sixty-one, sixty-three, sixty-five, and finally here I was at number sixty-seven, standing at the very door Jackie came out of every morning to go to school! I took a deep breath, tapped the iron knocker three times, not too loud, not too soft, and then cleared my throat, and took the envelope out of my inside pocket. After what seemed a fairly long wait – not a good sign, it always struck me, the slow answer to a knock on the door – I heard footsteps, a lock being turned, and the door opened. The woman before me struck me as rather ordinary to be the wife of Jackie – the sort of woman you could look at for a long time and a minute later be unable to picture in your mind. 'Good afternoon, ma'am,' I said. 'Mr Seddon gave me this message to bring to you,' and I handed her the envelope. 'Just a minute,' she said, and drew back inside. I heard her tear open the envelope – I wonder will she ask me in for a cup of tea and a piece of cake, I thought. She looked round the door, 'Thank you,' she said, 'that'll be all right,' seemingly eager to close the door on me. Could this be the end of it! 'Thank you, ma'am,' I said, and tried to walk off in a casual manner, but felt the flush come over my face, for it was a bit of a let-down all right. What a fuss I'd made over nothing! Thank God folk can't read your thoughts – above all your feelings.

Higher Swan Lane! – pooh, who do they think they are! I wouldn't live here bloomin' rent free! Apart from two women and a window-cleaner the place was deserted, not like our street, where there would always be a half-dozen youngsters playing in the gutter, making mud pies in shoe-polish tin-lids, a hawker or two, a street-singer, and women going back and forth in their shawls to the corner-shop. And yet I could see the odd woman peeping at me from behind the curtains – blooming toots! Call it a street, where you didn't see a woman or two in shawls; they and the kids made a street, not just a row of houses. As for Jackie and his wife adopting me – no, thanks, if you don't mind I'll stick at home. Could it be that I was overseen, as they said, in Jackie, and that he wasn't quite the figure I thought him to be, but just an ordinary teacher, who happened to have been to War, and had come through with that extra strand of character that civilians lack?

I was at a bit of a loss what to do with myself, when it struck me on the way back that I might slip into High Street baths and have a swim. I had neither towel nor drawers with me, but since I had some money I could hire them, a penny each, which would make fourpence in all. It wasn't cheap, but I felt in need of a good soak, one that would wash away any traces of the clout, and also I hoped I might be able to swim a full breadth of the baths on this occasion, for I had only just learned to float in the water. It was an ideal time to go, the schools would all have left, and few workers would be there. The only snag would be Jim the attendant.

To make Jim and his kind understandable, I must tell of a certain boorishness of the day that appears to have died out. I speak from personal experience in daily life and gained from various jobs over a dozen years and more, of the domineering attitude of those whose position allowed them to exert authority on the unfortunate ones under them. Among employers and supervisors there was a belief that the only way to get the most out of the work force was by animosity and intimidation.

Our May often came home with stories of certain overlookers in the weaving shed yelling loud abuse at a weaver for some fault in the loom for which she was not to blame, and cut-lookers – the men who inspected the finished cloth – reducing a woman to tears with their abuse over some defect, and then imposing a fine to be extracted from her wages (an illegal act). I had known a neighbour call in to tell my mother of how some boss in the cardroom had so sworn at her daughter in front of the others, that the girl had lost all confidence, stayed in all weekend, and always dreaded going to work on Monday morning.

No doubt but that fear – fear of disfavour, down-grading or the sack and disgrace – is a handy goad for keeping a work force on its toes. There were a few good employers such as Magee Marshall, the brewery and pub owners was one, noted for their paternalism (a word unknown at the time), but so eager were people to get work at such firms that the employees tended to be drawn from the same families. Tootal, Broadhurst and Lee had a good name in textiles, they employed a nurse and looked after the welfare, but such firms were rare. It was an accepted thing that a man – it was almost all men in those days who were in charge – who was a foreman, spinner, tackler or boss of any kind, to be good at his job had to be crabbed and unpleasant, authoritarian and difficult to please. Most workers had it drummed into them what a favour the firm did by giving them work. And yet so peculiar is the human mind that over the years such a petty tyrant might eventually take on the role of being a 'character', whose bark was worse than his bite. Fortunately there was a vital segment of artisans, spinners and others so skilled at their jobs that they were virtually irreplaceable, and this fact, combined with that of North-country mettle made them ready to cock a snook at any boss. Very few of such spirited men would be offered promotion, and some would not accept a job that alienated them from their old workmates, for 'a boss's man' was a contemptible figure.

The bossy stance taken up by most men in charge appeared to permeate the entire society, so that anyone in a situation, domestic included, who had obtained the least mastery over another, tended to play on it. An indication of an efficient boss, it appeared, was to be heartily disliked by all that worked under him. The typically successful gaffer, usually not the best worker himself, but a thruster of sorts had few friends, and so little to lose by unpopularity; a man who was unhappily married, probably hen-pecked, and eager to pass on his own state to those who worked under him. The more a foreman was detested by the workpeople the more the management appeared to see it as proof he was doing his job well, for a popular boss was not wanted, a measured antagonism between 'staff' and workers being preferred. This created a social attitude in which there was an instinctive dislike of all authority. The police, for instance, were intensely feared and hated. They would charge youths for kicking a football in the street, for spinning coins or playing cards in a backstreet, for putting a tanner on a horse with a bookie's runner, or even for standing at the corner of the street, if you didn't move on when they ordered you to. Policemen were almost never friendly – as may commonly be imagined – but seemed to be selected for their size, weight, bullying manner and scowling demeanour; any policeman under fifteen stone appeared to have little chance of promotion.

Another dreaded figure among working-class parents was the 'school board' – an attendance officer, wearing a bowler hat and long dark coat, who called on houses where children were off school, and often threatened the parents with court action and dire penalties. Dole clerks behind counters became autocrats when dealing with applicants for the dole, demanded to look at a man's hands to see if there were signs of his having been at work; small wonder that many of them suffered black eyes for their snooping tactics. Nor can I exclude certain Catholic priests who employed a front of ill-temper and an air of sacerdotal aloofness to advantage in dealing with parishioners. Fr Leighton was one, a stern and unsmiling man, quick to criticise, difficult to meet, a priest who managed to reduce the church debt, but who never once visited our home, or, it was said, any of those in the poorer areas. The most crusty and difficult priest of all, however, was Fr Chronnel of St Edmunds, noted for never being able to keep a curate. He spoke down to his congregations with a mixture of acidity and condescension, was nicknamed 'Timothy Tightarse', and it speaks much for the understanding of the parishioners that they recognised his good qualities, overlooked his bad, so that not only was he held in respect, but attracted a genuine loyalty from them. In essence, I imagine, all this was none other than a squalid kind of *hubris* – not exercised as in Ancient Greece by the high and mighty, and incurring the retribution of the gods, but by any Tom, Dick or Harry who had a position which allowed him to show gross disregard for the dignity and rights of others. Such humiliations could not fail to cause rancour, and despite the notion that vandalism did not exist in those days, there was hardly an old-fashioned street lamp that at some time or other did not have its glass shattered by a stone.

Since it would never even occur to me to deface a wall with obscene or other writing, damage property of any kind, fail to take care of library books and school books, or play jokes on householders or others, as was common, I feel that some explanation, even apology, is required for this high-minded stance, since it cannot but smack of a certain priggishness – a word and concept of which I was unaware at the time. Attempts at self-improvement of some kind or other were not uncommon. Groups of youths would rent a cellar for sixpence a week, and club together to buy weight-lifting equipment and boxing gloves, and would gather in the evenings for physical culture; others would join the Bolton Harriers, and take it more seriously. Although readers of the intellectual type were few they were vocal, and could quote Marx and Engels. I had a pal who worked as a side-piecer in the cotton mill, Harry Crowther, who was keen on poetry and philosophy, and stumped me more than once in an argument by quoting Bishop Berkeley, who was too abstruse for my own mind at the time. I have told how Harry, when deprived of his nightly read in bed because there was no candle, would close his eyes, and memorising one of his favourite Wodehouse books, would begin to read from the top of the page to the bottom, and turn pages over in his mind, so keen was his memory of his favourite author.

In Bolton of the day there was a distinction to be drawn between those who could look you straight in the eye, and those who couldn't. And this judgement was exercised in every walk of life down to the streetcorner. I always strived to be among those who could look anyone straight in the eye – although at times I had to put on a bit of an act. All the popular boys' magazines of the day, *The Magnet* and *The Gem*, telling of the happenings at various public schools where the boys boarded, divided the 'decent chaps' from the 'rotters'. Much school poetry extolled the public school spirit, 'Play up, play up, and Play the Game!', and 'How Horatio saved the Bridge' and 'The Charge of the Light Brigade' and dozens more.

There was the teaching of English Catholicism at school with its accent on sin, drummed into us morning and evening, and at home the Irish kind, more forgiving and understanding, but present in some form or other, thanking God for every meal, for the weather, good or poor, for health of course – the one exception being the Irish, 'God bless the work!' a sentiment my father could not summon for his work at Brackley Pit, often mixed in with ancient Gaelic incantations that surely preceded Christianity. Any child of the least spiritual could hardly fail to be imbued with its influence in the home – much of it that may have seemed to others a superstition, but to me a mystical dimension that enriched daily life, which I treasured – and was to do so for the rest of my life. And blended in was the hard-headed ethos of Lancashire Methodism, appealing to commonsense as well as to Christian principles. Inspired or goaded on by such influences it seems surprising I was not a more affected boy. I should stress, however, that in my youth and maturity, my idealistic aspirations were no match for my instinctual drives. Looking back I realise I was no better morally – probably worse – than most men around me, many of whom may never have given a thought to their spiritual selves.

CHAPTER 16

The Clogger – Sam Yick – Swim Baths

Among my more distasteful duties was that of going to old Howarth the clogger, with my father's pit clogs to have new irons put on. He looked disgruntled at the best of times, as well he might, in the dark and sunken den where he sat, among heaps of smelly mill clogs, hammering irons on to the soles from early morning until eight o'clock in the evening; I would sit there patiently, often for twenty minutes or more, waiting for him to finish what he was working on, before he even spoke a word to me. There was always an outburst from him once he picked up my father's clogs, and found that the wooden heel had worn down: 'What the bloody 'ell does he think I am!' he would roar at me. 'It'll tak' ten minutes an' three-ha'porth o' leather to balance it up. Why didn't he fotch 'um when the bloody heel came off!' I sympathised with the clogger, for it looked a tricky job putting on the extra packing, yet I couldn't tell him that the heel-iron might have come off at the start of the night shift, and the wood had got worn down. But he was a good workman, and although he did not charge extra, the clogs never left his last until they were near perfect. And once he had let out his temper, it seemed he calmed down and felt better for it, and his manner toward me would soften, although it was beyond him to lift the sullen look of one hard done by, which had become ingrained in his character.

There were other encounters that proved something of a trial but which were not so intense or drawn out. One was with Sam Yick, the Chinese laundryman, which often occurred around Saturday teatime. Most Mondays on my way back to school I had to take my father's stiff collars to Sam Yick's in Derby Street, when a flimsy piece of coloured tissue paper would be handed to me, to be presented on the following Saturday when I went to collect them. Although I was careful I was equally absent-minded, and by Saturday that fragment of paper was often missing. 'No tickee no collar!' Sam Yick would yell at me when I tried to explain, and then he would start serving other customers and leave me standing there beside the counter. But I had memorised the code, marked in indelible ink in the inside of the collar. After he had served all the customers who were waiting, I would venture 'Please, Mr Yick, the initials and number inside the collar are B.F. 27.' (The exact ones, I may say.) Sam would fling his hands up in the air, 'No! no! no!' he would cry out, '– I have told you – *No tickee – no collar!*' What I could do then was either to go out and walk up and down Derby Street for ten minutes and try again when his temper had cooled, or watch for his wife, an Englishwoman, to whom I would whisper the code words and she would soon find the collars.

Public institutions, such as libraries, were far from welcoming. Outside High Street library was a large notice board, stating the opening times and departments, below which was the name of the chief librarian, Archibald Sparke, F.R.S.L. At the top of the steps was posted a bearded attendant in uniform, who would first ask, 'Are you a member?'; if you hadn't a book, then you had to show your ticket. Boys were put off joining the library by the entrance form, which had to be signed by that mysterious person, a ratepayer. 'What's a "ratepayer", Dad?' I once heard Ernie Fairclough ask his father. 'A ratepayer?' said Mr Fairclough, '– I'm buggered if I know.' 'You're a ratepayer,' said Mrs Fairclough, 'you pay your rent, an' that includes rates, so you're a ratepayer.' 'Get off!' said Mr Fairclough. Next your hands had to be held up for inspection, to make sure they were clean enough to handle a book; after which you were sized up generally before being allowed inside the portals. All this created an antagonism in boys, and Archibald Sparke, Fellow of the Royal Society of Literature was defaced to, 'F…, Rotten, Stinking, Liar.'

I found myself outside the swimming baths, but I hesitated before going in, for it was not inviting in any way. There was the forbidding turnstile which barred the way of all until they had paid over their twopence. Further, no boy was made welcome by Professor Grundy, the manager, who appeared to hate being disturbed. Both the library and the baths, signifying cleanliness and culture, made it clear that they were reserved for more deserving clients than the likes of me. I've got to force myself to go in, I thought, or else I'll never learn to swim, and with that I stepped inside the door with its narrow entrance, and up to the turnstile. I looked inside the payment office, the sixpence now ready in my hand, and saw the professor seated facing me, reading the *Daily Despatch* – a newspaper my father abominated because of its partiality and right-wing views; Grundy was a man with a long face, thinning hair parted in the middle, with a quiff on either side, and to match he had a small black moustache, waxed and neatly smoothed down, also on either side. I knew he must have seen me, but as he had made no move after two or three minutes I summoned the temerity to tap quietly on the window. He looked up at me annoyed, turned back to his newspaper, then after another minute got up and opened the small window: 'What do you want?' he asked. He must know what I want, I thought, but found myself saying, 'Please, Professor Grundy, could I have a towel and drawers?'

I had been tipped off by one boy that he liked to be called 'Professor'; if so he showed no pleasure as he took my sixpence, slapped down the towel and drawers, as they were called: 'That'll be fourpence,' he said, passing me twopence change, and slamming the window shut. I made to go in, but the turnstile would not give way to my pressure, and I realised he had not yet touched the catch to release it, which he now did, and I lurched forward, almost falling over. He was an expert at such tricks, and I could see his look of satisfaction as I shoved open the heavy swing door that led into the big pool and the baths proper. I was struck by the dense silence that enveloped the place. There was not a splash, not a voice, it was deserted, and I was the only customer. As I saw the attendant Jim walking round with a bucket, that this was exactly what the professor and he wanted – perfect peace.

I had never been to the baths without witnessing a row between Jim and some man over the state of the water in the footbath 'I'm not made of bloody hot watter,' was Jim's standard reply to requests for more water. There were two tiled baths known as footbaths for the patrons of the plunge – the 'slipper baths', in which one had a bath alone, cost sixpence, and no one I knew could ever afford that amount. Each footbath was a five-foot square, eighteen inches deep, but the water was seldom filled up more than half that depth. Jim would never use more than one bath, except on Friday evenings and Saturday afternoons, when the crowd of customers demanded it. On my previous visit I had been one of five lining up in the draughty area between the baths to go in, but a man in front would not go in, and insisted on Jim being found – which was always difficult, for he would hide out of the way. At last he came along, 'What's up now?' 'Bloody hell, Jim,' said the man, 'tha doesn't expect us to wash in this bloody lot! It stinks – an' it's cowd.' 'Then I'll warm it up,' said Jim, taking out his big spanner key and turning on the steamy hot tap. 'I only filled it five minutes back.' 'Aye,' said the man, 'an' there's been three miners in, an' one chap from t'bloody brick-kiln – the watter's bloody red as well as black. Howd on a minute,' said the man, 'tha'll have it too hot.' 'It's too cowd one minute – too hot the next,' said Jim, 'no pleasin' some folk.' Jim was an ex-naval man, proof of which was the tattoos displayed on his arms; and he had the pig-like stubbornness of the dull-minded, that can defeat all reason. Jim won every bout because only he had the key to turn on the hot water, and the only patrons that were made welcome were the star swimmers and water-polo players, of whom Jack Grundy, the professor's son was one.

I went up the iron stairs to the benches on the top, where all juniors were sent, as they were not allowed to use the dressing cabins on the side. I undressed, put on the drawers – which held one leg, the other was contained by the tapes at the side. It was clear that the professor had given me a pair of men's trunks, much too large, but I lacked the pluck to take them back. I was rather enjoying the silence of the place, although it was a bit eerie, and I went downstairs to the foot-bath. There was a film of dark scum over it; I put my hand in and found it barely lukewarm. There was nothing for it but put up with it, for one thing was certain, I dare not risk an exchange with Jim, who by chance came along the moment I had just put my foot in.

'Hy,' he called out to me, 'tha can't go in theer, lad – it's not been changed since dinnertime. Tak' thy foot out –' I could hardly believe the fatherly tone that had somehow crept into his deep and grating voice. He took out the heavy plug and I watched as the dirty water ran out; then he used his special key to turn on the hot water, and fairly rinsed the bath round, replaced the plunger, and began to fill it. 'Them drawers are a mile too big for thee,' he said. 'I'll go an' get thee another pair.' And he went off, and returned with a pair that was just right. 'Try it now for warmth, lad,' he said to me. I tried it, and said it was perhaps a bit too hot. 'We'll soon put that right,' said Jim, turning on the cold tap. Then he turned and got a few squares of soap, 'Tha might as well have some fresh soap whilst I'm at it,' he said.

I found myself lying in a large footbath of lovely hot water – the first time in my life I had enjoyed that solitary pleasure. It was unbelievable – the feeling was so heavenly. How is it I could be so lucky on my birthday, I thought, shutting my mind against a lingering lightness around my left eardrum. I then had the best all-over wash I had ever had, although I dodged the large stiff brushes that not only scoured off the skin, but were said to be spreaders of disease. I had just got out to go under the cold shower when the squat figure of a miner came up: 'Howgo Billy lad,' he said. 'By gum, don't say I'm going to have it all to myself.' It was Bob Lee, one of the regulars at the Big Corner at weekends. I felt a particular respect for Bob, because on one occasion I had been playing pontoon with him and others, and he had remarked, 'That was a very *subtle* call of thine, Billy.' 'Subtle' was a word much used in boys' fiction, and although it was a word I had never uttered, I always pronounced it mentally as *sub-tull*; but the instant Bob said 'suttle' I knew that must be correct.

'Clean water an' plenty of soap,' said Bob, '– tha musta bribed old Jim or summat.' He began washing and singing, and when I came from under the shower he called to me: 'I say, Billy – I don't suppose tha'd like to scrub my back, would tha? I'm often here with Tommy Fairclough, an' we scrub one another's.' 'Yes, Bob,' I said, 'I'll scrub it.' I picked up the heavy scrubbing brush, rubbed soap on to it, and when Bob bent forward I started scrubbing. I had seen the backs of my miner cousins, Willie and John, but this back seemed so thick, hard and strong that it almost frightened me to be in contact with it. 'I'm not hurtin' you, am I, Bob?' I said. 'I were just thinkin',' he said, 'tha'll have to put a bit more bant into it to get the dirt out – tha has a touch like a midwife.' And so I laid it on, and as the soapsuds were rinsed away I saw his broad back was marked with numerous scars. 'Good lad thee, Billy,' said Bob. 'Ta very much.'

I went to the plunge, decided not to dive in, since I had once nearly knocked myself out that way. I went down the steps at the side, rested my back against the pipe that ran round, and looked to the far end of the bath, where the diving stands were. 'Will I ever be able to swim that far? I thought, as I pushed off into a float and began to move arms and legs in the breast stroke. By some fluke they seemed to move in perfect unison, and as I had nothing to distract me I kept going. I began to get nervous as I moved into the deep end, but calmed down, and finally, breathless but triumphant, I pulled myself out of the plunge at the far end, feeling like what I imagined Captain Webb must have after swimming the English Channel. No one could call me a liar now if I said I could swim.

CHAPTER 17

Clogs and Shawl

On my way back home, feeling so fresh and clean, and gratified that I could swim a length, I couldn't help but think a prayer of thanks, and the next thing the half-past five mill buzzers began to blow, and soon the streets were alive with men and women going home from work. They might crowd one off the pavement but somehow I enjoyed to be among them, for a more lively or spirited lot than women millworkers in their shawls and clogs could not be found. But then as I took more notice I saw that fewer of the women were now wearing clogs; just as well, they might keep out the rain but they were noisy and hard on the feet. And when I looked closer I could see that fewer were wearing shawls – almost none of the young ones. Could it be true, as our neighbour Mary Ann had said, 'Shawls are goin' out of fashion – an' same as they say, You might as well be out of the world as out of the fashion.'

The Shawl – I could not understand how any sensible woman would choose to wear a coat or what they called 'a costume' in place of a shawl. To me a shawl was the most lovely thing any woman could wear – as soft and as comforting as the sound of the word itself, free of buttons and no ugly square shoulders. Deep within me, almost like some instinct, was a memory of the warm and comforting wool smell of my mother's shawl, for under that old shawl I must have been carried for many an hour; during the illnesses of childhood, when I was restless, she had only to cover me with her shawl, and the ancient smell of wool and of Mother, would calm and console me, so that I would soon slide into a peaceful sleep.

A shawl was the most essential garment in homes such as our own, for whatever else a family lacked, no mother was without her shawl. Visiting my mates, how often had I heard the mother's cry, as she prepared to do battle with some hawker in the street, 'Where's mi purse? – where's mi shawl?' I also remembered an occasion during the early years of the Great War, myself a small boy going home from school, and ambling along in my absentminded fashion, when I suddenly found myself amidst a flock of women, all weavers, pouring out of Kershaw's factory gates. Although it alarmed me at first, it soon seemed as though I was being carried along by this great female army, helped by friendly hands guiding me, and encouraging voices, 'Come on, love – keep goin', or else you might get trod on!'

What a pleasing pageant that swinging sea of shawled women had made compared to the ill-assorted mishmash of figures on the street now – with coats either too big or too small, too tight or too loose, and not a one that looked cosy and comfortable like a shawl did. That was the handy thing about shawls – a shawl would fit any figure, and soften the outline of even the most unshapely woman, and there were quite a few of those around. Another blessing of the shawl was how it always blended itself in with the woman wearing it – you never heard, 'That shawl doesn't suit you.' At the same time a shawl enhanced the personality of the wearer, for you would see a more spirited woman, often with a splendid head of hair, wearing her shawl down off her shoulders, her head held high, a sort of Carmen, that would fascinate any man – even a hard-headed Boltonian. Yet the same woman could use her shawl to play a humble role, when going off to the pawnbroker on a Monday morning, both her face and her bundle hidden by it. And how snug it felt for a small boy when on a cold day his mother took him under her shawl. There was almost no purpose a shawl could not serve, even to being put on the bed on cold nights for extra warmth. True enough, a shawl did not exactly go with The Bob – the hair-style that had become fashionable after the War, much less with the new Eton Crop that was coming in; 'The old order changeth, yielding place to the new.' All I hoped was that it would be a long time before my own dear mother put aside her lovely Irish shawl.

When I got back to Our Street – oh what a comfort those two simple words held for me! – I could sense certain changes that had come over it since 1918. During the War no family had moved from there, except the rare fly-by-night, who had stayed a few weeks, paid no rent, and then done a 'moonlight flitting' on a handcart. I had a fixed impression that once a family settled in Unsworth Street they were there until death did them part, with neighbours and all their kids gathered in homage and curiosity around the front door. A street like ours was our very own, and just as you would never walk down another such street, you didn't want anyone come snooping down yours; if ever it happened folk would call to one another, 'I wonder what yon chap wants!' No woman, of course, would trespass in that fashion. Roads or thoroughfares were open to everyone, but streets were private. In fact, although I lived in our street for years, and walked countless times up and down our own side of the street, I scarcely ever walked the full length of the opposite side. Nor did any of the other tenants – you kept to your own side, and it would have been thought cheeky not to have done so. Charlie Howarth, for instance, a spinner in his twenties, lived in the adjoining Thomas Rostron Street, and invariably walked to the bottom of his own street, and turned into Birkdale Street, on his way to and from work – never once did he think to take what might appear to be a short cut down our street. Yet his sister, Ada, a weaver, going in the same direction, came along our street four times a day; but that was only because she had a workmate living in our street, and went with her. It was all right once folk got used to you – what you didn't want was the casual visitor. In fact, I even felt uncomfortable when driving a top along the other side, and did it only because a good top-and-whipper was expected to make the circuit of the street. Yes, we were an orderly lot.

Now about the street itself – Unsworth Street was made up of two rows of small, back-to-back houses, fifteen in each row, facing across a sloping roadway, the setts worn down to slippery cobbles over the years from the iron-rimmed wheels of various horse-lorries. Along both sides of the street ran a flagged pavement, known as 'the sidesett', and it was the regular weekly practice for each housewife to sweep, mop and stone her 'front'; that is to scour and dress the surface of an area of a yard or two outside her doorstep with a rubbing-stone, and the window-sill as well. It was a custom that rather baffled my own mother – but of course she would try her best to do as was expected of her. Yet I should not claim that on a Friday dinnertime our own front had quite the same gleam as that of certain others on the street; nor would my mother stone beyond what she could reach from inside the front door – unlike some women who would be almost off the pavement, stoning away. It seemed a vain task in Bolton of the day, giving but a brief hour before the many clogged feet marked it, and all the time the atmosphere, heavy with soot from numerous mill chimneys, and more from house fires that were banked up all night, let fall a mass of harsh black particles, making a film of grime on every surface. But as I often heard said, 'At least folk can see it's been done.' The standards of domestic cleanliness and order demanded by what would be regarded as the best Bolton housewife were so taxing that only a woman with some obsessive need to clean and scour could hope to satisfy all of them. Yet there were surprisingly few backsliders, since that meant a loss of face for the mother. Only three in our street of some thirty-two homes decided that they weren't up to it anyway, and gave up the doorstep stoning business altogether – and most neglected such doorsteps looked beside the others.

It seemed to me that once a woman set about her weekly washing in the back kitchen it was as well not to upset her. Even my own mother, the soul of good temper at most times, was not quite herself on washing day, and I was always careful not to interrupt her. But this was nothing compared to women like Mrs Barker, who took washing in. One holiday Monday I was in their backyard with Harold and I got a glimpse of his mother, and she seemed to me almost like a woman gone mad, the way she darted about the little back kitchen, possing, scrubbing and mangling: 'I think we'd best not go through the back kitchen whilst mi mam's like that,' said Harold, and we actually walked right round the street to get into their front kitchen. It was that same evening, about nine o'clock, when Harold and I were playing ludo, the smell of starch and a hot smoothing iron in the air, and his mother was hanging up the last of her ironing on the indoor wooden line, with its four bars across, that I saw her slowly relax. Then she pulled up the line by the rope pulley, looked up at all her spotless washing, the shirts stiff and gleaming, sheets, pillow-cases, covers, all beautifully laundered, that she let out a long sigh, and her normal face took over from what had seemed a possessed one.

CHAPTER 18

Social Distinctions

Every single street in Bolton, and of course each neighbourhood, had its own social placing, perhaps a little higher or lower than a nearby street or neighbourhood. It was the same, it seemed, with every person – the family you came from, their standing, and everything to do with them, all this combined to sum you up for what you were. It was no use trying to put on airs, or wriggle out of what was your social identity, folk wouldn't stand for it, they liked to know where they stood with everybody. Signs of the standing of a street were often subtle, and would only be spotted by a native. For instance, if you saw a notice in a window, '*Stockings knitted and re-footed*', this meant that some spinster or widow knitted stockings, a skill which few mill girls got the chance of acquiring, so that one never saw such a notice in a street like our own. Knitting or needlework or anything beyond darning a sock or sewing on a button was not a part of working-class domestic culture, and signified a more genteel upbringing. Another indication to my keen nose was to get a whiff of washing liquor on the flagged pavement outside a front door – a sign of the house-proud spirit not met in the poorer class streets, or in those streets which were above such a lowly form of cleaning. On the window of almost every good barber's shop was a notice, '*Umbrellas re-covered and repaired*'; most mornings, and all day Monday, if they were short of customers, he had this as a sideline, but not such a barber as Rag Bob, he filled in the spare time by rag-and-bone collecting. Of course, I'm only talking of the less obvious signs, and could make a list of hawkers and others, such as the crumpet man, hot pea and salt seller and others, who kept to certain streets, but I'll tell in some detail of how the fairly respectable tone of our street was betokened by the weekly visit of the Italian organ-grinder – for had we been a better-off street nearby, where they had parlours, they would not have opened their doors, considering it beneath them, or not proper to have any contact with such a one, and poorer streets, while they would have enjoyed his visit, would not have contributed enough to satisfy him.

Every Saturday dinnertime, come hail come sunshine, as it was approaching ten minutes to one, an odd stillness fell upon the street, and it seemed everyone could sense the air of expect-ancy – or at least I always could – as the barrel-organ was seen arriving outside Forrests', pushed by a tall woman and a swarthy man of short build. He would rest a moment to recover his breath and poise, then he would take hold of the organ handle and, his head tilted to one side, rather like a conductor listening to an orchestra, he would begin to play. He liked to start off with a Strauss Waltz, and at once the street would come to life, for he was a superb performer. He would play only one or two tunes before allowing his wife to take over, as he picked up the greasy collecting cap and got going with the more serious business of getting the money in. He rarely exchanged a greeting, much less engaged in talk, as he went from door-to-door. No musician, and there was seldom less than two a day, would dare to knock on a door. Indeed there was one old man who played an instrument said to be a Chinese one-string fiddle, and he did not consider it even fitting that he should appear in the front street, and instead would choose a backgate doorstep, just inside the backstreet, and sit humbly upon it and play away, his body stooped and his upturned cap on the pavement, mutely pleading for the odd coin. Mother would always hand me a penny to give him, and tell me to say 'Thank you', at which he would smile gratefully, and then I would go home, and stand in the back-yard listening, for his rendering of 'The Last Rose of Summer', would bring a lump to my throat. He would often give us a full half an hour at a time, as though for pleasure, and neighbours would stop their weekly washing just to listen to the beautiful strains of his music; in fact the poor chap was so simple as to turn up on a Monday afternoon, when people were not in a giving mood, yet would go away seemingly contented with perhaps two-pence ha'penny from the entire street.

It was said of the organ-grinder that he was the owner of three houses, but this nobody minded, for to give a penny to a man of means seemed more satisfying than to hand one to some bleary-eyed street singer, who would most likely spend it within five minutes on drink. And from the manner in which some hard-up neighbour would put a penny into that cap, receive a patronising nod, and appear well satisfied, it was clear that to make contact with affluence was more pleasurable than with privation.

Another trait that was approved of was his reliability (I keep to the singular, since his docile wife was so overshadowed by him that she was never even mentioned). He would even turn up when the snow lay thick upon the setts; whether this was prompted by an obligation not to let us down or a need to get hold of the pennies, I cannot say, but cups of tea would be handed out to them, and a helpful shove or two given to set them off on their way. He gave an impression of his calling being one of urgency, like that of a doctor on his rounds, and neighbours would talk as though the organ might be loaded with food for a starving populace: 'Hy, just look at t'weather,' they would call across the street to each other, 'an he's half an hour behind time, an' still has all his customers up Daubhill to serve. But I'll bet you he doesn't miss a one!'

Around the end of the Great War, and for a year or so after, it seemed that most families had some money, and he would get a copper at almost every door. In 1921 unemployment set in, there was a three-month miners' strike, and soon there were few pennies to spare. He was not a man to take refusal lightly, and had devised certain tactics, such as knocks, poses and expressions, to exercise moral pressure on defaulters. His usual knock was firm and confident – our street was not posh enough for door-knockers, but he had stout knuckles, and he had the excuse of needing to knock hard so as to be heard above the music – and as he stood there on the pavement outside a front door, waiting for his penny, he gave the impression not of a man in a hurry so much as of one whose time was valuable but who would condescend to wait; certainly not like someone to be kept waiting or a person expecting a favour, but a man requesting payment for his music that was spraying itself merrily on the street air. So powerful was his personality as he stood outside, that it seemed to radiate through our door, and should Mother for some reason decide not to answer it, I had not grit enough to remain in the front kitchen, and would slink into the backyard. He had it timed to about six seconds, and then he would knock louder, and add a further *rap-rap* at the end. Then his face would darken even more, and outside the door he would give a display for the benefit of watching neighbours of a man losing faith in human nature – there was his music for everyone to hear, yet some folk were not paying up.

Often a harassed mother might yell out to one of the children – 'Tell 'im I'm not in.' A small girl – girls seemed to fib easier – would appear at the door, 'Mi mam's not in,' she would say. He would not depart at once but stand there for a moment, fixing his stare on the child, and although not exactly calling her a liar, he made it clear that he was not one to be repeatedly fobbed off by such bogus excuses. He would always remember at which door he had had a refusal, and on the following Saturday would make a more challenging knock. There were few who could remain unperturbed at the sound – the loud music heightened the tension —and to relieve the strain of the waiting seconds it would often happen that some younger member of the family who was working, would give a penny, and it would be handed over, but with ill grace. There had been rumour that with some folk keep ducking their weekly dues it was getting that it was hardly worth his while coming to our street, and that he might have to consider abandoning us, and there were efforts to avoid such a slur on our street, and we were spared the threat.

My mother had given a weekly penny to the Italian organ-grinder, rather as a matter of course, and observing her usual custom of fitting in with the neighbours so far as possible, although neither he nor his music was quite to her taste, which was most rare, for she seemed drawn to every singer or beggar that came to the street. My father would sometimes remark as I came from the door after handing over the penny, 'That man picks up more money in five flamin' minutes, from turnin' the handle of a bloody ould barrel-organ, than a miner half-a-mile under the earth, stripped down to the waist an' workin' away with pick an' spade, an' the sweat pourin' out of him, would earn in an hour. Have the people no sense at all, givin' money to a rogue like that!'

There came a most difficult time when my father was laid off work with the miner's disease of nystagmus, and apart from the money shortage the impulse to give may not have been there. There was an occasion I remember well, for I was caught reading comics in the front kitchen when there came the first knock, and I hurried to Mother for the usual coin, but it seems there was no penny handy, and she nodded to me to ignore him. She must have expected him to take the hint but he didn't, and there came the second very loud knock. Mother walked briskly to the door, opened it wide, faced him, and said in a loud clear voice: 'Nothing for you today, sir!' I caught sight of him, and for once he was taken aback. She stood there smiling, and then he touched his cap – it was a rare gesture on his part – and went off. Whether it was a challenge of nerve or not and the Italian lost his, I cannot be sure, but he never knocked on our door again. He may not have fancied another encounter, or it could have been his way of returning a snub. Mother did not forgive him and would pass him in the street with the coolest of nods, and sometimes not even that. I always regretted that silent feud between Mother and the organ-grinder, because such was so unlike her, and she may have felt that she was somehow failing the street and her neighbours.

I have told at length of the organ-grinder to give some idea of the orderliness of our street, yet over the years critics in reviewing previous volumes of this autobiography, have labelled this humble though well-regulated working-class society as *a slum*. 'A street, alley or court, etc. situated in a crowded district of a town or city and inhabited by people of a low class or by the very poor,' is how the Oxford English Dictionary describes a slum, '…a number of these streets or courts forming a thickly populated neighbourhood or district of a squalid and wretched character.' This misunderstanding has both puzzled and pained me, and I am saddened that an educated class could be so ignorant of the way we lived. 'Poor', 'crowded' and the like I accept, but 'squalid' and 'wretched' I consider to be a slur upon decent and hard-working people.

Indeed, the very antithesis of squalor would be the instant impression one got when opening a front door of one of those homes on a dark winter evening, to feel the sudden warmth from the glowing hearth, the coal fire with its soft murmur, the eye almost dazzled by the gleam of the blackleaded fire-place, the brass fender, the ornamental tongs, and above it all the mantelpiece, with its fringed pelmet, which concealed a lower shelf on which a pipe would be left, and the photographs displayed above, various mementoes, and beside the fender the homemade peg-rug. No home of that class would be without its aspidistra, with long leaves, green and glossy, sometimes streaked with white, and often there would be a canary singing.

Such homes, creating an air of cosiness and domestic felicity, were in a minority, of course, which was understandable with the big families and the poor wages of the day, for few wives, no matter how houseproud, could afford to give such loving attention to the home. The Forrest home was one in the early years, and so was Barker's, and the home of my pal Herbert Howarth. And our own home came close to it on a Saturday evening, with the front kitchen linoleum mopped, the doormat and hearth-rug fresh from a good shaking – Mother could not bring herself to beating even a rug – clean antimacassars on the sofa, the water changed in the goldfish jar, and the bees busy, the coalfire burning brightly, the surround tidy and everything polished. Almost every home had some individual characteristic that set it distinct from others, keeping pigeons, or a few hens, or having a gramophone or a melodeon. We had 'sacred' pictures on the walls, a pair that depicted the guardian angel – always a real if unseen presence in my own mind – guiding a child safely over a chasm, one of the Sacred Heart, another of the Blessed Virgin and one of St Anthony. (Just as some children feel comfort in clutching a teddy bear or other cuddly toy in bed at night, I always closed my eyes and drew on the imagination for my Angel Guardian, the Holy Mother or St Francis.) Alas, there were those very few homes which, through poverty and upbringing, and possibly a weakness of character, in which the mother was incapable of a home with its own particular identity, the only impression being that of poverty.

As for slums, Bolton of the day had many hundreds of streets of poor housing, with poky backyards and privy closets, factors all conducing to slum life, but in fact there were very few actual slum areas. The houseproud English disposition, combined with Lancashire stubbornness, would not allow it. As for our attitude toward ourselves, hardly any of us considered we were poor, let alone that we lived in a slum. 'No matter how badly off you are,' was a saying, 'you'll always find somebody worse off.' The 'poor' were those who had to appeal for help to 'the Guardians' – a terrible disgrace – to be given food vouchers.

I remember standing among a few of my mates at Unsworth Street corner in 1922, on a summer afternoon, when the question arose as to what we should do, go for a walk-up the Middle Brook, or fishing for prickbacks, when Ernie Fairclough said,

'I'll tell you what – let's go an' look at the slums.' Ernie's mother had been telling them that in town, behind Deansgate was Spring Gardens, an actual slum in Bolton. ('Slumming', a pastime of the fashionable London set, was getting an airing in the newspapers at the time.) Five of us set off on the venture – two were in bare feet – and we found the Gardens, a narrow single street, with a gutter flowing down the middle, and two or three ragpickers' handcarts. We were staring with pity at the way some folk had to live, when a tough girl of twelve came up to us and asked, 'What have you come tootin' round here for, eh? What're you skennin' at?' she said to Ernie. 'Go on – sling your hook, when you're told.' Rather sheepishly we retreated: 'I mean I weren't frickened of her,' said Ernie, '– but you never know with a girl like that.'

Back Cannon Street, I must admit, a single row of old houses, small and mean, could be described as slum hovels. The supposed front of the row, at right-angles to our street, were shut up, and never opened; many of the tiny windows were broken, pasted up with cardboard, the landlord refusing to do any repairs. The intended backs of the houses, facing the back of Cannon Street, with tiny backyards, privy closets and middens, about six feet from the door, now served as the fronts, where the tenants gathered and chatted. Yes, this was slum property of the worst kind, yet most of the people were far from being slum-minded. They were a spirited crowd who made the best of what they had. The tone of the street was lower than that of our own, and there was the occasional loud slanging match, when Mrs Heyes would stand at her own front door and hurl abuse toward some neighbour. Nothing like that would have occurred in our street. But there were four homes in Back Cannon Street from which men went to work down pit each day, and I should not have cared to tell one of these, Jud Burns, a handsome miner in his late twenties, that he lived in a slum. Jud, a man of some importance, carried himself with pride as well he might, a miner who never missed a shift at work, and who could catch a half-dozen rabbits in an afternoon with his whippet Squire. As for the Arpinos, who lived at the end house, they were an outstanding family. The eldest son, Louis, a miner, was a noted wrestler; Albert, a school friend of mine, became a champion walker, and his older brother, Ernie, one of my best pals, ran a marathon when he was seventy.

There were certain benefits to be enjoyed from living in a relatively poor neighbourhood such as our own. The streets where the well-paid workers lived, such as spinners and tacklers, were lifeless and uninviting. Such homes usually had a so-called parlour with a piano, used mainly at weekends, and on Sunday evenings accepted as the prerogative of the eldest son or daughter for courting – which often took the form of sitting side-by-side on the couch, reading the same book together, set on the lap of the girl. Instead of looking out at the world, the family ate in the back kitchen, and looked at each other or out on their own backyard. In this way they became withdrawn, and such streets wholly lacked a street life such as our own in which the girls played their games, skipping rope, hop flag, and rounders, and boys gathered at the streetcorner. On summer evenings some fathers would sit on the doorstep, wives on a chair, stool or box, and lively exchanges would take place. Such gregarious exchanges were not considered the thing by more respectable families, such as the Greenhalghs, nor would the very poor, who tended to keep out of sight, but all the girls would of course join in the games.

In the streets where these outdoor activities did not occur – I occasionally visited a home or two of that type – there was a lack of that spirit of neighbourliness so natural to the people of streets like our own. Not only was this seclusion the cause of much loneliness among housewives and the old, but the adolescents, never participating in the lively arguments and leg-pulling of the streetcorner, often went in for toy railways, collecting stamps and the like, and were inclined to a sedate manner I found rather dull. Whether privacy of that kind breeds enmity I cannot say – it certainly does not promote fellow feeling – and I recall an occasion when I went into a florist's to order some flowers for the school, and while I was standing waiting to be served my eye fell upon a card attached to a rather forbidding wreath on the counter. I was always curious about such inscriptions, and I read, 'He suffered long, he suffered well, He'll suffer more, He's now in Hell! With the remotest esteem from his neighbours in View Street.' View Street at the time was one such respectable street, and I could hardly believe what I read, and went over it a few times to make sure. In our street such a thing would have been un-thinkable, for there was always a door-to-door collection for a wreath for anyone that died. What particularly impressed my schoolboy mind was the adjective 'remotest'.

By the way, although our street and the Big Corner presented the most lively scenes of working-class exchanges, I must point out that these did not compare with those of more robust neighbourhoods, where miners' families were in the majority. At the far end of Isabel Street, for instance, there was a large dirt area, with pens and allotments, a long ginnel leading off, and the spectacle on a Sunday afternoon was a most exciting one, with a gathering of dozens of men and youths, pigeon-fanciers waiting for their birds to come in, many of them with their whippets, and gambling of every kind going on, banker, pontoon and other card schools, pitch-and-toss and much else. I was always a bit scared when I came through that way from a walk, but I had school friends in Kelly and Sykes, who would assure me of a safe pass, although so fascinated was I by atmosphere, and the fact that the pair of policemen dare not even venture there, that I was always reluctant to tear myself away from the scene.

CHAPTER 19

Our Street: 1914-1918

The twin row of houses facing our row, that is with the odd numbers – numbers, I had calculated, began at that end of the street nearest the Town Hall, with odd numbers on the left, even numbers on the right – was on the higher level, with double doorsteps in place of our single steps, the rents threepence a week more than our rent of six shillings and sixpence, and this, perhaps with the sense of elevation, allowed those who were that way minded, to fancy themselves being on the posh side. Our backstreet, combining with back Birkdale Street to make a regular backstreet, had the usual line of poky backyards, at the bottom of every pair an outhouse, constructed to provide two privy closets, one at either end, serving two homes. It was an ideal backstreet for boys to enjoy a game of football, mostly with a tin-can for the ball, also for playing swing-round-can, and being out of the way it was often the venue for various gambling games. At the rear of the opposite front row was Barker's skipyard; this meant it was less lively – the one pastime enjoyed there was that of making fires, owing to the abundance of bits of cane from the skipyard; beyond it was the Peace United Methodist Church – today a mosque. As for the front street, the sidesett on our side was always chosen for girls playing hopscotch, or skipping rope or ball games; and as our gutter took all the heavy rain, and the sewer grid often became blocked, it served the younger children for sailing their match-sticks and paper boats, and the sludge that was left was used later for making mud pies, the tops of blacking tins serving as moulds.

The opposite side also had the corner-shop at our end, the bottom end of the street, kept by the plump Miss Lancaster, white-haired and rosy-cheeked, who cooked roast heart for Thursday teatime, and roast pork on Fridays, and opened at halfpast seven every morning of the week except Sunday. On our side, at the top end was the Lads' Corner, set at the gable-end just under the street lamp-post. Over the years this was the usual meeting place for the younger lads from our and nearby streets. Most lads up to the age of sixteen, when perhaps they were mature enough to worm their way in to the Big Corner, could not get out of the house quick enough to join their mates, and many turned up eating the jam butty with which they had left the tea-table; no lad who had shared an egg would fail to leave signs of it round his mouth, to show off with.

I was much drawn to the streetcorner myself, and liked to get there early, so that I had a good seat on the pavement with my back to the wall, and could join in all the talk, the boasting, the telling of dirty tales and the laughter. There were many games played, such as 'Ride or Kench' and 'Jump o'er Back'. A novelty that came every year was that of awaking some wintry morning to a strange silence. No clogged feet heard clacking by, but perhaps the occasional sound of someone kicking off his clods against a wall – the heavy lumps of snow that gathered between the clog-irons. And then to get up and look out and see the first winter snow, with a wonderful white glisten everywhere. It was a joy to run out into it, but within an hour or two the immaculate whiteness would be seen to be darkening from the fall of soot from the air. Boys would soon make a slur – a long slide of icy surface along the sloping sidesett, which was an ideal sport for lads who wore clogs.

My happiest times, however, were on late summer evenings, when all the boys would start singing old songs, such as 'Nelly Dean' and 'Daisy, Daisy…' A lamp-post seemed to set off a streetcorner, and what made ours better than others was that bottles of homemade pop could be bought at Leylands', the end house opposite. Leylands were one of these good Lancashire families, ordinary enough in that they weren't particularly well off, with two children, Wallace and Nora, both rather older than myself. Wallace not only had an impressive name, but I thought him good-looking, with his brown eyes and rosy cheeks; 'Poor lad,' I once overheard a woman say, 'that high colour – it can only mean one thing around here, a bad heart.' And funny enough she was proved right. It was the Lancastrian families such as the Leylands – people who had that assurance of those that belonged – that helped our street to maintain its tone and character. Being the end house, adjoining Thomas Rostron Street, meant that the Leylands not only had an extra bit of backyard in which they ate their meals on sunny days, but they also had a scullery, the only one in the street. It was in the scullery that Aunt Emma brewed the pop, which she sold at three-halfpence a bottle, the cork neatly tied down with string to prevent it blowing out. I envied any lad who had an aunt living with the family – it was like having two mothers to play on. On Friday nights in summer, when the little-piecers had drawn their wages, handed them over to Mam, and been given their spending money of a penny in the shilling, they enjoyed nothing better than sitting on their backsides against the gable-end wall, and sending younger lads fagging for them to the corner-shop for caramel toffee, and then for a bottle of pop to wash it down with; the fag being rewarded with a few grumbles, a piece of toffee and a sup of pop.

Next to the Leylands lived the Forrests, a dignified family, and of some social consequence, for they had had three grown-up lads, and sons had the extra pull over a daughter – you couldn't threaten to bring your daughters if there was some trouble, but three sons carried some clout. Childless couples, usually both working, and there were two such in our street, might be tidy, respectable and well-off, but they did not add much to the life of the street, and seemed to fade away over the years; even those with one child seemed to lack what a street needs to give it character. The very poor, however, no matter how many children they had, hardly counted at all; that is, until those children began work in the mill, and then there would be a slow shift of attitude. The Forrest home was one of the early homes I visited when I was a small boy around 1916, and I was greatly impressed by what I took to be the magnificence of it, compared to the Irish home. They had a splendid glass-backed dresser with a huge mirror, and laid out on the highly polished surface above the drawers there were bronze horses, glass domes, and various other ornaments, and across from it was the iron fireplace, a cheery coal fire, and a brass fender and lovely brass tongs, even the poker looked spotless.

Mr Forrest was a nice but insignificant little man; the lads took after their mother, a big woman, a rather brooding figure in the dark shawl she wore. I was never to see her smile again after the news came that the eldest son, James, had been killed at 'the Front'. The two younger sons – they were also fairly big, Johnny, a brawny fair-haired youth, was a miner, and Joe, the elder, a spinner – were exempt on account of their jobs. There was also a daughter, Edie, a close friend of our May; a bonny girl was Edie, she looked just like a younger Gladys Cooper. The Forrests were Catholics, the only English Catholic family in the street – our family and Walshes across the road were Catholic, but Irish and Catholic were synonymous, and as such ten a penny, but the English Catholic family was not without a certain distinction, as indeed was any family that observed Sunday church-going. Next door to the Forrest family, at number 27, lived the Robertses – and with them the social tone came down a bit. It was not that there was anything wrong with the Robertses – they were a decent little family in whose home I spent many a Saturday evening, when Harry's Mam and Dad had gone out for their weekend drink. We were often joined by their Maggie, aged fifteen, who worked in the mill, and on Saturday evenings always seemed at a loss, often not having had the energy to wash off the mill grime after the Saturday morning work, and then helping her mother mop the flags and other jobs. Mr Roberts, a short man with a big moustache, was a Welshman – the only other man in our street besides my father that voted Labour.

What put the Robertses apart from those families that belonged in the centre and not on the fringe, as it did every other such family, was that they lacked that solidity of folk who were used to having a regular job with a good firm, and a bit of money at one side. Also, Mr Roberts, being Welsh, could never really belong in the way a family of good Lancashire stock might – folk who created the very character to the street, folk you knew where you were with. It was a look and manner that could not be put on, for it needed backing and time to cultivate. It was one I could spot at once, and only a few families in our street enjoyed it. The Robertses were not badly off during the war, with Mr Roberts working at Bessemer's foundry, and Maggie just starting full-time in the mill, but it took a few years to shed that vulnerable look, which comes from rubbing shoulders with poverty.

During the war, and for a year or two after, Bessemer's forge, a huge iron foundry in fact, was working night and day, busy making steel and iron for the war effort and later for the immediate peace-time needs, and as Harry was a good pal of mine I was roped into going along with him when his father was working overtime and needed an extra meal to see him through the evening; many workers depended on a few quick pints of beer for their extra energy, but Mr Roberts's drinking was mainly on Saturday evening. To keep up his strength after his dinner-time sandwiches – few work places had ovens in which meals could be heated up – Mrs Roberts felt that her husband, David, must have something warm and nourishing to eat in the evening, and I could see the fuss and care she went to so that the meal would be tasty but not too heavy on his stomach.

She was a big woman, wore clogs and a rather greasy pinafore, but a new side of her nature came out when she began to put the meal into the basket. 'I wonder would your Dad like an orange,' she would say, '– he left it last time.' 'I think he might miss it, Mam,' Harry would say. 'Aye, I suppose he can always leave it,' she would remark. It seemed odd to see this woman, always so sure of herself, fuss over what might please her husband. The hot dishes and blue can of tea would be carefully packed in a large wicker basket with a lid – of the kind in popular use by pigeon-fanciers to carry their birds – and with warnings to Harry not to 'sheed' a drop, he and I would set off in the early evening. Harry, a year older than myself, was shorter in height, with blue eyes and a smallish head and clean-skinned face, the head mostly close cropped – they owned a pair of hair-clippers, and Mrs Roberts ran them all over his head about once a week, always leaving a cowlick of hair standing up at the front. He went to Emmanuel School, was perhaps below average at school work, and in consequence suffered that keen sense of inferiority most boys did who were treated by teachers as stupid; this attitude, I might add, often being taken up by others, even a parent, to gain advantage.

I recall that first visit to Bessemer's Forge particularly, an autumn evening it was, how we went down Derby Street, the street slowly clearing of mill workers, droves of women in clogs and shawls, but the atmosphere still lively, both of us stopping to look in shop windows, admire cakes and fruit, and carrying the basket in turn. We were good pals, Harry and I, in that each respected, and perhaps envied, certain qualities in the other; myself noting the way when I took the basket from Harry he would often spring along for a few yards, rising up in the air, and with a half-turn clack his clog-irons below some window, causing bright sparks to appear. I envied his litheness, but even more his freedom of voice when he began to yodel. Such a popular sound in Bolton of the day was unknown among the Irish, and at first I could not take to it, but soon I became fascinated by the variations Harry could bring to the *Uraloyeettee*...His own natural boy's soprano, as clear as could be, would take off into falsetto, twirl about, and slip back again, as sweet to the ear and as compelling to the feelings; no Swiss away in the Alps, I felt sure, could have bettered Harry's yodelling, unechoed but not unappreciated, amidst Bolton's smoky streets. His singing spell over he would join me, take his turn with the basket, and when we got chatting he seemed to like to draw the talk toward school subjects, as though eager to learn. He was almost in awe of what I appeared to know; it struck me as odd how the boy who was the less bright mentally, no matter how advanced his other skills, would usually defer to his brainier companion – unless this turned to aggression.

At a junction known as the 'Wooden Blocks' – the name derived from the type of paving, pleasant in dry weather but treacherous in wet – we came to a dark and deserted area, and as we went past Flash Street Special School, for backward children, there was the usual autumn damp fog, and I became more aware of a loud throbbing in the air, measured and slow. 'Bill,' said Harry, 'can tha hear the steam hammer at Bessemer's?' I could – and didn't care for the sound of it. 'Wait till we get nearer,' he went on, 'it'll shake the ground under thy feet.' Next we were in Moor Lane, a depressing stretch, with pawnbrokers, pubs, a newsagent on the corner, some slum houses, a boarded-up stretch, and on the left the big gas works, with three huge gasometers to be seen towering in the grey mist. 'One good thing,' remarked Harry, 'we's't not go short of gas – th'ometers are brimmin' full to the top.' Good old Harry – he always looked on the cheerful side.

Harry now took the dinner basket, assumed a more serious expression, as he led the way to the right toward the foundry. Although I had seen it at a distance, I had never been close, and vaguely expected it to be a factory of sorts, but when I followed Harry I was taken aback to find there was no marking-off line between the inside and outside of the huge works, which was like a vast metal shed, the uneven cinder ground of outside becoming the floor of the forge, the whole place open to wind and partly to rain. My clog slipped into a large puddle of water, and as Harry led us towards the mighty furnace, a wave of heat struck our faces, but my feet felt wet and cold, and with the impact of the thudding steam hammer, rhythmic and earth shaking, I felt it was a foretaste of hell itself.

'Ah, there's mi dad!' exclaimed Harry, '– across yon'. He made a gesture toward a short figure, grimed in grey dust, with white sweat streaks on his face, whom I should never have recognised as Harry's father. Nor did he show any signs of recognition of us, no greeting, no smile, as he accepted the dinner basket with a quiet nod of thanks. How different, I thought, from all the excitement over putting up the meal. He didn't give us the coppers expected on such an encounter, or make a joke, or ask about Harry's mother, but seemed caught in some strange world of work and din. From the fearsome thud of the steam hammer I felt it would be some time before the real David Roberts came out.

'Mi dad never says much at work,' said Harry as we made our way out over the rough ground, '– an' mi mam doesn't like us talkin' or makin' a noise when he gets home – not till he's come round like.' The 'come round' reminded me of when I had fainted over at Mass and been carried out, so that when I came round, as they called it, it was as though I had been in a trance. Being a father in Bolton, and working to bring up a family, seemed a hard and thankless prospect ahead, and secretly I resolved to remain a single man if they would let me, and perhaps try to become a priest or something of the sort. It struck me that taking spiritual care of a flock who subscribed to one's needs every Sunday, listening to their sins and giving them Communion, seemed a much pleasanter way to heaven than toiling down a mine or sweating in an iron foundry.

CHAPTER 20

Our Street: Our Eddie

As I turned the corner of our street on the way home after my swim, I became aware that it was no longer quite what it had once been. The doorsteps and fronts were not as clean as they once were; right enough, it was Thursday, and only on Friday did the weekend round of cleaning begin, just the same it seemed women were not going at it as mad as they used to. Happen rubbing stones would go out of use one day – you never knew the unexpected changes that could occur in this life. It seemed that over the last year I had spotted much that I should not have noticed earlier – the fact was, there had been some crucial shifts in our street, literally so. Leylands' had gone to live in Doncaster. Folk couldn't understand that – fancy, a Bolton family flitting to Yorkshire of all places! Everybody said they'd rue the move – or at least most people did – but a year or two had gone by and they hadn't returned. The worst of it was, the family that moved in by the name of Rice, quite a nice bunch, hadn't the foggiest idea how to make pop, so that the top-end corner lost much of its attraction. I had already switched my loyalty to the Big Corner, in Birkdale Street, where I could listen to the chat of the miners and spinners and others, but had still enjoyed at least one or two weekly visits, listening to the simpler talk, telling a tale or two, but I missed Leylands' pop. A family called Browitt – of which I have more to tell – had emigrated to Australia, and Birtwistles had moved in, a rough sort, who seemed to lack that certain reserve our street expected of its people. The Barkers had emigrated to Canada – I missed my old mates Billy and Harold. (The family was to return two years later, telling of their trials, and swearing that there was no place in the world that could compare to Bolton.)

Such departures, which I took to be desertions, occupied my thoughts considerably, for I simply couldn't understand anyone from our street even wishing to flit to some perhaps larger house in a better-off street nearby, let alone going to

Australia. I knew every flag and nick on the sidesett on each side of the street, no doorstep or window-sill by which I could not have identified the house and family on our side, and many of those on the posh side; even the bricks below – which brick was a soft one, and which a hard, a dodge that helped me win a few games at marbles, when I placed my taw before the poor one and caught out an opponent. I even knew every yard of the riggut – the local name for the gutter – which were the handy spots for damming up the flood after rain, for sailing boats, made of bits of wood and paper. I often registered each family by the smell as I passed by, that of hides from Walker's tannery, where Mr Lever at number 2 worked, and on up with a variety of home smells going all along the street, such as that of spinners, miners, lobscouse, embrocation, leaking gas and poverty. It seemed to me that every living inhabitant of our street, including the cats and dogs, had Unsworth Street writ upon the soul, the same as I had myself.

Things had looked good just after the Great War was over and won, with plenty of work, the workers generally getting better conditions, but once the 1920s came in unemployment came with them, the mills on short time, or worse still, closing down altogether, the workers on 'the Bolsheviks' as the dole was called. I heard people talk about the country being done, 'kaput' as one ex-soldier put it, foreign expressions being in vogue after the war. There was a subtle shift in the social balance of the street around this time, with the bottom end becoming the more respectable. To get to know all that was going on in the street it only needed a mother like my own, in whom neighbours came to confide, and a sister like our May, who loved a right good gossip, and an inquisitive urge to learn more about the peculiarities of human nature, which was myself, together with the sly way I had of pretending to be absorbed in a book – 'Sure that man hears nothing at all,' I had heard my mother assure a whispering neighbour, 'when his head is down into a book.' What book, I used to think, is one-tenth as satisfying as hearing of the extraordinary things people get up to. I came to envy women for the daily chats they exchanged, which made me realise that below the surface there was the most interesting variety of happenings going on, of which no man appeared to have any idea. That is not to say that husbands didn't suspect something, which may have been the reason so many of them disliked seeing women enjoying a little gossip as they swept the pavement outside the front doors. What men did not understand was that wives, confined to home most of the day – at a time when there was neither television nor radio, in homes where there were no newspapers or magazines available, simply had to give rein to their lively intelligence by an exchange of news and views with others of a similar cast of mind. Without that release they became stunted, for husbands had a narrow range of interests, and in general were inclined to be dull compared with their womenfolk.

How the social change in our street had come about was in the following way: the Orrells had come to live next door to us at number 6, and Fred Orrell was the only office worker in the neighbourhood. Then on top of the Leylands' flitting from the other end, the lovely Edie Forrest, only sixteen, was to get in trouble, the father being none other than Wilfred, who lived just across the street to them. He was a tall soft-spoken man, with fancy spectacles, married to a lame woman, Amy, who, unwisely, had asked Edie to take his evening meal to the place where he was a firebeater – and the two of them being alone, that was how it all began. This was something my mother would hardly bring herself to listen to, so shocked was she, and sorry for the poor girl and the Forrest family.

The next thing I overhear Mrs Orrell whispering to Mother, 'Have you not heard? You'll never guess – they're expecting a visitor at number 4 – would you believe it!' I certainly would not have! It appeared that Florence, the daughter of the posh widow with the high voice, Mrs Challoner, an avid reader of library books, had somehow become pregnant by none other than Albert Heyes, the lodger, a collier in his late twenties, undersized and with a squint, nothing to look at and not a word for the cat. No one could believe it – least of all, it seemed, Mrs Challoner, who denied it vehemently up to and even beyond the wedding, right until the birth of what she insisted was a premature baby, weighing a good nine pounds. What a street, our street, for nourishing gossip!

I could go on endlessly about those families I knew so well during my boyhood, for had I been drawn to the writing of fiction I'd say there was a good novel brewing inside almost every front door in the street. Fiction – to take a leap forward some twenty years – which over many years had given me so much pleasure, lost its pull and vitality once I started setting down in detail so much that I had seen, heard and that had happened to me. On many a morning in that splendid Reading Room of the British Museum, I would turn from a story I was writing for the magazine *Lilliput*, to tell about some character or family from that street in Bolton I grew up in – later to put it aside among the millions of words that lie unread in dusty tin trunks in the loft of our present home. And truth to tell, no matter where I was to live in later life, no place was to make its mark on me anything like so deep and lasting as that of Unsworth Street, nor to turn up so often in my dreams some sixty years later. I had the notion that it had been ordained that our family should not only settle in Bolton – to see that name in print excited me – but in that very house, so much was it part of me.

Walking back home from school, or from having been on a long walk, perhaps as far as Barrow Bridge, or beyond to the moors, I always felt myself to be in a strange world until I turned the corner of our street, felt the familiar sidesett and cobblestones under my feet. No harm could befall me now, I was home. On one occasion I had paid a visit to a school pal, Eddie Guildford, who lived at 57 Rosamund Street up Daubhill. I pitied him and all his mates – no proper Corner or Corner-lamppost, no atmosphere of warmth and welcome, and certainly there had never been a door you could knock on with three-halfpence and get a delicious bottle of pop. As for fish-and-chip shops, it was agreed by all who knew anything about such matters that there wasn't one in the land that could compare with Bibby's, at the corner of Birkdale Street and Edward Street, later to become Booths', but the standard of excellence maintained. Some of the best meat pies, pork pies, and pasties could be bought at Ditchfields, a stone's throw away in Derby Street.

Although at times as I grew older I might find myself dis-enchanted with my way of life, especially so when I reached the age of fourteen and longed to join the Royal Navy and get away to sea, yet in my heart I was always to feel attached to our street – at times perhaps less happily than at others. And it seemed the same may have been true for the rest of the family, for Mother and Father were to stay there until death called them, God rest their souls. May was to marry and live a quarter of a mile away, and always a daily visit, and Edward, after spending some years in America and marrying there, returned on holiday with his wife, Catherine and son, Eddie in 1932, together with her uncle. She was a Bostonian, a Juno-esque figure in her dark dress, a good two inches taller than Edward; Mr Wood from next door was heard to declare that she was the most strapping woman he had seen in his life or was ever likely to see, and I actually put the penny in the slot when she stood on the scales outside Woolworths, to send the disc spinning round to 18 stone 4lbs, stamped on the ticket that came out.

Every morning of their visit, my father said, there had to be a new bottle of tomato sauce for the breakfast of bacon, eggs and sausages. At the end of the fortnight's stay, on a Thursday morning, they all departed for what was then the port of Kingstown in Ireland, from where they would sail on the Friday to America. This was much to the relief of my mother and father, I need hardly add, who were by this time comfortably on their own, no doubt relieved to be rid of all of us, but particularly Edward, whom my father could not stand, for he was too much like himself. On Saturday morning, however, he got a shock as he was reading the newspaper to see the front door open and in walk Edward, alone with his suitcase. His story was that he had actually been aboard the liner for America, but just as it was about to sail, he said that something made him change his mind, and he hurried off the boat as they were lifting the gang-plank. That was the last his wife and son were to see of him. My father always insisted that he must have had it all planned beforehand. 'The bloody schemer, knowin' well that they'd have no chance to get off themselves.'

What gave support to my father's belief was the fact that Edward had left certain articles of dress behind in the bedroom. Anyway, the back bedroom was no longer occupied and he settled in there as of old. Of course it was the last thing my father wanted, and not only did it create a difficult situation in the home for my mother, but his cooking and laundry gave her much more work; the Irish way, however, precluded their telling Edward to find another place. So once back he stayed on; Mother was to die twenty years later, and my father go on for another few years, living cheek by jowl with Edward. He remained in that house at 8 Unsworth Street for a half-century after his return, until the eve of the demolition men coming to raze the old street to the ground. Had it been an ancestral home, one could hardly have been more attached to it than that.

Should I in this memoir at times appear critical of Edward, I must point out that it was those very quirks and foibles which in memory endear him to me. Obstinacy of character, combined with a natural egoism – 'To thine own self be true' was our Eddie's rule – may not be easy to live with, but can often be amusing to recall. When the old home had to be vacated in 1976, and the street demolished, he was seventy, and in good health after retiring from his last job as an insurance agent, in which he cycled daily; also, for some years he had been a keen golfer. He was delighted with the comforts of the new council flat he had been allotted; and I was fortunate enough to ensure he would have no financial worries. To cap it all he met Joyce, an attractive woman almost twenty years younger than himself, who was devoted, loyal and selfless. He ate every evening meal at her table, and also those of the weekend. He told me he was confident of reaching the age of a hundred, and could not understand my saying that I hoped I had no such misfortune.

Alas, it was not be so, for in his late seventies he fell victim to Parkinson's Disease, as well as arthritis and an enlarged hernia. These were of course perfectly treatable in one who had taken such good care of himself, were it not that he distrusted medical practice generally, refused to take the prescribed medication, nor would he consider wearing a truss or having an operation. A priest from his old church of SS Peter and Paul brought him regular Communion. He would allow no one to have a key of his flat, and on one occasion when the warden couldn't get in the police had to be called, to find Edward lying helpless on the floor at the head of the stairs. I constantly appealed to him on the telephone to follow medical advice, and Joyce and others tried to persuade him, but he was set on going his own way.

One Wednesday afternoon I was telephoned by a health visitor from Bolton, who said that his doctor believed that Edward was no longer safe living alone, and that he should go to the Rehabilitation Ward of a hospital for a period of treatment, but this he had refused to do. In which case, she explained, the only alternative was to get a magistrate's order for him to be taken there, which they were reluctant to do, and would I talk to him. I was shocked at the possibility of a member of our family, one that in all its years had avoided offending against the law, should now have such an order imposed on him. After having had a heart attack myself, I did not feel up to going across to Bolton, not that I could have done much. He responded to my telephone pleas, and those of Joyce who was with him, repeating, 'I'll go next Monday – but not before!'

On the Friday morning, I learnt, the nurse had called to bathe and prepare him, Joyce also went round, the health visitor called with an order for a three weeks' stay. Finally, the ambulance came and Edward, sitting upright in a chair, defiant and tight-lipped, was taken off. Joyce visited him on the Friday and Saturday, and telephoned me to say that he was not taking any food. It was on Sunday afternoon, only two days after his going in, that a policeman called at our home to inform me of the death of my brother Edward in hospital in Bolton. I was shocked at the news, so vigorous had he sounded only three days before on the telephone. I then rang Joyce, under the impression that she already knew, but in fact I caught her just as she was setting off to visit him – apparently Edward had not put her name down as next-of-kin, and the hospital had been unable to contact her. She simply could not believe it, became distraught at the news, and broke into tears. Only now in my own old age do I understand the poignancy of that onetime supplication for a happy death – an entreaty in the very nature of our passing almost impossible to grant.

CHAPTER 21

The Browitt Family

Browitt was the name of the family that lived at number 25, next door to the Robertses, a lively family of four boys, all with pale faces and dark brown eyes. Two incidents about the Browitts stick clearly in my mind. One son was called Noah, a year or two older than myself, with a haggard face, and hair so thin around the temples that he looked as though he was going bald. Added to this he was known to be 'delicate' or, as some said, 'consumptive' – but for all that Noah could be a tough fighter. He not only enjoyed the privilege of staying away from school as much as he liked, but at the same time he could ignore the 'school-board'.

One day when I was away from school because of a sore throat, I met Noah and he started chatting to me at the street corner. Few things I enjoyed more than a right good talk – and if my mate was more interesting than I was, or had more need to get something off his chest, I was a responsive listener, nodding my head in agreement, never interrupting, and now and again during a pause, using the Bolton 'Gerroff!...' and tactfully asking a question if some matter was unclear. Being off school seemed to have sharpened Noah's wits, so that he knew everything that was going on in the street, what troubles each family had, down to what time each hawker or street-singer was due to arrive. It happened that on this day I had twopence in my pocket, not a sum to be sneezed at, and feeling in Noah's debt for all that talk, and not wishing to appear that I had brought nothing to the scene, I took my coppers out, one penny and two ha'pennies, and said I'd go and buy a penn'orth of toffee at the corner-shop.

I had spotted a quick gleam of interest in Noah's eyes as he saw the money, but he surprised me by saying, 'Don't, Billy, don't!' and putting a matey hand on my shoulder, 'tha won't get full weight,' he said, 'an' on top of that most of the toshy there is not fresh.' This concerned attitude of Noah's took me by surprise, since it was almost unheard of for a boy without money not to attempt to persuade a mate to spend any money he had. There's more to Noah, I decided, than the mere name. Then after a pause he turned and said, 'Tha knows Hodgson's toffee shop on Derby Street – I'm well in there, dusta see, with bein' off school – now don't tell anybody, but I can get thee a full quarter – that's four ounces, not a miserable ounce – of caramel toffee or treacle toffee for tuppence. That's if I go in on mi own an' old Daddy Hodgson thinks it's for me.'

To spend twopence all at one go went against custom, in fact the ritual of spending included a long look in the shop-window first before handing over even a penny, but the anticipatory sense of having a bag of caramel toffee weighing four ounces prompted a quick response: 'All right, Noah,' I said, putting the three coins in my palm, 'I'll come with you to Hodgson's.' 'Good,' said Noah, and off we went. Then he stopped suddenly: 'Hold on a tick,' he said, 'I don't want owd Hodgson to see thee. Same as I say, he does it as a favour to me, bein' off schoo' an' that. 'Ere, I know what,' he went on, smothering my intention of saying I would wait round the corner, 'give me thy tuppence, Billy – an' thee stay here – an' I guarantee I'll be back under five minutes. Now what dusta want – caramel or treacle toffee?' 'Will he let you have half an' half?' I said, poised with the twopence in my hand, which by now had assumed a hefty sum. ''Course he will,' said Noah, 'I'll talk him into it.' And with that he took the coins in his palm, waved to me, and set off hurriedly to Derby Street.

I stood there at the corner, not entirely at peace with myself, but seeking comfort in the large bag of toffee I imagined I would get when Noah came back. The minutes went by, a quarter of an hour, a half an hour and, yet I couldn't bring myself to believe that a boy who lived in the same street as myself, who was a mate, would go off with twopence of mine and be so barefaced as not to return. But finally with no sight of Noah, I had to accept that it must be so. The odd thing was, I didn't go round to his home and tell his mother, which would have been the usual response, I told no one, being more ashamed of having been fooled than I was of getting my own back on Noah. Noah kept out of my sight for a day or two, and it was the weekend before I saw him, and plucked up enough guts to accost him over the matter. 'Wot tuppence! wot arta' talkin' about? Oh that, well, to be honest, some lads came after me an' made me hand it over. But don't thee worry,

I'll see tha gets it back one day. Truth an' honest,' and he made the sign of a cut across his throat if he failed to.

The second incident had mainly to do with Noah's mother, when she and his father called in to our home late one Saturday evening in 1917. It must have been the first Saturday of Bolton Holiday Week, a somewhat festive occasion, for although no one would be going away from our street, there was a holiday feeling in the air. Every Saturday evening there was a gathering at our house when my mother's brother, Uncle William, her nephews Pauric and John Kirrane, together with Willie who lodged with us, got together to talk about Ireland, and exchange any news that may have come in letters – talk not to my father's taste, since he had no close relatives, and had served his time as a shopboy in Ballyhaunis. During all this the big jugs would be on the go to Nancy's off-licence, someone slipping out the back-gate, usually myself with him, to get the jugs filled up with beer, and a few bottles also bought.

The 1916 Rising was more than a year behind us, the Great War seemed to be turning in the Allies' favour, there was any amount of work for coalminers, which they all were, and generally there was a more optimistic mood around. Out of the respect Uncle William insisted we show toward our English hosts during the War, there was rarely any singing, or if so it had to be muted, but my father liked a song when he had drunk plenty. On this occasion he was singing his favourite patriotic song, 'Who fears to speak of Ninety-Eight'. The emotion rises in his voice, 'Who blushes at the name? When cowards mock the patriots fate, Who hangs his head with shame?' I am always moved by the song, but I can see it is hard going for him to inspire the Kirranes or Uncle William with a fervour the like of his own, for although decent and honourable enough, their world has been the more insular one of the peasant.

We have the Irish habit of leaving the door ajar, and suddenly it is pushed open and Mrs Browitt looks in, calling out as she does, 'Can anybody join in?' The singing stops, of course, and the Kirrane brothers rise to their feet to greet the visitor. She is a vivid personality, a rather slight woman with lively brown eyes, who calls to her quiet husband to come in, and goes round shaking hands with the men, and so obviously does she enjoy doing so as she looks up at the handsome Kirrane brothers, that it seems that with any encouragement she would be hugging and kissing. They are shy, but polite and cordial, and she gets a loud greeting from my father, who it seems does not mind his song being interrupted by an attractive woman.

The drink appears to have run out, as it is around halfpast ten, but my wily father has a habit of smuggling a pint bottle each of beer and stout to one side and now, perhaps to impress Mrs Browitt, who was getting surprising response from him, brings these out from the back of the built-in cupboard, although Mother has already put the kettle on for tea-making. My Uncle William, intensely fond of children, and especially so of young James, born in our Bolton home in 1915, at the end of our first year in England, insists that on Saturdays we should not be packed off to bed in the English manner, but sit around as children do in the Irish home, as long and as late as we wish. My sister May has already made off quietly to bed, and so has Eddie, who is not taken up by the Irish scene at all, but I am still up, and would stay up until I have almost to fight it out with my father, so much am I drawn to company and chat, which I can never get enough of. James, eighteen months old and weaned, has become fretful, being in need of sleep, and Mother has taken him from Uncle William so as to placate him, but he still grizzles. I know what he wants to settle him off to sleep as I watch his hand groping around her bosom – and so does she of course; James will go off to sleep in her arms so long as he can have a hand resting inside her blouse, but modesty does not allow that Mother give him this comfort with the present company around.

His cries get louder, so she rises to her feet with James in her arms, to take him off upstairs, when suddenly Mrs Browitt intercepts her with a swift movement: 'I know what the child wants,' she calls out with a laugh, taking him from mother and crooking him in her left arm, 'he wants some titty. An' I've still some milk left from my last one.' And without more ado she has the front of her blouse unbuttoned and open, and she fishes out a large, white breast. I am beside her, and it startles me to see such a small woman pull out such a big breast, so white and bouncy: 'Here y'are, luv, –' she says to James, pressing the nipple to his face, 'suck away at that.' And she turns to the company, displaying her bosom as she attempts to get James to put his mouth to the nipple.

Of course I had been around when Mother would breast-feed young James over a year or so – for any mother not to do so carried shameful reproach among the Irish – but she always turned her back on us children, and fed the babe with such discretion that none of the breast was ever visible. From Mrs Browitt's flaunting exposure – she is clearly proud of what is on show – I can hardly avert my gaze, and indeed it seems to be so with my father, for when I half-turn I spot him. Irish good manners, however, forbid any show of disapproval to a guest, although the Kirranes are stunned to an embarrassed silence. But for Uncle William it is a bit too much; he stands up, and putting on an air of the coolest politeness, turns to Pauric and John, 'Come on, gents,' he says, and addressing Mr Browitt but avoiding looking in the direction of the wife, he goes on, '– you must pardon us, but we'll have to hurry to catch the train.'

At that moment the baby James, who has been caught off guard, and silenced by the unexpected, finds his voice, and lets out a bawl of distaste seemingly of both Mrs Browitt and her breast. With that he almost flings himself to Mother, who comforts his sobs. The gathering breaks up, with Mr Browitt hauling off his wife, who is reluctant to go. With the Browitts gone, the atmosphere changes at once, and Mother whispers to Uncle William to stay the night. I should have liked to stay up, but my father calls out, 'Willyeen! will you go up to bed – or on the verth of my oath I'll –' I feel I'd better not try him out further and I go round and kiss everyone goodnight and then off upstairs to bed.

Later I am lying awake in bed from all the excitement, Ed and myself at one end, and May at the other, both of them asleep, and I listen intently to Mother upbraiding my father for encouraging the woman, and he saying how he could not speak a hard word to a guest under the roof, and the poor woman couldn't be blamed for hadn't she drink taken. But strange for one so long-suffering in other respects, it was clear that Mother will not forgive such impropriety as she may have thought my father guilty of, and the whispered argument going on as I fall asleep.

CHAPTER 22

The Sound and the Seedy

There was one family which lived at number 9 at our end of the street, that was becoming more sound and respectable all the time, until it became a puzzle to some people why they should stay on – although not to me – since they were so clearly a cut above the rest of us. I speak of the Greenhalgh family, that of the onetime Scots Highlander, Frederick Augustus, who had long returned to civilian life as a commercial traveller.

'Yerra, amn't I after bein' in the Ram's Head there, in among the men in the taproom,' I once heard my father say, 'an' who should come in the door but your man Greenhalgh, in the same brown raincoat he wears winter an' summer. What does he do but stand himself up at the bar among the toffs, where they pay extra for every drink, an' what do I hear him call out but "A large John Haig", that's a Scotch whisky, a double, an' I see him put a thimbleful of water into it, pick it up, an' shlug it off! He never speaks to a soul, won't pass the time of day, or even give one a nod, for fear he might get himself in a round. I thought he must be in a hurry, but then don't I hear him call out again, "A large John Haig!" As God's my judge, while I was drinkin' my one glass of beer I saw that man down his two double whiskies!' In spite of himself my father couldn't keep out of his voice the note of admiration he always had for a drinking man: 'An' the next thing he wipes his jib with a big handkerchief, an' goes off like one who had never tasted drink in his life.' My father sighed, 'To think that a bloody ould commercial traveller, or whatever he is, can drink two double whiskies, while a poor miner the likes of myself has the one glass of beer – that's the state of the world today.'

Mrs Greenhalgh was a tall woman of lean build, with greying hair and a swarthy complexion; it seemed odd that in those days not one of her daughters took on her own humble Christian names of Sarah Ellen. She went about her work in a determined manner, avoided chatting in the way most women did with a neighbour – it had been whispered that 'The Mester' didn't approve of it. The eldest son, Fred, into his twenties, was a spinner, and had the same manner as his mother. Next to him came the eldest daughter, Doris, who had been courted by Wilf Edge, the son of the widow, Betsy Edge, who lived three doors away. On Sunday evenings, when it was darkening around halfpast-eight, the couple would stand in the accepted way of engaged couples of the time, cuddling away on Greenhalgh's doorstep across from our own. One evening after we had all kissed my father goodnight as he was going off to pit – 'I'd have to go tonight if I was dead,' he used to say, 'so that the road is clear for the datallers coming on in the mornin',' – he opened the front door, suddenly closed it again, and then turned and went out the back way. I asked my mother what was the reason for the sudden change: 'Musha the sight of those two on the doorstep,' she said, 'so embarrasses the poor man, that he hasn't the courage to cross the street.'

Edward, a miner, came next to Doris, then Beatty, a plump, good-humoured dark girl, Phyllis next, then the youngest, Hilda. The question that puzzled me – it was not one that was aired, since such were private matters not to be pried into – was how such a large family contrived their sleeping and toilet arrangements, in a house that had two small bedrooms, a single cold-water tap in the back kitchen, and an outdoor privy closet. Yet a cleaner and more presentable family than the Greenhalghs could not be met anywhere. After a lifetime's work in the coalmine, Edward, unmarried, set himself up in the corner-shop, and Hilda was to marry a man called Greenhalgh, and settle there until the demolition. This may give some idea of the affection our street inspired in us inhabitants.

There was, I have to admit a seamy side also to our street life. There was one home in which a miner in his early fifties had married a widow with a daughter of twenty and it was whispered of his having sexual relations with his step-daughter. A more unhappy situation was in a family of two brothers and a sister, all in their thirties, the home ruled by the eldest, Bill, a violent man of whom the other two went in fear. One evening the small son of the unmarried sister – rumours of incest went around – suffered a grave injury from a fork flung at him by Bill. Everything was known among the neighbours, to whom the sister would confide – but there was no prosecution. People avoided having anything at all to do with the police, a man in a police uniform spelled trouble, and as Bill was the wage-earner they may have felt it would only make matters worse if he were sent to prison. The younger brother, known as Happy Albert, was suspected of being a child molester – for which offence he was later to serve a term of imprisonment. This family, I should point out, whilst capable of doing menial tasks in cotton mill and warehouse, were somewhat feeble-minded, and such people often suffered from a psychosis that went unrecognised until the person was taken off in the 'yellow van' – a sight that drew onlookers, and one I witnessed more than once.

Now I must return to say a necessary word about Betsy Edge, always a good friend of mine as a boy, since she, and those like her, personified a trait that I much admired. Betsy was one of those sturdy Lancashire women who, no matter what happened around or to her, stayed just the same. She wore the same old-fashioned dark-blue skirt, always clogs and shawl during the week, and shoes and a coat on Sundays. And even though her son Wilf became a petty officer in the Royal Navy, and later a policeman, she still retained her broad and homely Lancashire accent. For those who may imagine that this was merely a form of dialect, I should like to point out that it was much more, for it indicated a certain singularity of character, a north-country disposition to which it gave expression, and this meant that in exchanges with someone who spoke the same idiom, you knew where you stood; you may not think alike, but you usually felt alike.

In Peace Street, for instance, a better class of houses than our own, with parlours, but allowing for Barker's skipyard in between could be said to be back-to-back with Betsy Edge, lived the Halliwell family. This was a fairly prosperous home. Fred Halliwell, the father, was an overlooker at Kershaw's factory, the sons and daughters working, and I was to become matey with young Fred, who was my own age. Mr Halliwell was reputed to be one of the finest cornetists in the North of England, and to my ear he played so lightly that if he was in their parlour and I was with young Fred in the kitchen, it sounded to me just like a mellow violin. In his own way, Fred Halliwell typified that Lancashire individuality in a more expansive way than Betsy Edge. On Saturday evenings, when he was dressed up, perfectly groomed and shaved, his skin glowing, about to take Mrs Halliwell, a stout woman, for a drink to the nearby Ram's Head, he looked the most impressive figure, a more handsome Lord Derby. In fact he might be said to have looked even grander than the peer, for Fred sported an *imperial*; and for those unacquainted with such, since they are far from common, Fred Halliwell's imperial was a small, pointed beard, just below his lower lip; the name said to come from Emperor Napoleon III, and it suited the man to perfection.

Now to come to the point, Fred Halliwell, despite his being an overlooker, and with a distinctive flair for the stylish touch, always spoke the broadest Lancashire dialect. To hear the rich cadences, the rolling vowels and stressed consonants articulated by a man that had been born and reared to them, was a joy to my ears. And yet Fred and his sort, even though they retained the common touch, would not permit managers and the like to attempt any familiarity by lording it over them with a mixture of fancy talk and the odd 'thee' and 'tha' slipped in: 'Don't thee "tha" me,' he would tell them, 'thee "tha" them as "tha's" thee!'

CHAPTER 23

Adolescence and Antipathy

That the dictum 'Cleanliness is next to Godliness' should come from John Wesley, the founder of Methodism, seems fitting in that this religion above all made its mark on the prevailing moral tone of Bolton and its people. Even though only a small minority were active members, Methodists were articulate and socially active, their teaching accepted if not followed, except by the few. Above all, there seemed to be an affinity between its simplicity and the Lancashire character which neither Catholicism nor Anglicanism could quite meet. Although my own heart was imbued with the Catholic faith beyond all chance of straying away, I could not fail to recognise in Methodist teaching a required stringency with regard to daily life which Catholicism wholly lacked.

The Methodists' disciplined and sober manner of living appealed to me, in that though the weekends might be less celebratory, it ensured that weekdays had fewer difficulties and problems. Their aims were less concentrated on the future, and more practical in that they set out to improve conditions in the present life, whereas the Catholic message from the pulpit was the good time awaiting us when we were dead – if only we stuck rigorously to the teaching of the Faith. The hope this set up may have been comforting at times, but seemed to wear thin by each Monday, let alone Thursday.

There was a move on at the time by a section of the Methodist church to get young people to attend meetings, not services, in schools; and on wet winter evenings this gave the opportunity for a few mates to keep together under a roof, and at the same time enjoy a free cup of cocoa. Although I was not supposed to go to such gatherings, I went along a few times, and found the atmosphere quite novel. A regular speaker was Charles Brady, a short, hunchbacked man, known locally as 'Humpy Charlie', who kept a newsagent and tobacconist's shop in Derby Street. His appeals to avoid the evils of drink rang as half-baked to me, in that he clearly knew much less about them at first-hand than I did; that my own father, a knowing man in some respects, should choose to spend his hard-earned money on beer every Saturday evening, to wake up with a bad head and a bad temper every Sunday morning, struck me as yet another of those daft habits of most men, such as smoking, that was impervious to reason.

What caught my interest most from those meetings were the booklets they handed out to boys only, inviting them to join the 'Alliance of Honour', which involved promising faithfully never to indulge in the vicious habit of 'self-abuse'. This was a subject avoided by our own priests from the pulpit and understandably so, but on rare occasions was hinted at during confession, and was regarded by the Church as a mortal sin. Teasing accusations were common among the older youths at the Big Corner – there was an almost inescapable sense of guilt about it among most boys – and there was a variety of low colloquialisms, from 'pulling your wire' to 'bashing your bishop', and others less euphemistic.

I hid the booklet in my drawer, and in secret studied it over and over again. Among other things it told of how the body supposedly took four ounces of blood to make one ounce of precious semen, and that 'self-pollution' not only caused debility and general weakness, but could lead to blindness and idiocy. This was a fairly common opinion of the day, and it was many years before medical science came to the conclusion that masturbation – a word I never heard used – was a relatively harmless impulse, one which could alleviate adolescent sexual tension. However, since my secret ambition was to develop into a Eugene Sandow, whose handsome face and figure was displayed on various boxes in the window of Skinny Nancy's sports' shop, the Alliance of Honour warning gave me a scare, and made such a deep impression on me that a natural avoidance of anything that smacked of being 'sinful' became something of a phobia. Although this intensified a certain inherent nerviness, it simplified my sexual inclinations, in that all auto-erotic impulses became repugnant, and in time ceased altogether. In their place it seemed there came a longing for the company of some special girl or woman, with an idealising of such a relationship, so that I was constantly in love with one virginal girl or other that I might see as fitting the role. As I got older this puritanical streak kept me perpetually sensitive to the sexual appeal of women; good looks as such did not impress me so much as the female self. The voice, laugh, smell, smile – I longed to become close to and hold to me some mysterious soft and rounded figure of a woman or older girl.

Distorted sexual attitudes may have had something to do with the antipathy that seemed innate between the sexes at the time in Bolton – and possibly all the industrial North. (Curiously enough it did not exist among the Irish, where male supremacy was accepted as a fact of life.) In Bolton families it was an understood thing, from childhood onward, that girls did not like boys, particularly their own brothers – possibly this aversion proved a handy inhibition in such crowded homes. All boys were expected to scorn girls and any activity in which girls might share: 'Go on, get off with thee,' a boy who was being a mardy or difficult would be told, 'an' go an' play with the wenches.' Wenches were avoided by most boys from the age of five, their paths in life seen as contrary and mostly in conflict. This resulted in there being almost no shared interests among adults, and it was rare to see a married couple go out together, except on Saturday evening, when a young husband might be seen grudgingly taking his wife into town, often for a stroll round the market hall or possibly a visit to the first-house pictures, while clearly longing to get back to his mates. Once they had children even that gesture ceased and the wife was tied to the home.

When the family had grown up, a forceful wife of some manual worker might insist on her right to be taken out – on the other hand many wives said that they were only too glad to get him out of the house – but going out together often meant that the husband saw his wife to the room at the back of the pub, usually the kitchen reserved for women, whilst he stayed with his mates in the taproom, paying for the occasional bottle of stout to be sent in to her; this, by the way, often suited both of them so far as company went. Most husbands found it as well not to upset their wives at weekends, since Sunday morning was the only occasion they could enjoy a lie-in together, or Sunday afternoon go to bed for an hour after midday dinner.

A satisfactory sexual harmony between husband and wife was most difficult to achieve in the cirumstances of that place and time – I should imagine it is not easy in any social group – when parents often had to share the bedroom with children, and no home of our kind had a bathroom. Nor did conformity lead to a normal understanding between the sexes, in a society where it was considered improper for male and female to even enjoy swimming together – they had to be segregated and go on different stipulated days. I would surmise from what I heard later in life that not one husband in a hundred had ever seen his wife naked, or she him – he would have been considered extremely odd even to wish to do so, and not altogether a nice man. Not that either of them was likely to have missed much, for with the undernourishment, going to work in the mill at the age of twelve, and the endemic children's bone disease of rickets, brought about by a lack of vitamin D, physically attractive adults were rare exceptions.

As for sexual pleasure, what many a man most enjoyed far more at the end of a day's work, was to rest into the rocking-chair after tea, clogs off, feet up on another chair, and snooze for a half-hour, happily remote from life and its problems. At bedtime the one thought on the mind of most wives was to rest her weary limbs. Even at the best of times the sexual act was more one of relief of tension rather than of pleasure, for in the absence of modern contraceptive methods it had to be coitus interruptus withdrawal, known locally as 'getting off at Lostock', a railway station before the main one. This method was known to be unreliable, and so for both partners the sexual act became fraught with anxiety, and for the woman something to be endured rather than enjoyed. All in all, sex could hardly fail but to have a bad name in Bolton of the day, since it was the cause of so much misery, and gave but a brief and limited enjoyment. It served as the subject of endless jokes, and one that summed up a not uncommon attitude was of the young woman who finally yielded to the advances of her boyfriend, and at the climax remarked, 'Now a fat lot of good that can 'ave done you, I must say!' And I rather think that standing up against a privy-closet wall in a backstreet, where most of such hanky-panky went on, he would have been inclined to agree. Had it been possible, I believe that many women would have had sex done away with altogether, for what little pleasure they got out of the exchanges, and the worry associated with it.

Much female antagonism toward men in general could hardly fail to be aroused by an absurd assumption of superiority on the part of the males even to the government denying women the right to vote until 1918, and then only when they had reached the age of thirty. Any time I happened to be bemoaning my own lot in life I could always console myself by imagining what it would have been had I been born a girl instead of a boy – not a life to be envied. Although it was obvious that every home revolved around the mother – 'Where's mi Mam?' was the first question on the lips of anyone who came home to find she was not on hand – yet few mothers were openly accorded that special respect and affection that was their due. They might be indispensable, and indeed much loved, but the Lancastrian is not one to display tender feelings, let alone flatter or even praise.

All mention I have made of these minor marital frictions, however, must be understood as being of trivial account compared with that deep dependence, loyalty and unspoken love that years of struggling along together through hard times created between husband and wife. Although few widows of the day would consider marrying again, women could somehow bear up after the loss of a husband, but it was truly pitiful to see the helpless state most men were reduced to once they lacked the guiding presence of a wife. I have a memory of making a visit to Bolton in the 1950s, a year or two after the death of my own mother, and first I went to the home of my sister May, where I would stay the night, before going to see my father in Unsworth Street.

'Now don't be surprised,' May said, as we were having a cup of tea, 'if Dad doesn't recognise you when you go down. He's not been quite right in his mind lately, he keeps talking about getting back home to Mother, as though she were still alive, and a few times he's been found wandering off. Once some nice people brought him home in the car, and twice the police have brought him back.' She had hardly finished talking when the back door opened and in walked my father. 'Bill!' he cried, '– musha, how are you at all, at all! B'jaze but I'm glad to see you.' Although he knew me instantly, I'd almost have had difficulty in recognising him, so changed was he, looking inbelievably haggard and thin. But his mind, I saw at once, was as sharp as ever. We embraced, and slowly it became clear to me that living in the home with Edward, but without Mother there, was so painful to him that he simply went wandering to get away from it.

CHAPTER 24

A Feel for Money

'Hasta got thy balance?' said Charlie Scarlett.

We're back on course after those various social asides on Our Street – and it is still that same day, June 12th 1924. (No happenings related here are inventions, all are factual and dates correct, nor have I taken liberties with the weather; the speech is set down as faithfully as such can ever hope to be accurately recalled. Indeed, so abundant is the material once I begin to tap memories, that the problem has been cutting down. Once I have struck some chord of memory, others open up, and much that I imagined had been forgotten flows out – faces, places, names and countless moments, as fresh as can be. This happens most often when I am lying awake in bed in the middle of the night; I always keep large notebooks beside the bed and write down such recollections as they come to me; finally I get up and make myself a pot of tea as a reward. What I felt to be permissible, however, was to compress certain minor incidents, mainly to sustain a narrative flow; on occasion I have made particular that which I remembered as being usual. In fact, I have simply written it in the sequence it has set itself in my mind.)

I am astride Charlie's Rudge Whitworth bike, the firm leather saddle creaking under my crotch, and Charlie holding on to the frame. I can't believe my good fortune – he's letting me have a ride on his bike; but the fact is, I haven't yet learned to ride a bike, but Charlie has told me that all I need is confidence. 'I think so, Charlie,' I said.

'Tha'd better be sure so,' said Charlie, '– because I can't run beside thee, I'm outa puff as it is.' We had come up the hill of Cannon Street, and were now facing down High Street, a fairly broad thoroughfare, that had smooth setts in place of cobbled ones, and with a slight slope ideal for a bike. 'Right,' said Charlie, 'all tha needs remember is that tha has two good brakes. I'll just give thee a push – here goes – off wi'thee!' and the next moment I found myself sailing along, my heart beating wildly with excitement. For the first hundred yards I was too tense to enjoy it, but as Charlie's advice came to mind, and I became confident, I could hardly believe the feeling of pleasure there was in riding a bike.

I found myself simply gliding along, past Redmond's billiard hall on the right, the library and the swimming baths, and again I became tense as I approached the road crossing at Bridgeman Street, but all clear, and I went bowling effortlessly along, the fresh air caressing my face, a heavenly sensation. 'Rudge it – Don't trudge it,' said the advertisements, and how right they were! Why hadn't I thought of getting a bike before – the pleasure I had missed in life! I pressed on the brakes and slowed down as I went along by Heywood's Park, and not daring to venture a turn on Charlie's new bike I came to a halt beside the pavement. Then I got off, crossed the road, wheeled the bike a few yards, then decided to risk getting going by pushing off from the pavement. On the third attempt I succeeded, and there I was actually pedalling the bike along.

I found Charlie sitting on the narrow pavement at the back of the Ram's Head, resting against the wall of what I knew to be the women's lavatory. His legs were bent up under his chin, the bony knees sticking up in the long trousers, his round shoulders slumped down, head sunk forward, and in spite of his toffee and new bike, Charlie was not the picture of a happy lad, and I felt a stab of feeling for him, and tried to keep hidden my own high spirits.

'Charlie,' I said, keeping my voice down, 'that's a champion bike of yours.' 'You managed it then,' he said, 'without fallin' off?' 'I went as far as Lever Street,' I said, 'but I didn't risk turnin' round. Chey, you don't fancy a Vimto – across at Drinnan's temperance bar, d'you?' Vimto was a famous drink for pepping one up, and it seemed Charlie needed just that. Also, I felt very much under obligation to him for most lads would charge a penny for a ride round the street on a bike, or twopence for one round the wooden blocks. Whilst Charlie had actually let me learn on his new bike.

'No, ta,' said Charlie.

'Or an ice-cream or summat?' I said. 'No, but ta all the same,' said Charlie, slowly rising to his feet. His lips looked pale but he had a patch of red colour on either cheek. I turned the bike round for Charlie, expecting him to go down Derby Street, 'It's all right,' he said, 'I can just coast home from here – down all the back streets, an' I won't have to pedal at all.' And so I turned the bike the way it had been, beside the edge of the sidesett, and in a weary fashion Charlie put a leg over, and rested on the saddle.

'Ta, Chey,' I said, 'ta very much.' I felt like giving him a shilling, or at least a tanner, for that lovely ride, but same as they said, there was nothing in this life Charlie needed – except perhap a bit of extra wind. He just waved to me, and I stood watching as he went down the narrow backstreets, and a forlorn figure he looked on his Rudge-Whitworth bike. Although I had no idea of it at the time it was to be the last sight I was ever to have of Charlie Scarlett.

A year earlier I would have hurried off to the Big Corner to join all my mates, to argue and tell tale, and listen to the talk of the men, but since I had got hold of some money it was no longer the same fun and enjoyment. The fact was, I could no longer be my true self, the spontaneity had gone out of my behaviour, and I found myself sort of acting. Any boy known to have cash in his pocket would be worked upon by his mates, 'If I had some money I'd buy summat good an' whack it with my mates', until he had spent it on toffees in which they could share. If he resisted their overtures, he could expect taunts and snubs. It was clear that there could never be real friendship between a boy who had money and one who hadn't – the presence of money upset it, unless it was shared. For a time I had had sex on my mind, women's legs and busts, but now it was money. I preferred the feel of the money.

Clearly there were two kinds of people in the world – those who had some money and those who hadn't. I often felt like treating my mates but if I had taken one to the pictures I'd have had to take the lot. The same as it was said, it was easy to be generous when you had nowt, but it was a different matter when you had some money. No doubt but that once Money got you in its grip you had a hell of a job on to break free. You couldn't forget about it – it wouldn't let you.

And so I made my way home, slipped quietly into the deserted back kitchen and opened my drawer. I carefully got out the book in which I hid the money, pressing the covers tightly so no coin would fall out, and was creeping quietly to the stairs when our May came in. She looked at me, looked at the book, but said nothing. May had sharp eyes, and I felt like saying, 'What are you skennin' at?' but thought it best not to. I went upstairs, turned into the back bedroom, closed the door firmly, went across to the bed, and turned the book over, letting all the coins jingle softly on to the top blanket. Half-crowns, florins, shillings, and a few sixpences – what a lovely sight! You've become a right old miser, I thought, but that was one sin the Church appeared to overlook, providing it got its share.

This getting hold of money, and becoming enthralled by it – for such was its hold on me – had begun one Wednesday afternoon a year earlier, when Joe Harrison and I had been chatting on our way home from school – Dear old Joe, with his little bright eyes and big ears and warm smile! 'Hy, I say,' one chap had stopped us in Derby Street, '– you two lads wouldn't like to earn yourselves a shillin' apiece would you?' Joe and I looked at him with surprise – and interest too, for a shilling was a lot of money on a Wednesday. Even the word 'shilling' itself was impressive, not like a 'bob'. A shilling was a good amount even on a Friday, but on a Wednesday, with everyone skint, it seemed like a small fortune. 'I've a sofa I've promised faithfully to a woman in View Street,' he went on, 'an' I've been let down by one chap. Now there's a handcart, and it's nobbut a half-mile or so, an' although it's goin' up a bit of a brew, it should be a doddle to two likely lads like yourselves.'

'I'm gam',' said Joe, '– what about thee, Bill?' I was ridiculously self-conscious, and disliked being the subject of any stares in the street but felt I ought not turn it down. 'I'm with you, Joe –' I said. The three of us got the sofa on to the handcart, 'Which of you is goin' to drive?' asked the man. 'In the absence of a mule,' I said, repeating what I'd heard ex-soldiers say at the Big Corner, 'the senior N.C.O. will take the shafts.' And with that I got into them, fastened the pull rope round my chest, and with Joe shoving at the rear we set off.

I kept my embarrassed face turned to the ground to avoid the looks from passers-by, yet at the same time I enjoyed giving scope to my fairly muscular arms, and found the pulling back of the shoulders a good exercise. 'Hy,' shouted a horse-carter to us, 'can't you see you're on the wrong side of the bloody road! You're goin' agin the traffic – folk have to pull round you – you should be across there, on the left, you pair of numb buggers.' A funny thing, but it had never struck me that the flow of traffic must keep to the left, at least not for handcarts. 'He's bloomin' right,' said Joe to me as we wheeled the handcart across the road, 'that's what we are.' Even so, an hour later there was a nice flush of feeling to be going home with a shilling in the pocket. 'I'll be late home,' said Joe, 'but mi Mam won't mind when she sees this bob.'

Once I had got hold of that extra shilling it seemed that I had some capital I could work on. I'd heard it said that money draws more money to it, and I could now see that this was true. Various scarce cigarette-cards, and pictures of footballers given with a magazine called *Champion*, could be bought at the Big Corner for a penny or twopence, and would bring up to sixpence from some collector at school. I also enjoyed a gamble, and had a system that so far had never failed me. There was a game called 'Heading', played on the dirt ground opposite the Big Corner. Some older youth in need of a gamble would place two pennies, tails up, along the forefinger and middle finger, and take bets on whether, after spinning them high up in the air – they must rise above the head – they came down heads or tails up. Heads up he won, tails up the punter won, one of each and nobody won. My system was to wait until the pennies had been headed three times in succession, and then start betting, for I believed that the law of averages inclined the toss to tails the more often there had been two heads up. And so far it had never failed, and I had won a few bob that way.

It so happened that from then on I was often approached by others in need of a handy lad for a few hours. Over the summer holidays I went with Bert Greenhalgh, who drove a Handley's bread van, and soon became quite good at carrying five two-pound loaves on one arm. He paid me a shilling a day all through the month's holiday, helping him from halfpast eight in the morning until halfpast four in the afternoon. A man called Corlett opened a new provision shop in Derby Street, and paid me five shillings for helping around every evening and at weekends. This gave me no spare time among all my mates, and I was relieved when he told me that he had been reported for employing a schoolboy and that I would have to finish.

I imagine it was my neat appearance, always washed and fresh, with celluloid collar, that prompted Farmer Akky to pick me out of a bunch of lads standing at the streetcorner, to help him with the milk deliveries. I did my best for two weeks, but I lacked the dexterity it needed to turn the can with one deft movement and pour the milk clean into the jug held by the woman customer. 'Tha'rt sheedin' more flamin' milk than tha'rt puttin' in,' he would say to me. Also, as I was lacking in balance, I could never easily spring on to the rear step of the milk float as the horse was trotting briskly along. Finally, one Saturday there was a loud clatter as I made a desperate attempt and tumbled in the roadway, with three milk cans bouncing along the cobbles. Farmer Akky drew the horse to a halt, helped me to pick up the cans and then turned to me with a solemn air: 'Here's a shillin' – I'm payin' thee off. I've nowt agin' thee, lad, I've no doubt tha does thy best, but tha'rt a bit of a slowcoach, tha hasn't enough spring in thee,' he said, 'an' so far as deliverin' milk goes, or any job that needs a pair of nimble feet an' hands, I'm afraid th'art neither use nor ornament.'

I counted the money as I replaced the coins carefully in the box, putting each one tight up against the stiff binding, from which it could hardly move, and reckoned I had just thirty-one shillings. Suddenly I felt an enormous sense of relief, a release from the grip of money, for I had decided after that enchanting ride on Charlie Scarlett's bike, that I simply must have a bike of my own, even if I spent every penny I had. The pleasure and independence of having money wasn't worth the sense of hypocrisy that went with it, when I was among my mates or at home – and it seemed to have taken the comfort and meaning out of prayers. After all, I could hardly be said to be 'mourning and weeping in this vale of tears' the 'Hail, holy Queen', one of my favourite prayers – if I had thirty bob safely tucked away in a drawer. It had been my habit when I felt sad and unhappy to whisper a prayer – the Holy Spirit, once caught, could always bring a smile to my face – but since the money fever had got hold of me I tended at such times to put a finger in my vest pocket and feel the milled edge of the silver coin with my nail.

I had seen a cartoon in the comics, of two men stranded on a desert island, one saying to the other, 'If we don't get help soon we'll starve.' The other has a hand in his pocket, 'How can we starve,' he says, 'I've got a fiver!' I thought to myself, that's just how I should have felt. I liked to think I was a devout Catholic, but at the same time I didn't fancy taking it as far as St Francis, and I wanted to have both God and money. Anyway, I resolved I must get myself a bike for June Holiday Week – no matter what happened. Then I tiptoed downstairs, the back kitchen was empty, and I crept across to my drawer, opened it, and put the book safely back in its place at the bottom, and piled the other books and papers carefully around it, and closed the drawer.

CHAPTER 25

The Last Day at School

'Wisha isn't it a great thing altogether, my fine scholareen,' said Mother, as I was about to leave home, 'that after all the long years this should be the last day I'll see you go off to school!' It was a fortnight later, Friday, 27th of June 1924, the day which would bring the start of Bolton Holiday Week, and the end of my school life. 'I'll be makin' fresh tea now for your father,' she went on, indicating she wouldn't stand there waving me off round the corner, for he disliked any fussing between herself and us, and with that she kissed me and off I went. In the Irish home so much had to be implied without being spoken. I could feel my face glowing from the good wash I had given it, and sensed that my black hair, parted from the side, was well damped in place with tap water, but my Eton collar now felt on the tight side from all the neck exercises, and I thought, it's as well I'm leaving school, or else I'd need one-and-sixpence for a new one. In my pockets, spread about, was around two shillings in all, and with the money still in the drawer it was hard not to feel full of myself.

'Ee hello, Willie!' I heard a woman's voice call out. It was Mrs Orrell, our next-door neighbour at number 6, who was holding the two-year-old infant, Sam. Orrells' house was one of a block of three, which must have been added later to the original row, for they were of glossy brick and a more fancy style than the rest of the street. The house-front was set back about eight feet from our house, with a small flagged area, a sort of imitation garden but without so much as a blade of grass or a privet leaf, bounded by a three-foot high wall, which was topped with a rounded brick on which boys would sit in the evening. But this front show meant that there were no backyards, only a narrow strip to the shared privy closet.

I always walked by Orrells' gazing straight ahead, but having been greeted I turned and stopped: 'Oh hello, Mrs Orrell,' I called out. 'Hello, Willie,' said Mr Orrell. 'Good morning, Mr Orrell,' I said. Fred Orrell was a nice man, a clerk in the mill office at Crosses and Winkworths, and that he was a cut above our street could be recognised at once by the quieter tone of voice, not to mention the suit, trilby hat and walking stick – the stick on account of his having lost a leg in the War. It was whispered that he had married beneath him, Mrs Orrell having worked in the cardroom – for 'staff' to marry 'worker' was almost unknown; but Fred was a simple man, no snob, and seemed more than satisfied with his wife, who still retained the lively wit and voice of the mill girl, and also the pallor. That was the way it was in Bolton, your face and your manner gave you away as to what you were, before you even opened your mouth. The couple were enjoying a regular morning scene of Mrs Orrell and Sam seeing Dad off to work.

'Wi-Wi-Wi-Wi-ee!' cried Sam, who was now held by his mother as he stood on the wall. He stretched his arms out for me to take him, but she held him back: 'Say that poem mi dad learnt you for Willie,' she said. 'Come on, "I'm a navvy…" ' Sam began to recite with her, 'I'm a navvy – I can wheel a barrow up a brew – An' when I get to'top, I can sup a bottle of pop – An' I'll work till mi shirt's wet through!' 'Good lad you, Sam!' I applauded, although I resisted his outstretched arms, for I didn't want to get mussed up on my way to school. 'Ta ra,' called Mrs Orrell to Fred. 'Ta ra,' called Fred. 'Say ta ra to your Dad,' said Mrs Orrell. 'Ta ra,' called Sammy. 'Say ta ra, to Willie,' said Mrs Orrell. 'Ta ra, Wi-ee!' called Sam. 'Goodbye,' I called back, and went off feeling that they might have started Sam's poetry on a higher level, yet at the same time I found 'I'm a navvy –' kept repeating itself in my mind as I made my way to school.

I stopped in Derby Street to watch the deliveries from Magee Marshal's big brewery turning out, the barrels loaded on the horse-lorries, drawn by powerful shire horses, their coats glossy, hooves raising sparks from the cobbles. I'd love a job at Magee's, I thought, but not the remotest chance, for it was one of the firms that rarely took on strangers, but always members of the same family – a 'job for life' firm, they said. They would only sack you for dishonesty or drunkenness, for they would always find you a job that suited.

I was looking forward to this day at school, the break-up for the summer holidays was always a pleasant one, with a relaxed atmosphere. Boys would not be caned by Mr Smith in the schoolyard for arriving a minute or two late, clogs would not be examined, neither would there be any inspection for dirty necks, and catechism became an easygoing affair. And with the change of attitude of teachers towards the boys, there was a corresponding response from them, with lads smiling to one another, and whispering away, and it seemed that at a stroke the spirit of severity and chastisement was gone and in place of tension and temper there was peace and amity. The transformation puzzled me, that it should be so simple, almost as much as it pleased me. Then after playtime, around eleven o'clock, the entire school would gather in the basement, for a sort of farewell concert. At the end of which the school song would be sung, with Mr Smith conducting, and then he would address us all, but especially the schoolleavers.

'Don't forget, you boys who are leaving the old school, going out into the world, that the acquaintances you make there will not stay in mind like your old schoolfellows – those will remain in your hearts until you are old.' I always enjoyed that talk of Old Smithy, which would often bring a lump to my throat. On top of that we usually got an afternoon's holiday. As for Jackie, I resolved that somehow I would find the opportunity to tell him that my year in his class had been the happiest in my school life.

First I had my final morning's duty of checking, were there any letters to be picked up at the Infants' School. There was the usual hush in the playground as I entered – they had all gone in and I could hear the young voices at prayer. How innocent they all sounded – and to think I had once been like that, before I had become tormented with sexual feelings, and with grasping thoughts about money! All the same, I'll bet there are a few unhappy souls among them – infancy, the state when you are at the mercy of everyone. When I turned into the broad corridor that led to Sister Edwardine's room I put on the expression I had used on every occasion since she gave me the whack across the lug. It was beyond me to be impertinent or discourteous in any way, and although my temper might flare up, I could never put on a peevish look, or even a cocky one. It seemed to me that the only way I could get even with her, and preserve some self-esteem, was by never giving a hint of anything except a polite detachment. I reasoned that as she was Irish herself she would get the message. Every day there had been the two encounters, morning and afternoon, when carefully retaining my snubbing distance of some six feet from her, I would put on the remote voice, 'Are there any letters, Sister?' I could not quite understand what was going on between us that gave me the feeling of superiority over her – apart from the fact that she had been the one that had lost her temper, and was bound to feel some guilt over it – but from the gentle way she responded, trying different touches, sometimes appearing to be waiting for me, and calling out, 'Oh nothing today!', it seemed I was slowly wearing her down.

On this last morning she was talking to Miss Devine in her room, but when she saw me approaching she broke off at once, turned to the desk on which there were a few letters, picked one up, and came to meet me, 'Oh there's one here,' she said with a smile, and I felt for a moment she was going to say 'William'. I let her come to me, and as she gave me the letter our hands touched, and the feel of her long firm fingers seemed so intimate that I could hardly resist the impulse to smile back at her, but somehow my training had been so intense it would not allow me to give way. 'Thank you, Sister,' I said, bowed slightly, and went off, flushed, and uneasy at having gone against my own nature. It took a minute or two before I could say to myself, it serves her damn well right! And yet I had to admit that the dinger she gave had done me good, for if I was not taken down a peg or two now and again it seemed that I became right smug and self-satisfied.

During catechism Mr Smith came to our class, and had a word with Jackie, and then turned to us: 'I'm afraid there will be no breaking-up concert today,' he said. 'The education officer has been in touch with me, and in view of the visit to the Wembley Exhibition this year, and the school time missed, the usual half-day's holiday has to be forfeited.' There was a groan from the class – but my disappointment was too intense to come out. The day seemed all messed up after that, and lessons went on in an orderless fashion until half-past three.

I had been expecting Jackie to come round to the few of us who were leaving, and particularly so to myself, and say a few parting words of advice, or indeed anything, just to show a little feeling, which would allow me to respond, and tell him of my gratitude, but nothing of that kind happened. Jackie simply addressed the class after prayers, 'Now be sure every boy takes home his school bag and returns with it laundered and ironed on the Monday after the holiday. And about any outstanding raffle tickets – will any boy with money owing for tickets be sure to hand it in at Sunday nine o'clock Mass to the teacher in charge.' And with that he put on his old trilby hat, gave a quick look round, and hurried off, without so much as a wave of the hand. I felt set down that my good teacher, my hero of sorts, should take off in such an uncaring manner, without even a handshake. I did not join in the quick exit from the classroom, but looked down at my desk, and around the room, unable to reconcile myself to the feeling that what had become so much a part of me I should never again see.

Then out I went into the schoolyard that was full of hurrying figures, and the next thing I found myself almost being borne out of the place by the crowd of lads making their wild rush through the narrow alley that led to the way out. I turned on one or two, and even gave a jab with my elbows, but no boy took any notice. It seemed an unbelievable liberty for them to take, one that had never occurred during the past twelve months, when the juniors had always known their place, behind, or if in front to give way to the seniors, and above all to the Cock of the School. But here I was, being hustled and shoved around as though I were a nobody. And there was simply nothing I could do about it – the sharp look to which they had all submitted was now ignored. Could it be that they were glad to see the back of me! I was bowled out through the open door and on to the street. What a school – you give them nine years of your life and this is the thanks you get! Not one of my old mates had troubled to come and shake my hand – what a miserable lot! 'Are you goin' down to the Education Offices, Bill – for your school-leaving papers?' I turned and saw Jackie Relph beside me. 'Hello, Jackie,' I said, as I remembered that I had my birth certificate in my inside pocket, ready to go for my papers, which I had completely forgotten. 'Yes,' I said, and went off with him. We made our way to town before the offices closed, and got our papers. He was chatting away to me, but I was somewhat unheeding of his talk, finding it difficult to suppress my sense of disappointment – of which I should have been glad to confide to a closer mate.

On the way back we were parting at Fletcher Street, and I was about to say 'So long,' to him, when he stopped and faced me, his hand out. 'Well, Bill,' he said, 'I've enjoyed these years in your class – and I've always looked on you as a good mate. If ever you get into any kind of trouble – not that you're likely to do,' he went on, 'or if ever you need a good friend, you know me, you know where I live, and I'll always be glad to help you.'

I couldn't speak for a moment, I was so touched by Jackie Relph's words, and the concerned look on his face: 'Thanks, Jackie,' I said, as we shook hands, 'thanks very much. An' the same goes for me, if ever you're in trouble.' It seemed to me that as Jackie went off he had a lump in his throat, and I felt ashamed that it had taken someone like him to do something which I ought to have done myself. I watched him going off for a time – surprised that those few words of his had somehow wiped away all mortification. My spirits rose as I remembered I must hurry home, look in the *Evening News* 'Articles for Sale' column, and see if there was a bike going. Then get all my money out of the drawer, and surprise all my mates at the Big Corner.

CHAPTER 26

A Sudden Setback

I had sensed the holiday spirit being held under in the morning, but now signs of it were springing out all over the place. Women, mostly in shawls, were hurrying into a shop across the street, 'Number 66A', always referred to by its number, a draper and handy goods store, and beside the entrance stood the proprietor, a small man, Myer Goldstone, of sombre but civil mien, a man my father always greeted warmly. Three men were standing looking in Pikes', gents' outfitters, hesitant about going in. Few working men would enter shops, it was always left to the mother, and later to the wife, to do such – and indeed as I was passing in hurried a woman in a shawl, with the confident air of someone who knew exactly what she wanted. Further up the street I saw men hurrying into Fairclough's barber shop – everybody wanted a haircut for June Holidays – and it would be midnight before the later arrivals got out. Rag Bob too would be doing roaring business.

My eye was drawn to every bike I saw – to make a calculation, would my thirty shillings buy it? To think that Charlie Scarlett, a lad who had never said a Hail Mary in his life, had a Rudge Whitworth, and there was I, who rolled them off my tongue from morning to night, and I hadn't even an old boneshaker. It made one wonder about the power of prayer. At the corner of our street I saw Jim, my ten-year-old younger brother, eating a jam butty and talking to his street mates. 'Hello, Bill,' he said, coming to meet me. 'Here y'are, Jim,' I said, and slipped a penny into his hand. It was a form of largesse I had begun to give him over the past year, a sort of easing my conscience over having money of my own when those close to me were without. 'Oh ta, Bill,' he said, pretending to be surprised. He and Edward had almost no brotherly contact, and he often turned to me, 'Dad's home from drawin' his wages,' he said, 'but he might be gone to bed by this.' Jim was a goodnatured boy, but like any younger brother did not impress me. 'So long, Jim,' I said, walking up to our front door, and thinking as I went that with Jim out of the way, May not home for another hour, and Dad going to bed, there would be a chance to get my money out of the drawer.

My father was much like I had seen him on countless Friday afternoons over the years, after going to Brackley Pit to draw his wages. He was working on what he called 'the roads' – a form of piece work, in which himself and two mates had contracted to keep the roads clear for the day shift. Some weeks they had extra amounts to draw, and from the flushed look on his face this had been one, for it was obvious that he had drunk a few pints of beer. 'That flamin' Ramsay MacDonald an' ould Snowden,' he said, '– shure now that they are in aren't they as bad or even worse than the bloody Conservatives. They won't give the working man anything at all.' Ramsay MacDonald had been a hero of my father's when he became the leader of the Labour Party in 1922, and great things were expected from him after the 1923 election, but he proved a cautious prime minister, and although Snowden took the tax off tea – 'a free breakfast table' – this was far from enough for my father, who wanted his own simple pleasures, a pint of beer and a pipe of tobacco, reduced in price. 'Arra, why don't you give yourself a half an hour's rest, woman,' he said to Mother, 'after goin' around the house all day.' He would never say 'after all your work', but on Sunday afternoons when he had had a few drinks, and May and I often went off to the cemetery to put flowers on Uncle William's grave, and on Fridays after drawing his wages, he would suggest it. My mother hesitated, and not being one to disagree, said, 'Maybe I could manage a few minutes,' and looked at me and went off upstairs after him.

It was just the opportunity I needed to get hold of my money, and I bolted the front door just to make sure, in case Mary Anne or Mrs Orrell popped a head in. Then, I tiptoed into the back kitchen, deftly opened the difficult drawer, put my hands down into the corner, and got the book out with my savings pressed between its pages. It was comforting to lay hands on it again, for I hadn't touched it since my birthday, yet I felt an odd sense of misgiving as I went back into the front kitchen, for there was something about it that didn't feel just right. I went across to the table, on which my mother had replaced the green chenille tablecloth after my father's meal, and turned the book over to let all the coins fall out.

There was no heavy jingle as I had expected, but a sort of weak clink or two, as out came a few shillings and sixpences, not a single heavy half-crown or two-shilling piece. I could hardly believe my eyes – but there it was. I shook the book, riffled the pages with shaky fingers, and then tapped hard on the spine – but *nothing*. I counted the miserable coins – twelve shillings in all. Jesus, Mary an' Joseph – my life savings nearly gone! In a sweat I hurried to the back kitchen, feeling that maybe the coins had slipped out. I actually took the drawer out and searched every corner of it, but not a single coin did I find. Then I remembered the last time I had taken the book out – how May had seen me with it in my hand. Our May, it struck me with a sense of certainty, she must be the blooming thief!

I was waiting in the front kitchen when a half an hour later I heard Mother coming down the stairs. She stayed in the back kitchen for some time, washing and changing herself for the evening, as she liked to look different on a Friday. I was preparing myself for when she came in. 'Mam,' I said, and there was a break in my voice, 'I've been savin' up like mad this past twelve months, to buy myself a bike, an' I put the money in this book –' I kept control on myself, for it was a situation too serious for tears – I was not after sympathy but my money, and I held up the book, '– down at the bottom of my drawer it was – an' now I've just gone in to get it, an' most of it's gone!'

'Arra wisha who would take your money out of your drawer!' said Mother, 'after you savin' up for the bike! This is a terrible thing altogether, agraw,' said my mother, 'that you couldn't be sure your money wouldn't be safe under this roof.' 'It's our May,' I said, 'I'll get at her as soon as she comes in.'

Mother stood there at the hearth, 'D'you know,' she said, 'I feel I know a better way – one that will save any trouble or upset, bein' that it's the holiday week anyway. Maybe the poor girl only borrowed it.'

'*Borrowed* it,' I said, '– to go down in my drawer an' into my book – without askin' me!'

'Make out you know nothin',' she said to me coaxingly, '– say a hard word to her – don't upset the poor girl's feelings after her week's work. Now she'll be comin' in home with the two weeks' wages – an' maybe it was her intention to put it back without you ever knowin' a thing about it. An' won't it be the same thing at the heel of the hunt, so long as you get your money.'

I was persuaded by her manner, and grumbling away I put the money back, and put the book into the drawer. I didn't exactly relish an encounter with May, because no matter how right I was, she had a way of putting me in the wrong and winning every argument. 'Now go off out before she comes in home,' she said, 'maybe go to the library an' read a book an' compose yourself – or to church to say a few prayers for comfort – but don't come back until after eight o'clock when she'll be off to see one of her friends. How much did you say was in it?' 'Thirty-one shillings!' I almost yelled, but it seemed my voice broke with emotion, and off I went, striving to look normal.

CHAPTER 27

Holiday Week Euphoria

The pleasure of drawing two wages at once was such that it showed on every face I saw, except perhaps for those of the spinners who gave nothing away, as I walked along the streets, now bustling with mill folk. Little thought would be given to the following Friday, when there would be no wages, and even worse the Friday after, no wages again, for that week would be withheld as the week in hand. Most of the working class had so many problems in just keeping going that they had little thought to spare for what lay ahead: 'Ee, it doesn't stand thinkin' about,' was what most folk said about the future. Catholic teaching, with its stress on this world being only a temporal trial, and the next an eternal one of heavenly bliss, could hardly fail to give consolation to its people. Yet those outside it kept gloom and ill spirits at bay with a natural good humour, expressed in the exchange, 'How arta goin' on, Bob?' 'Hearty but poor.' Yet so uncomplaining were the Lancashire workers that it was rare one heard the valid comment, 'It's no holiday – it's just the bloody sack for a week. It gives 'um chance to sluch out the lodge an' chip the boilers.' Those were two jobs which proved handy for oilers-and-greasers and other underpaid workers to earn some money and make up their wages during the period the engines were stopped.

I decided to occupy an hour by walking to town and amble around in the novel holiday atmosphere. Groups of lads from poor homes, wearing tatty old scarves and clogs, were watching at the town terminus near the Flag Hotel to catch holidaymakers getting off the trams, a short walk from Trinity Street station: 'Carry your bag, sir!' 'Carry your bag, missis?' went up the cries. I should have enjoyed joining them, and talking to people, and earning a tanner or two myself, the recognised tip, but unfortunately I was in a class just above that, which I felt to be a pity. Although the big crowds would not be going off until Saturday, with long queues forming, taxis were already busy, arriving at Trinity Street station every minute, for the better-off folk who were getting away. These were of the 'staff' – people who had had their taxi ordered perhaps weeks ahead, and had their cases all neatly packed and labelled, put aside in the parlour for days, folk who could afford that extra change of clothes that made life so much easier.

Although no entire family from our street would go away for the week, considering themselves lucky to enjoy day outings, it was strictly required of this class to do so; but they went mostly to Southport, Morecambe or the Isle of Man – not Blackpool, which, although recognised as the best place, was said to be 'common'. There were some lively bunches of young men in flannel trousers, excited at the prospect of the midnight sailing from Liverpool to the Isle of Man in the famous old ship, the Ben-My-Chree, to stay at Cunningham's Camp – thirty shillings all found for the week. The long sunny spell had broken, and the weather was unsettled, threatening a rough crossing, yet it seemed nothing could have damped their spirits. The annual figures for the pay-out of savings clubs had reached a quarter of a million pounds, a record in spite of creeping unemployment. Nor did the patient Bolton holiday-maker ask for much more than getting away from work for a week, a daily walk along the front at Blackpool, and return with some colour in the cheeks, and of course, a few extra pounds in weight, and some funny incidents to tell friends about.

There were various girls going off, in twos and threes, all mill workers – their sharp voices and pale faces told all – among whom was Maggie Schofield from our street. None of them would come back with faces tanned, let alone bodies. 'Oh you should see how red her face is after that week in Blackpool!' was about the most that could be expected, or exceptionally, 'All the skin came off the top of her arms with the sun!' (A town near Glasgow had a holiday week coinciding with that of Bolton, and many attachments began that flowered into marriage. Maggie was to meet a Scotsman, marry him, and our evenings were enlivened by the music of his xylophone; two others from the street, a youth and a girl, were to find Scottish partners for life in Blackpool during holiday week.)

I had no envy of those who were going away, nor had I a wish to go anywhere, for I preferred the feeling of being left out. Lads in big groups were too noisy for me, for then I never got chance to sort out my thoughts, which I liked to get clear in mind, and follow up. The Big Corner crowd was different, because they were your close mates, and you could always slip off unnoticed if you wished. When I felt I had had as much as I could comfortably take, I turned and made off for the familiar Corner – that beats all their Blackpools, I thought. I walked at a good pace up Derby Street as far as Cannon Street, so that I could approach the Corner from a short distance. Even before I actually got there I could hear the murmur of the voices and the laughter in the air and when I came to the open space there was the Big Corner crowded as I had never before seen it. There was an enormous gathering of men, youths and lads, all around the wall. The sight set my heart beating fast, and I forgot my worry about the money. They were the most animated crowd, swopping opinions, one shouting the other down, cracking jokes and laughing, all seemingly in great good humour. I went quietly across, for you had to be ready for some leg-pulling if a mate spotted you, as they would always pick on something they could make fun of, above all should you be wearing something new. They were talking away so heatedly that nobody even noticed me, and I was able to take a good look round.

There was the usual bunch of the regulars, the miners, Jud Burns, Louis Arpino, Gilbert Clegg and others, not down on their hunkers, there wasn't room, but standing against the wall; beside them were those from the spinning mill, Jimmy Fish, Nog Hosky, Bally Selby, Jimmy Seddon, Charlie Howarth, and a few others. It seemed that the stocky physique of the miners, and their robust manner was nicely toned down by the lighter build of the side-piecers, with their faces pale, a shade greasy, but their wits and tongues as sharp as could be. Adding to the holiday crowd were some men that came only occasionally; Bobby, a man in his late twenties, a graduate of Manchester University, who seemed to enjoy just being in the company of the young men, and settling certain of the arguments that sprang up. Billy Marsh was there, plump and womanish, with two gold teeth, and beside him his special friend, a young chap called Nicholas, who I remembered well as an older boy of my own school. There was Horace Farnworth from Swan Lane, a well-dressed young man, hunch-backed, lively and with plenty to say. 'Howgo, Eddie!' he greeted me – for some reason he always mixed me up with my elder brother, whom he knew as another spruce dresser like himself

– 'how's your knees an' things, eh Eddie!' and he laughed loudly. There was something infectious about Horace's high spirits, and his warm greeting rather cheered me up.

A man from a nearby street was going by, something of a dandy with his smart cap and trim moustache, 'Here's the bloody fancy man,' said Charlie Howarth. Horace called to him,' 'Howgo, Fred! – aren't you havin' five minutes?' 'I've other fish to fry,' said Fred. Mrs Winstanley was just picking up one of her grandchildren and she called after him, 'Don't forget, Fred – Nature gelds you but never tells you.' There was a burst of laughter from Billy Marsh, 'Ee my Christ,' he lisped, putting his hands under his chin, 'I hope she doesn't geld me just yet!' and with that he gave his friend a push in the side and said, 'We're off to Morecambe tomorrow – aren't we, Joe?' I couldn't understand much of it, but that may have been what kept it stored in memory.

Even the pressing thought of my stolen money went out of mind as I listened to arguments going on about various matters, the British Empire Exhibition at Wembley, the Olympic Games – would Nurmi, the Flying Finn, repeat his earlier Olympic victories in a month's time in Paris. Jud Burns was on about the town of Bolton. 'Takin' it all round,' he said, 'Bowton is generally considered to be one of the finest towns in the land.' 'How dusta mak' that out?' asked Joney. 'For a start,' said Jud, 'tha's got the pits to the south theer – so we're sure of coal – the damp climate, ideal for spinnin' – why dusta think they've built all the mills?' 'Aye, an' half of 'um are shuttin' down,' said Joney. 'They'll come back,' said Jud, '– don't thee worry –' 'I'm not,' said Joney, 'I bloody left the spinnin' to go down pit – but I doubt they'll ever come back on full time.' 'Then there's all the beauty,' said Jud. 'What beauty?' said Joney. 'All t'moors to the north theer.' 'Folk 'ud go mad down South if they'd moors like ours,' said Knocky Bolton, who was married to Jud's sister. 'Aye, an' thee walk o'er 'um,' said Joney, 'an' a bloody keeper will come up an' tell thee to piss off.' 'An' there's the Bolton people,' went on Jud, 'reckoned to be the most friendly folk in the land. Thee ask any visitor – an' they'll all tell thee the same.'

No matter how heated an argument became, no one would take offence in such a way that could prompt him to raise a fist or make any kind of challenge. There was never the least sign of a fight. That's what I found most comforting about it

– the English way of not starting up a fight. Whatever the Scots or Welsh would do, one thing was sure, the Irish couldn't have stood a single night of joke and leg-pull of that kind without trouble breaking out. Politics and religion, however, were subjects never mentioned. It was an understood thing that matters of that kind, or family affairs, must be avoided, but all else was fair game at the Big Corner.

Forty years on I was to have two plays and the film *Alfie* running in London, and I frequently dined at various clubs. The only one I became a member of was the Dramatists' Club, a condition of the invitation to join being that a member must have had two plays on in the West End that ran for no less than three weeks. It may seem to be stretching things a bit when I say that whether it was the Garrick, the Savile or the Reform, I instantly felt at home and at ease, for I always got an echo of the Big Corner in Birkdale Street. Even at the Athenaeum – where I was invited twice on Guest Nights – the atmosphere to me was oddly reminiscent of the Big Corner – a sort of male haven, to which men could escape, and relax and regress, free of female presence.

CHAPTER 28

Saturday Morning Scene

It was ten o'clock on Saturday morning before things were quiet enough to give me the chance to slip into the back kitchen, take the book out of the bottom drawer, and sneak upstairs with it held close to me, and go into the back bedroom. I closed the door firmly behind me, then went to the unmade bed, and emptied the contents on top of the blanket. Now that looks more like it, I thought as the half-crowns and other coins tumbled out. I counted it carefully – thirty-two shillings! A shilling interest – that wasn't too bad, but not like our May to make a mistake. I felt a mild sense of relief, but no more, for the way it had been occupying my mind had by this time got on my nerves, and I was almost fed up with any thought of money – getting the bike was what was now on my mind.

I began to pocket it – spreading the coins out over my various pockets; that was the luxury of a waistcoat, there were two extra pockets that could hold a few coins without making a jingle. Slowly the warmth of possession invaded me – money in the pocket was like having extra clothes on, the more you had the more protected you felt. When I had it all balanced nicely about myself, I looked into the mirror, and tried to make my face look natural – not easy, I found, with all that money on me – and went downstairs. Mother was in the back kitchen and we looked at each other and I just nodded to her, for I had a feeling she didn't want to talk about the money. 'Here y'are,' she said, dipping into her purse, and handing me a shilling, '– your spending money.' 'No, don't bother, Mam,' I said, 'after all I've got all my savings.' 'Here y'are,' she said, thrusting the coin on me, '– you'll need the other for your bicycle, when you get it.' 'Ta, Mam,' I said, giving her a kiss. 'I'll go off now an' see what I can do about getting one.' And I went out into the street.

Just as I was turning the bottom corner I came face-to-face with our May. I had been rather avoiding any exchanges with her, and now I didn't know quite what to say: 'Hello, our

Bill,' she said, and added, '– you'll speak when your money's done!' and she gave me a look. May could put a lot into a look, and that look was certainly not one of a person who has been found guilty. That set me thinking: Had our May spotted me, then told Mother, and between them they had discovered my secret savings, and on Thursday or Friday had started 'borrowing'? There had been a relaxed and prosperous atmosphere of chips-and-fish at the Friday dinnertime table. I thought of myself as the closest one in the house to Mother, but I somehow knew that such an understanding did not compare with the intimacy between Mother and daughter – they were closer than any pair of thieves. I had learnt that certain things in life are no better for being thought over too much, and this it seemed was one of them, so I decided to start thinking of something else, and to keep my mouth shut.

I could already smell the holiday week literally in the air. Firebeaters had ceased stoking up in the mill fire-holes, and with the fires out the dark smoke no longer rolled out of the high chimneys and the air felt fresher; the faces in the street looked different, relaxed in a way never seen on an ordinary working Saturday morning. The Big Corner had a few miners squatting against the wall – no spinner could attain that particular form of rest – and others standing around, but the action had moved across to The Dirt. This was an open space that abutted on the bottom end of Back Cannon Street. At one time it had been enclosed by a hoarding, as though the developer intended to extend it to two more houses, but over the years the boards had fallen down and never been replaced, and now it was a dirt square adjoining the gable-end of the Arpino home. It served well for small children playing games during the day, also in the evenings for lads playing 'Jump o'er back', and the occasional game of cricket, but was not big enough for football except heading a pig's bladder; at weekends gambling often went on, unless they felt it safer to play in our backstreet, pitch-and-toss, crown-and-anchor and cards.

I stood to watch a fierce game of handball, known as 'knock-up', between Jud Burns and another miner called Gilbert. It was an exciting game to watch, and what surprised me was the speed the seemingly slow-moving miners could move at, and the skill with which they drove the ball so hard yet so accurately against the wall with bare fist or closed hand. There was scarcely a single brick on the entire gable-end that did not show signs of being struck by the ball. Suddenly the figure of Mr Arpino appeared, standing in the backyard, looking over the wall at the players. He was a short, spare man with a lean face, small grey eyes, a fierce expression, and a violent temper, and was known among his family as 'Old Nick'.

I saw him pause to take a breath before he let out a roar that stopped the game instantly: 'Eenough!' he yelled, 'ee-bloody-nough!' He kept his gaze on the players for some seconds until they were still and silent, then, not being a man to waste words, he simply put his head back and ran a thumbnail across his throat, as a warning to anyone who dared knock another ball against the wall. Jud and Gilbert, a tough pair, both eager and sweating, as well they might be, for they had money on the game, looked at each other, uncertain as to what to do. Then Louis Arpino, the eldest son, a miner himself, came casually across from the Big Corner: 'I told you he were in, didn' I, before you bloody started,' he said. 'If you don't want to see blood an' skin flyin', you'd best pack it in.' Reluctantly the players decided that perhaps it was the wisest thing to do.

The Dirt was quiet for a minute or two, but then Tommy Burton began a game of 'heading'. I watched as Tommy put the two pennies on his hand, tails up, and stood there taking bets. It was the simplest of all gambling games, and the most open. Tommy took the bets, all in coppers, up to a shilling, and then sent the two coins spinning in the air – should they come down a head and a tail the betting was void, two heads he won, two tails he lost. I was certainly not joining in any gambling game. Tommy was unlucky, and after losing on three occasions he gave it up. No one else would take on as the header, until Jack Dalton turned up from his mother's home in Back Cannon Street. It was four years since I had last seen Jack, when he had been on the run from the army, and had hidden in our coalshed to dodge the 'tecs. They had caught up with him later, sleeping in his mother's back bedroom, and it was known he had done a spell in the Glass House, the military prison, before being shipped off to India.

Jack looked a much different figure from the lad of nineteen he had been then. He was wearing his tight-fitting army trousers and braces, the trousers belted round his firm waist, his skin was scorched to a reddish-brown leather look, and he stood as stiff as a board. All this I could not but admire, but what almost frightened me, and what set him apart from all the others, was his manner and expression. He never laughed or even smiled, and the young face I remembered, so boyish and lively as he told my mother how he hated the army and longed to be back home with his Mam, was now frozen into a set look, and the lively blue eyes had no life in them, so that one would never know what he was thinking or feeling. It seemed that as that hot Indian sun had been burning him outside, something else had been freezing poor Jack inside. He seemed utterly indifferent to anything that might happen.

'Nob'dy headin'?' said Jack '– I'll take it on.' And he got two pennies out of his pocket, casually displayed a few crumpled-up pound-notes – backers liked to feel there was ample money to pay them – and called out, 'Any more for any more?' The sight of the notes seemed to have tempted some of those around for now the bets became bigger, with sixpences going on. Jack let all see the two tails on top, and sent the coins spinning up in the air with the skill of one used to heading. Although I enjoyed a gamble, I felt that nothing would have induced me to join in, so fixed was my mind on getting a bike. Jack had a nice little run of luck, for between a few mixed drops he had turned up three lots of double heads, without once tailing both pennies. I had a couple of threepenny joes in my pocket that easily went missing, and I half-thought I might put one of those on, or even two, for this was when I usually had a bet, but something warned me against it, and I resisted the impulse. A good job too, I thought, as Jack came up with another pair of heads. Just then Tommy Fairclough clomped up, tall and clumsy, his lively blue eyes, with traces of coal-dirt clinging to the lashes, agleam in the long face, with its bony, broken nose, glowing under his check cap. A silk handkerchief was knotted round his neck, and he was wearing a blue serge suit and heavy pit clogs, the gear of a collier ready for anything that might turn up.

Tommy was a voluble young chap, with a ready flow of words, mostly of an earthy kind, with which he liked to give vent to his every feeling. Four-letter words were used by only a few youths at the Big Corner, these mostly miners, but those that had the habit uttered them repeatedly, often in a single sentence. They would not use such language if a woman was within earshot, of course, although occasionally they slipped up. Some women would ignore it, or give them a look, others would call out, 'Go home an' wash your filthy mouth out with

Condy's fluid!' or the ironic, 'I suppose you feel a lot bigger now, after usin' that sort of language!' I never swore, and had no impulse to do so, for when I was aged six I had been given a scare, the memory of which had stayed with me. I had been making a fire in the backstreet with a boy called Fred, younger than myself, over whom I could take on the role of being boss, when he upset the box of matches on to the damp ground. The day before I had heard Tommy Enty, a man who it was said had been in prison, use a word that had caught my imagination, for it sounded so English, and I wanted to shed my noticeable Irish accent and pass as English, and now I shouted at him, 'You daft cunt! look what you've done!'

I felt rather pleased with the ugly force of the word, and the feeling it gave me of using it. A minute later there came up to us Mr Barker, who owned the skipyard, a kindly old man but now looking most severely at me – over making a fire I imagined. 'I just heard what you called your friend here –' he began in a stern voice. 'Aye,' said Fred, 'he called me a daft cunt!' 'Yes,' said Mr Barker, 'I heard him. And at seven o'clock tonight, when I close the yard, I shall go straight round to your front door and knock on it – and tell your mother and father about you using such foul language.' Then he added, 'And I always thought you were a nice boy.'

I wanted everyone to think I was a nice boy, and to see Mr Barker looking at me with such distaste quite upset me. What could be so wrong, I thought, about such a short word? I went home at once, feeling sick in my stomach – what had I done? It was not something, I felt, I should tell my mother, for this would only give me away, and she kept asking me was I all right. Then my father got up to get ready for the night shift, and I kept waiting to hear the dreaded knock on the door. The thought had struck me that it might be a good idea to gain sympathy by running away, but I lacked the courage. The knock didn't come that night although I kept expecting it to, and not until weeks had passed without hearing from Mr Barker did my guilty feelings lift. It had proved a lesson I should not forget, and I became most discreet about my use of words I did not know the meaning of.

Hearing bad language, however, in no way upset me, for I felt I could act as my being the innocent audience. If they want to blacken their souls in that manner, I would reason, let them – I'm not responsible. God might forgive them, where He wouldn't me – who should know better. Although there was a monotonous repetition of a certain word, the users varied the inflection, sometimes forceful and again light, and the spontaneous rhythm with which the words came off the tongue of a good swearer, together with giving vent to his feelings, made it a rounded performance that was often comic.

In my setting down the words verbatim, however, which the incident I am telling of demanded, I met up with a snag. The spoken word, perfectly meaningless, and flung thoughtlessly into the air, disappeared forever without trace, but the typed word on the page, arrested the eye, and took on a false significance. Then it struck me that I could replace it with a popular euphemism, just as meaningless and as monotonous, making about the same impression on the reader as the original one on the hearers.

CHAPTER 29

The Big Gamble

Tommy went up to Jack, 'Flippin' headin' 'um, arta Jack?' he said. 'Aye, I flippin' am,' said Jack, picking up Tommy's rhythm. 'How much dusta want on?' he added. Tommy said, 'What's thy flippin' limit?' 'No flippin' limit,' said Jack. 'In that flippin' case,' said Tommy, 'I think I'll have a flippin' tanner on –'

Jud Burns turned sharply on Tommy, 'Howd on a bit wi' that sort of talk, Tommy,' he said, 'wi' young Billy 'ere.' The attention embarrassed me, 'It's all right,' I said to Jud, 'I don't mind.' ' 'Course it's all flippin' right,' said Tommy. 'Too flippin' true it is,' put in Joney, another miner, 'an' of course Billy durn't mind. I'll have a flippin' bob on this throw mysel' –' and he handed Jack a shilling.

'Any more for any more?' asked Jack, 'before I spin 'um?' This is the best chance to make a quick shilling by having a bet, I thought, for after four headers in a row he's almost bound to tail them. 'I'll have a shilling on, too,' I said, dipping into a vest pocket and handing Jack a shilling. After all, if I was standing there listening to bad language, I felt I should make it look as though I had a right to be, that I was one of the school, and every shilling would come in useful over the holidays. I wasn't one to turn down money for jam.

Jack looked around. 'All done?' he said. 'Make up your minds.'

'Make mine a bob,' said Tommy Fairclough, appearing as though he didn't want to be seen putting on less than a school-boy. Jack took the extra sixpence, then put the two pennies in place on his hand, and sent them spinning in the air. I felt my heart give a flutter as down they came on to the dirt.

'Bloody hell,' said Tommy Burton, '– two bloody heads again!' Bad luck, I thought, but it's now even more sure to come tails before it comes heads again, I reasoned, so then I'll get my shilling back; after all, what is a bob out of thirty-two bob, and I've a few more spread about me! Jack showed no pleasure, no interest even, just wiped the two pennies with his army handkerchief and looked around to start taking bets again.

'I'll have another flippin' bob on this time,' said Tommy. 'Me too,' said Joney. 'I'll have another,' I said, and I handed a shilling to Jack. 'An' that's my flippin' lot,' said Tommy. Jud Burns, who would never use that word, gave Tommy a reproving look, 'I've told you once,' he said, 'an' if you don't mind – after all it's not a nice word to use before a young lad.'

'Give o'er, Jud,' said Tommy, '– tha ought to hear his old man down flippin' pit – he flippin' blinds away like a flippin' trooper –'

The remark of Tommy's gave me a sudden shock. I felt almost sickened – that my father should be brought into this scene on The Dirt. Our home, I felt, was utterly set apart from all that went on outside, and I couldn't bring myself to think that my own father, who sat alone at our table every evening, and always blessed himself as a Grace before eating his meal and drinking tea, whom I still kissed going off to pit, and for whom my mother knelt and prayed that he return safely, would ever soil his tongue with such a word. 'Not my father,' I said, but I found I spoke so weakly that I wished I hadn't opened my mouth.

The next three tosses each came down one head, one tail, and on the fourth Jack headed the pennies yet again. 'Flip me,' said Tommy, 'but in for a penny in for a flippin' pound, so's I'm 'avin' two flippin' bob on this next spin.' 'I'll have two on as well,' I said, getting a florin out of my waistcoat pocket. 'Any more for any more?' said Jack, taking the bets from me and Tommy Fairclough, and a shilling from Jud Burns. 'All done before they go up –?' Then up they went. A head and a tail – then a tail and a head – and then sharp-eyed Tommy Burton called out, 'Two bloody heads!'

Four shillings gone – four weeks' spending money – twenty-four large ice-cream sliders.Things were looking serious – but surely he couldn't go on heading them! 'Any more for any more?' called Jack. If I go away now and he tails them I'll feel a right quitter, I thought. 'I'll have four bob on,' I said, and they all looked at me, a school lad putting on all that money! 'An I'll have flippin' four bob on too!' called Tommy Fairclough. 'I'll get mi flippin' money back if it flippin' skins me!'

Jud Burns turned on us, 'Hy, what sort of game d'you call that – doublin' up!' he said. 'Play the white man!'

'It's all the same to me,' said Jack Dalton, holding out his hand, '– the more the merrier.'

'Aye, but they're bound to soddin' win sooner or later,' said Jud, 'if they double up. I know I wouldn't stand for it if I were 'eadin' 'um.'

'Now I always back a bob a throw – but I could get my full six bob back in the next spin if I wanted.'

'Thee try it,' said Jack, 'if tha fancies it.'

'I soddin' will,' said Jud, 'now tha puts it that soddin' way,' and putting a hand into his pocket he counted out six shillings and handed it to Jack. If a determined look could influence the coins there would surely be two tails this time. I could feel the tense air all round as Jack placed the pennies ready for tossing, tails on top, and then sent them up in the air. Down they came. I looked down near my feet – *two heads*.

Tommy Fairclough let out another vivid mouthful, felt in his pockets and brought out an empty Woodbine packet, 'Giss a flippin' coffin nail, somebody,' he said, and Joney obliged. Tommy lit it from Joney's cigarette, took a deep draw, and although I never had a desire to smoke I felt that as I watched him, and saw the relief it gave him, I shouldn't have minded a draw at that moment myself, after having lost eight shillings. I could walk away and leave it at that, but not only would I be eight bob short, but it would take a long time to live it down – Death before dishonour. They had all dropped out skint, except Jud Burns, Tommy Fairclough and me.

'Any more for any more?' said Jack.

'Jack,' said Jud, 'can I have ten bob on the next toss?' They all looked at him – that was by far the highest stake ever made on The Dirt, more than the full pay of a night's work down pit.

'Tha can have what tha wants,' said Jack, 'so long as tha has the money. It's all the same to me – I'll stand up to a fiver.'

'Here tha art –' said Jud, handing Jack his ten-shilling note. 'An' win or lose – that's my last soddin' bet.'

'Jud,' said Jack, 'dusta know what a sod is?'

'A sod, aye,' said Jud, 'a sod of grass. Why?'

'Tha'd know different, mate,' said Jack, 'if tha'd done a spell with the army out in India.' But what that difference was he didn't say, as he went on, 'Any more for any more?'

'That –' said Tommy Fairclough, 'is my flippin' last half-dollar –' as he took a half-crown out of his pocket, 'an' flip it.' Jud looked at him, 'Tommy, I durn't like to keep tellin' thee about that tongue of thine – but wi' Billy here –'

'I tell thee I can't hold a flippin' candle to owd Naughton,' said Tommy. 'Why, tha shoulda heard him lettin' out a coupla week back int' flippin' Plodder mine.' Tommy got excited at the memory, 'There was this big fall of flippin' dirt just as they were ready to go off – an' they had to flippin' clear the whole of it for the day shift –' When Tommy said that I suddenly remembered my birthday morning, and my father coming home late. 'He were sweatin' that flippin' much were old Naughton, that it were runnin' down t'handle of his flippin' spade,' went on Tommy, 'an' he had to keep wipin' it so's he could grip it. Talk about th'air bein' blue – it were flippin' purple – he were flippin' an' blindin' everythin' an' everybody undert' flippin' sun – down to Lord Ellesmere, the mineowner, even Ramsey MacDonald –' The moment I heard Tommy say that I recognised the unmistakable truth.

'Billy, arta not on this time?' said Jack, as he got ready to send them up. 'Aye, I'll have eight bob on,' I said, recovering quickly, '– if it's all right wi' you?' I wasn't going to see my money lost like that.

'Everythin's all right with me,' said Jack, holding out his hand. I counted the eight shillings hurriedly – I didn't want to miss this toss. It was painful to imagine my father down the coalmine, the sweat pouring off him, so that he couldn't hold the spade. Jack sent the two pennies spinning steadily in the air – then down they came. God in heaven – make 'em tails up.

'Two heads –' called out Tommy Burton, '– he's bloody done it again – eight times on the bloody trot –'

Tommy Fairclough let out a burst of flippings, and I almost felt like squeaking in with one or two of my own to relieve the strain I felt inside me. It seemed my whole little world was coming to nothing – my father – my money – my soul even – everything! All I had now was sixteen shillings. I wouldn't get a bike for that.

'That's me soddin' finished,' said Jud. 'He's on a winnin' streak – he'd skin the soddin' Aga Khan.' And off Jud went. Tommy Fairclough was desperate, 'Anybody lend me a quid? – ten bob? – a dollar?' The situation was serious when Tommy didn't use his favourite word. He looked around but they only grinned at him – they were all in the same boat. Jack was the only man with money – but it was known that no winning

171

gambler would think of giving away his luck by lending out. An odd silence came over The Dirt. 'Don't say I've skint you all,' said Jack. He looked at me, 'What about you, Billy lad?'

I could feel all the eyes on me: 'If it's all right by you, Jack,' I said, 'an' you don't mind doublin' up, I'll have sixteen bob on this time.' I thought I heard a gasp or two around me – but my tongue felt so dry, and my heart so unsettled, it seemed that I couldn't hear very clearly.

'It's san fairy Ann by me,' said Jack, 'so long as you've got the rowdy.'

With shaky fingers I gathered the sixteen shillings together from my various pockets, the others watching me curiously. Now I felt light, and a bit lost without my money. 'Here y'are,' I said, 'just count it to make sure.'

'I don't have to,' said Jack, putting it into his bulging pockets. 'You're a gambler after my own heart, Billy boy – shit or bust, is what I always say.'

There was a tense feeling of excitement all about as Jack calmly wiped the two pennies, and with deliberate care placed them along the slit between the index-finger and the middle finger of his right hand. Has he got some secret way of spinning them so that they come down heads? As I watched I felt I would have given anything to be as cool as he was. To think of all the hours I'd sweated to get hold of that money – the loaves I'd carried Saturday after Saturday – and then put my weekly shilling away in the book like an old miser – and now if the two coins came down heads again it would all go into Jack's pocket and I'd be a poor lad once more – no bike, no nothing. Blessed Virgin – please help me – I'll try not to be so greedy again. No, She said, it serves you right!

'Any more, for any more,' asked Jack, 'before I toss 'um?' Tommy Fairclough was looking more desperate, 'I could be back in five flippin' minutes, Jack,' he said, 'with some money from the old lady.'

'Sorry, Tommy,' said Jack, 'but I can't hold up the game for one.' He gave one last look, then he tossed the two coins into a swift, high spin, and I watched them turning evenly in the bright air, and then come down to earth. One rolled just beside me – I looked and saw a head, *I'm done – I'm finished!* My heart sank – what'll I tell Mother when I get home! 'A tail o'er here,' called Tommy Burton. Thank God, I thought. I began to breathe once more. Jack took up the coins and wiped them again, and up they went and down they came – a head and a tail, and Jack picked them up in an almost bored fashion. Up they went and down they came – I could see one tail. The other coin was rolling on the ground toward me, I drew back, it stopped, then I watched it drop over. And I saw the helmeted figure of Britannia seated beside the shield, holding the trident. *Tails up at last!*

'Oh hecky pecky,' said Jack Dalton, 'so I've tailed 'um'. He gave a yawn as he counted out the thirty-two shillings and handed it to me. 'A bloody relief to get rid of that lot,' he said, 'it were weighin' me down.' It felt a bloody relief to me to get hold of it and put it back in my pockets.

'Art takin' over the heading?' asked Jack.

'I don't think I'll bother,' I said, 'mi dinner'll be ready.' And I went off, feeling sick from excitement, and whispering Hail Marys of thanks.

CHAPTER 30

Buying the Bike

The atmosphere in the home was pleasant that dinnertime, the way it always was when my father was out, with young Jim seated opposite me at the table, a large slice of buttered bread on his plate, and a small basin of chips beside it, from which he was taking chips one at a time, and laying them evenly across the lower half of the bread. When he had it covered with chips, he delved down into the basin with a spoon, came up with it full of mushy green peas, dabbed them over the chips, put his hand under the top half of the bread and neatly folded the bread over, opened his mouth wide and took a big bite. Whilst he was chewing away, he picked up his mug of sweet tea and had a good gulp, then added another spoonful of sugar. Mother had often tried to persuade him to first cut the bread with a knife, but as Jim said, 'Sorry, Mam, but a chip butty doesn't taste the same if it's been cut – you seem to let half t'flavour out.' So delicious was the succulent taste of a chip butty, with home-baked bread and a half-dozen or more crisp chips between it, spiced with vinegar and salt, and tanged with burnt bits of scraps, that I could never understand how no one had thought of opening a shop that would sell nothing else. Of late I had adopted knife-and-fork table manners, and I found my chips and peas didn't taste half as good once I started eating that way.

'Yu'know what, Mam,' went on Jim, for he was something of a compulsive talker, '– Faircloughs' have chip butties for breakfast.' 'For breakfast!' said Mother. 'Aye, Mam,' he said, 'I've seen 'um. She buys 'um the night before, an' warms 'um up in the fryin' pan next mornin'.' 'God save us,' said Mother. Although she let us eat what we fancied, she sometimes went on about how it wasn't right food at all, and that one day we'd need to learn to eat a good dish of bacon and cabbage that would put some stomach into us. We had just finished the meal when the door opened and in came my father. At once there was a change, a lowering of voices, for none of us children liked him, although May could handle him, mostly it seemed because she reminded him of his mother.

(I shall point out that any lasting bitterness rarely occurred within Irish families, although there might be feuds between families. The reason may be that despite the touchiness and quick temper of the Irish, even to the point of blows being sometimes struck, the cool and cutting word had not to be spoken, for that could not be forgotten. In our adult years all that early antagonism had no place, and we were warmly reconciled with Father. Jim became most attached to him, and was often surprised at his wit. He told me of how he had once visited Dad in hospital, and had been asked by him what was the time; seeing the clock was at five minutes to three, he casually answered, 'Three o'clock!' Then Dad happened to see the clock himself, 'B'jaze, Jim,' he said, 'you were well out there – for couldn't I have seven men hanged between now an' three o'clock!' May's home was a haven where he was always welcome and cared for; and there came alive in me on my visits to Bolton, a true love and understanding of him and his nature, an appreciation of all he had done for us and for me. We used greatly to enjoy each other's company, and nothing I liked better than that he and I should be alone together. By that time, I am glad to say, I had learnt that the only good that ever came my way from another – and as a writer that has been immeasurable – has been by accepting that one exactly as he or she is; 'You've got to take folk as God made 'em,' is a Bolton saying I should have taken to heart much earlier in life. Finally, I was always to bear in mind Mother's words whispered to me during her final illness, 'Will you be sure that when I'm gone, ye'll all look after Dad.')

On that Saturday my father had on him what I took to be his usual 'four half-pint mood' – for he was careful not to drink too much at Saturday midday lest it spoil the evening session. He liked to talk of the different public-houses he had been in (he would never use the colloquial 'pub'), and four half-pints gave him enough optimism to believe that the horses he backed would win; any more and his control began to slip. Saturday night he would drink eight or nine half-pints or occasionally more – the Irish did not drink in pints. Mother would often have a pint bottle of Magee's Crown Ale put aside for him when he came home from pit on Monday morning, knowing he would be in need of it. Over a full week his average drinking would be around twenty pints of beer, mostly mild, and although a fairly substantial amount it would certainly not be regarded as excessive for most miners. Yet despite the relaxation and pleasure he got from drink over the years, it seemed to have an insidious effect on his character. He came to depend on it, and needed it for every occasion out of the ordinary – no matter where he went his first thought was to get a glass or two of beer. He would be flushed and noisily cheerful when he had drunk plenty, and pale and morose when in need of it. During the two long strike periods in the 1920s, when he would have to forego his appetite for drink, I would get a glimpse of another man – a quiet and highly intelligent one, the man he might have been had things been different. Together with his fondness for a pipe of tobacco, and the drink, it left him, and even more so my mother, extremely short of money at times.

I gave a look to Mother that I was going to slip off, and she winked at me, 'Willyeen thought he might go off to see would he be able to buy a bike for the holidays,' she said. 'D'you think would you have enough money?' she asked me. I shook my head at her, so that she would not attempt to coax money from my father, since it almost never worked. 'Urra what would he want a bike for – isn't every street thick with them! sure he's better an' safer on his two feet!'

'I'll be off, Mam,' I said, and I gave her the usual kiss, quickly got out of the house, the money safe in my pockets and my mood one for spending it; I had come to realise that money could cause one almost as much anxiety as trouble it could solve. I now told myself I didn't care what sort of language he used down pit – it was all the same to me. What had I been so upset about! I made off for the Big Corner, thinking what a blessing a good corner was compared with having a regular pal. I had tried it a few times but did not like making arrangements, and felt at ease only when I went by the mood – and could go to the Big Corner or not go, and nobody minded or missed you. Indeed, close mates were not all that welcome there, where you all had to be one.

I was taken aback as I got near at the sight of so many bikes around. Some lads were doing trick turns on the pavement, others had their bikes upside down, oiling them, others leaning on them. Ernie Arpino had one, Jimmy Naylor and his brother Pierce both had bikes, Joe Fish and others, each one with a bike. It struck me that although I thought I was canny over money, they could lose me. That's the Boltonian all over, I thought, all supposed to be broke, but on any big occasion they won't be left out. I got in among them, and asked did anyone know of a bike for sale. 'I'll tell thee who wants to sell a bike,' said Jimmy Naylor, 'if tha'rt set on buyin' one – Sammy Hart in Edward Street.' 'Aye,' said Joe Fish, 'an' it's a fair old bike.' 'Right,' I said, 'let's go an' see him.' Edward Street was only a couple of hundred yards away, beside the Emmanuel Church, and I walked alongside them as they rode their bikes. I knew Sammy Hart vaguely, a quiet lad, with a mop of thick black hair falling over his dark eyes; but I was on good nodding terms with his father, Ben Hart, the roadsweeper, a tall man, well over six feet, with a thin body and long legs, who could often be seen in his corduroys and enormous clogs, sweeping the streets.

We got to the house, and Jimmy stood at the door and called out, 'Sammy! Sammy!' A boy never knocked on the door to make his presence known to a mate, for this would have been thought out of place, as a knock might disturb the family – nor could it be recognised in the way a voice could. When Sammy came out and heard what we had come about, he wheeled the bike out on to the pavement to be inspected. Then fastened his dark eyes on me, the prospective buyer, and at once I realised he was no ordinary boy. There were quite a number of families known to be just a bit barmy, and Harts' seemed to be such a one, but in every family of that kind there was usually a sensible member, who from living in such a home appeared to develop a sort of dual intelligence, so that he could hop from one to the other when it suited him. Sammy was clearly the sane one in the Hart family.

'How much arta askin' for it?' asked Jimmy. 'Thirty bob,' said Sammy, at the same time never taking his intense gaze off me. 'An' well worth it,' said Joe Fish. 'I should think it is,' said Sammy, 'especially at June holidays. Folk are goin' mad to get hold of a bike – they're payin' pounds.' I had a feeling that Joe was on Sammy's side, and that Jimmy was on mine. The bike had recently been done over with black enamel paint, but had an old-fashioned look to it. Jimmy said, 'I see there's only one brake, Sammy – a front 'un.' 'Who needs a back brake with a front 'un like this –' said Sammy, demonstrating by pushing the bike then putting on the brake: 'See, it'll bring thee up dead.' 'Now about that chain,' said Jimmy, 'it doesn't look like an ordinary bike chain.' I said nothing, but it did look rather heavy and clumsy. 'It's not!' said Sammy. 'Nowt ordinary about that – it's a special inch-pitch chain, made to last. Just look at it – it's twice as strong as an ordinary chain. Tha'll have a job to get one of that quality these days. It'll live us three out – I can guarantee that!'

I had an uneasy feeling as those two eyes of Sammy's held me in their grip that I was about to be bamboozled, and that unless I ran off at once there would be nothing I could do about it. Sammy Hart, I felt, had been looking for someone like me, and it seemed to be in the nature of things that he should not be deprived of his victim. The less fuss about it I made the sooner it would be over. Escape seemed impossible.

'Is there a lamp to go with it?' I said, for knowing nothing about bikes, it was the only thing I could think of. 'A lamp!' smiled Sammy, '– what dusta want a lamp for at this time of the year! It doesn't go dark till nearly midnight – an' it's light again in two-three hours! Besides, if tha had one it would only get pinched.' Then he said, 'Here, why not have a ride round t'church block – tha never wants to buy owt afore tha's tested it.' 'I've never had a bike,' I said, 'an' I can't ride properly – I mean I can't catch on.'

'Nob'dy can till they've had a bike a bit,' said Sammy understandingly. 'I'll put it up against t'sidesett for thee.' Obligingly Sammy stood the bike beside the pavement, 'an' I'll hold it whilst tha cocks a leg o'er.' I cocked a leg over the cross-bar and rested on the saddle. 'No hurry,' said Sammy, 'just get thy balance, then I'll give thee a shove off. Tha couldn't have found a better bike to learn on if tha'd searched Bolton,' he went on, 'it's solid, an' it'll stand some knockin' about.' Sammy didn't give me a shove off so much as run beside me, holding the bike by the back of the saddle, and the next thing I was off on my own.

The bike may not have felt as comfortable as a Rudge Whitworth, but the lovely sensation of gliding along, the breeze on my face, was the same, and I got nicely round the church and along by Cannon's factory and back to Sammy without mishap. He was waiting for me, a greeting smile on his face: 'Well if tha hadn't told me tha were a learner,' he said, 'I'd sworn tha'd been ridin' bikes all thy life – the way tha came round that corner. I'd say that bike was just thy bottle – it coulda been made for thee.' Then he went silent and just looked at me once more.

Jimmy Naylor came to my rescue, and as Sammy was putting the bike on the pavement he whispered, 'Offer him twenty-five bob for it.' Sammy turned and looked at me, but didn't speak; I had never before understood how compelling silence can be, when accompanied by the look that was in Sammy's eyes. It was like some mute appeal from heaven – hard to resist. 'I'll give thee twenty-five bob for it, Sammy,' I said, softening it by my first use of his name. Sammy at first looked pained, as though I had insulted him, then seemed to consider it, 'I know what,' he said, 'bein' as tha'rt a mate of Joe an' Jimmy here, I'll let thee have it as a special favour for twenty-seven an' a tanner! An' that's final!' The way Sammy said 'twenty-seven an' a tanner', he made it sound even less than twenty-five bob, and to show his good faith he held out a small, dirty hand to shake on it.

There was nothing for it but to take that hand, feel down in my various pockets, and count out the money, watched closely by those two dark orbs, and then hand it over into the waiting fist. The moment he took it from me he dropped his pose, and before me was a pair of the most cunning eyes I had ever seen. I had an impulse to blurt out, 'I'll sell it thee back for a quid, Sammy!' but I couldn't get the words out, and besides, I had a feeling he would refuse. Then, with my pockets feeling strangely empty, I got on the bike – my bike! – and Sammy gave me a push off and away I went. Somehow, I felt I had had more than enough of life for one day, and what I wanted now was to ride off alone out to the country, and think things over by myself.

CHAPTER 31

Biking to Blackpool

'What a bloody boneshaker!' said Ernie Arpino when I first turned up at the Big Corner with the bike. 'Inch-pitch chain!' said Jimmy Seddon, '– it musta come outa the bloody Ark!' 'I'll tell you one thing, Billy,' said Jud Burns, 'if that chain breaks tha'll never get a replacement – they musta stopped makin' them fifty year back.' 'What – tha paid twenty-seven an' a tanner for that,' said Albert Greenhalgh, '– he musta seen thee comin'!'

Their remarks didn't upset me much, for after four days of ownership – I had been shy of taking it to the Big Corner – I found I had become much attached to the machine, feeling that somehow it had now shed Sammy Hart's possession of it and had become mine. The wonderful thing about having one's own bike was not just that singular pleasure of actually *riding* – now I understood how Billy Burton would ride to pit early morning, ride home in the afternoon, have his dinner and an hour's sleep on the rug in front of the fire, then a good wash, and come out to the Big Corner on his bike, although he only lived a hundred yards away, and pedal around on it most of the evening – but the fact that I could dodge all the encounters to be faced in our neighbourhood, 'Hy, where arta off?', that interrupted my flow of thought or daydreaming and could slip away on my own, for no one could detain you once you were on wheels. Together with this feeling of being on one's own, was that of enjoying fresh air, which it seemed I not only loved but needed. The holiday weather so far hadn't been good, little sunshine and a fair amount of rain, but I had had some good rides on my own. One day in the rain I had come down the fairly steep brew (as it was always pronounced 'brew' I cannot bring myself to write 'brow', or 'brough' as some would have it) from Chorley New Road which came out at the cemetery gates and went along Gilnow Road, a stretch we had sometimes used for trolley races, and the pleasure and excitement had been so intense that it brought me out in a sweat. I found that a clumsy touch of the front brake could send the bike into a dangerous skid, and so I had had to risk going very fast, especially round the bend at the bottom, but I had greatly enjoyed the experience. Unlike all my mates, I never wore a cap, and I also liked to be out in the rain, and the feeling of the fresh air and drizzle had reminded me of being back home in Ireland. What I still had to learn, however, for I sorely lacked a sense of balance, was how to catch on – get my right leg over the crossbar whilst moving; so far I had always to get against a pavement edge and do so before moving off, which I felt made me look a bit ridiculous.

'Hy, chaps,' Jud Burns called out to those around him, '– what about a spin up over the moors to Belmont?' The older ones did not agree to this at first, for it was the thing never to take up someone else's idea with any show of enthusiasm, no matter how good it seemed, so as to give the impression of doing him a favour – and it also allowed for some carping in case it did not turn out to be a good one. But after a time, some half-dozen or more of them grudgingly took up the suggestion, and off they set on their bikes, leaving us, the younger end, at the corner. Then Ernie Arpino, who was fifteen, and a bit of a leader, said, 'What about it, lads – come on, let's join 'um.' Then they all got on their bikes, and I quickly went to the edge of the kerb and got on mine, and on I followed, the last in the younger group.

They had gone down Cannon Street, and along Deane Road, but they could be seen and heard from a distance, for they didn't go along heads down, grim and determined like some cyclists, but sat upright in their saddles, chatting, calling out to each other, and even singing, and taking up a good half the width of the road as they went four or five abreast, giving way to no traffic except the tramcar. Then our bunch caught them up, and I swiftly tagged on at the end, feeling proud and excited to be one of such a spirited cavalcade. We went over the High Level, along St George's Road, up Bridge Street and along Blackburn Road, and what a noisy and confident crowd we were, anyone would think we owned the road the way Jud Burns and others told horn-blowing motorists what to do with themselves. That was what was so exhilarating about being one of a big gang, you had all your mates and you felt safe and secure, and what was even more, there was a sense of being carried along by the company of young men, so that you sank yourself into a mood in which the pedals seemed to turn much easier.

Next we turned up Belmont Road, up the big hill that led to the moorlands, and my bicycle-chain began to creak rather ominously, so that I was relieved when Jud Burns decided we'd be as well to walk up, pushing our bikes. The talk was incessant, with a lot of leg-pulling going on, and my heart was beating fast from the exertion and the feeling of adventure. When we reached the fairly level stretch we had travelled but five or six miles from the streets of Bolton, but already we were in what seemed a new world, with the heady fragrance of moorlands, tinged here and there with the smell of new-mown hay. The procession of bikes came to a halt at one peak point at Belmont, and Bob Lee pointed to the far horizon: 'Con you see it, chaps – Blackpoo' Tower?' No one believed him at first, but the air being clear it proved to be true enough, some thirty miles away there was what looked like a misty finger pointing upwards.

'Hy, lads,' called out Walt Mayo, 'what about makin' for Walton le Dale, near Preston?'

A number agreed, but Jud Burns suggested taking the return route by Rivington and Horwich. The big party split up, Jud Burns leading the homeward group, but I joined the ones going on to Walton le Dale, being drawn to the name. There were about a dozen of us now, and without Jud Burns in the lead the gang shed some of its authority on the road and motorists took advantage of this. It was hilly, often a matter of wheeling the bikes up one steep slope and careering freewheel down the next. I was feeling a little tired, but there was a new strange smell in the air which seemed to draw me on. At last we reached Walton le Dale, a disappointment to me after the barren moorlands which I loved. It was agreed that we would ride back the easy way, along the main road to Chorley, when Ernie Arpino suddenly spoke up: 'Hy lads – who's gam' for Blackpool? It's nobbut another nineteen miles, if that!'

The older ones were against it, pointing out that we had no lamps on our bikes, and that it would be dark on the way back, but Ernie took a vote on it. 'What about thee, Bill?' he said. Ernie, a onetime school pal, was a lad of character, and although I felt tired I was always optimistic, could not resist a challenge, and also there was that strange smell which seemed to lure me on, but which no one else appeared to have noticed.

'I'm for Blackpool,' I said. 'Right,' called Ernie, 'all them for Blackpool follow me.'

And so the party split up once more, four or five making for home, and seven of us, the youngest bunch, setting off for Blackpool. I still was unable to catch on, and each time had to look round for a curb or some mound or other from which I could set off. Now we were all shouting and laughing, calling out to each other as we went along, for it had become a boys' party. I found I was tiring a bit, but was comforted by the thought of having some money, one-and-ninepence in the general pocket and a half-crown in my secret pocket, and somehow a bit of money always kept up my spirits. Then mile after mile we drew nearer to Blackpool, and the country gave way to built-up areas and busy roads, and I felt myself becoming depressed and unhappy, until suddenly there was a breeze and I got a deep lungful of the mysterious smell that had been almost haunting me.

'Con yu' smell it, lads,' called out Ernie Arpino, '– the sea!' And it was the sea! And after my long years of breathing in the smoky and soot-drenched air of Bolton, that stirring tang of the open sea struck some deep response in me, and I pedalled faster and with more spirit to reach the source of that powerful smell, to see it and taste it! Finally, around seven o'clock, after travelling the busy main roads, we came to the long, wide promenade of Blackpool, and the sea. I had expected to see big waves breaking on the sand and all the holiday makers standing by watching, but although people were now coming out for the evening, all washed and spruce, many from Bolton judging by the faces – I could always recognise a Bolton face – not one even gave a glance at the sea or the deserted beach. As exciting as the first smell of the salt air had been, now I was secretly wishing it were the Middle Brook, and that we were nearer home, so that I'd be sure of a bacon butty and plenty of hot tea. The ride had taken more out of me than it had the others, who were lively enough, arguing about where to get something to eat. And although I tried to put on a bold face to the world, in my heart I was still a mamma's boy. Although my mates and I fitted comfortably in our own surroundings at the Big Corner, it was clear from the looks we got as we leant our bikes on the rail, that we were out of place in Blackpool.

I felt that the first thing I must do was to go to the edge of the sea, and it was a strange and lonely feeling to find myself alone on the vast stretch of deserted sand. I walked stiffly toward the bobbing waves, and when I got to the edge I stood there, and let the water lap over my boots. The evening sun had sunk behind a mass of cloud, and being weary I sat down on the cold sand. I sat there feeling rather chilly, until I heard my mates calling me, asking what the hell was I doing. I got to my feet with some effort, and I tried to put on my hypocritical smile, and as I got near forced myself to straighten up as I hobbled along. Not one of them seemed to have even looked at the sea, but more important had found a fish-and-chip shop, I was told, but that there was a shortage of money. Pierce Naylor said he hadn't a penny, his brother Jimmy said he had a tanner, another said he had twopence, and some sort of pooling of resources and sharing out of funds was being mooted. Now I have my one-and-ninepence, I thought, and the secret half-crown, but there's the rest of the holiday week to be got through, so I think I'd best keep mum about that half-crown. I took out all my money, except the big coin, and offered it to Ernie Arpino who was the treasurer; it was a good enough sum, which would buy six rounds of fish-and-chips in Bolton.

'I've a tanner-meg,' said Joe Fish, bringing out the sixpence and a ha'penny from his pocket, and I saw Ernie give him a dubious look. Various other amounts were handed over, but mine was the most toward the kitty, which eased my conscience over keeping quiet about the half-crown. Then three went off to get what they could, and when they returned there were groans of disappointment when it was seen that all they had got were a few paperfuls of pale and greasy chips, not to be compared with those of Bibby's, and a large bottle of lemonade. They were all complaining loudly: 'What a bloody swindle – they sell nowt less than threepenn'orths of chips, an' little bloody dollops of fish at a tanner a time!' The chips were eaten, and the lemonade drunk as we stood there on the front, with people staring at us as they went by. 'Come on, lads,' called Ernie, '– they haven't given us a good welcome here – who's for gettin' back home?' 'We've only been here ten bloomin' minutes,' said Joe Fish. 'Ten minutes too flamin' long,' said Jimmy Naylor. 'What will tha do if tha stays on?' said Ernie, '– go dancin' or summat in the flamin' Tower?' So that made it final, and each one got on his bike, complaining loudly of Blackpool being a fraud, and declaring that there was no place on earth like Bolton. I was behind for I still couldn't catch on, and with the motor traffic pressing up to us it was clear that our happy outing had turned sour.

I had no sense of direction, could never remember strange roads, and I clung to our little group, led by Ernie Arpino. At one spot I attempted to put on a spurt, but felt the pedals swing round, and I had to dismount to put the chain on. By the time I had got it on, the traffic had separated us, and I realised I had lost them. The sensation of being alone so far from home was not a happy one, and not only did I miss their company, but without a group it seemed that the pedals became harder to turn. On I went alone for a few miles, and the traffic eased as I reached the countryside, with fields and hedges. I found this pleasanter, but a new threat came in the form of darkness, and there were calls to me of 'Lights!' and 'Where's your lamp?' I'll just have to go on like this until I get home, I thought, and a good job I didn't give 'em my secret half-crown, it struck me, for they've sloped off and left me. The darkness itself I found soothing, except for the flashing of occasional motor lights in my eyes.

It must have been around ten o'clock when passing a country spot beside a farm, at which men were chatting leaning against a gate, I was prompted to stop, get off my bike and walk back: 'Excuse me,' I said to them, 'but have a few lads passed buy here on bikes?' 'Aye,' said one, 'about five or ten minutes back.' I was about to hurry off when another called out, 'I've a feelin' they might have farmed just here for the night. Why dussent ta go an' see?' This was exciting news, and wheeling my bike I turned down to the farm entrance in a side lane. At that moment I saw a man closing the door of a barn, and I hurried across to him, 'Excuse me, sir,' I said, 'but have some lads farmed here for the night?' I thought I'd use the same word as the man, and at once there was a burst of voices and laughter from inside the barn: 'Is that thee, Bill?' 'Let him in, mister, please!'

I had never been happier to hear the voices of my mates, and I felt a great flush of relief. 'Tha's no matches on thee?' said the farmer. 'No, sir, I haven't,' I said, for I never smoked. 'Aw reet,' he said, 'I'll lock you all in for the night, an' come an' open the door at six o'clock tomorrow mornin' an' let you all out.' He opened the barn door and in I went to the greetings of my mates, and we all called our thanks and goodnights to the farmer, and they began to make fun of me: 'Have some lads *farmed* here!' they kept calling out. It was totally dark inside, with bales of hay around the place, and lots of loose straw, and I was glad to rest and relax. The calling out and laughter went on for a long time, but finally they all quietened down. I pulled some straw over myself, and thanked God that he had so clearly directed me to all my mates, who now seemed most dear to me. I thought of home and Mother, and how she would be worrying about me and wondering where I was, until at last I fell fitfully to sleep.

CHAPTER 32

A Sorry Coming Home

We were all awakened early by Joe Fish, who was the first to wake up, and who started talking and waking up everyone else at once. It must have been around four o'clock – no boy had a watch of course – now it felt cold, with the dawn light coming in through the door cracks. The others began to test their bikes for the journey home, at the same time calling out to each other what they would like to eat for breakfast if they got the chance. I felt down in the corner of my pocket to make sure I still had the half-crown, and I found the solid feel of the large silver coin most comforting. We were a long time messing about, waiting for the farmer to come and let us out, when Ernie Arpino tried the door and found it open: 'It musta been open all bloody night!' he exclaimed. They all hurried off to the gate, flung it open, got on their bikes and went off down the road. I tidied the barn a bit, closed the door, wheeled my bike through the open gate, then closed it carefully. I liked to feel that I should always leave a place knowing I could call there again. I found a wide stone on which I could stand, so as to mount my bike, and then set off after my mates along the silent and deserted road in the early morning.

I caught them up, and the morning turned out sunny, and I found I was no longer hungry. We had a lot of fun calling out and overtaking each other, and yelling to cyclists going in the opposite direction: 'Goin' to Blackpool? – you'll bloody rue it!' It was mid-morning when Ernie Arpino spotted a secluded cottage, and decided we should approach it and ask for a drink of water. A simple countrywoman came to the door, and Ernie asked her, and went on to say, 'We're from Bolton, Missis, an' yesterday we set out for Blackpool. But they didn't welcome us there, an' we've slept all night in a barn, and had nowt to eat or sup.'

'Sit down there on them seats,' said the woman, 'an' I'll see what I can do.' She went inside, and a few minutes later came out with two large steaming jugs and a big plate of currant cake slices. 'Try this lemon tea, lads,' she said, 'made with our honey, and a bit of my currant cake to go with it.' I was very fond of making a lemon drink at home, and nothing could have suited me better, for the hot sweet liquid seemed to clear my throat and chest, and the currant cake to revive me. We all thanked her warmly, 'If ever we can do as much for you, Missis,' said Ernie, 'we will. God bless, an' thanks very much.' And off we went on our way, feeling in good spirits.

We got off the fairly busy main road after Preston, and kept to the moorland road we had come by. Because of the faulty chain on my bike I found myself some distance behind my mates for most of the time and I was pedalling hard up a rise, trying to catch up with them, when I heard a snapping sound, the pedals swing round, and the bike stopped. I looked down to see that the chain had actually broken and I got off the bike and picked it up. There was nothing for it but to wind the broken chain around the crossbar, and walk the remaining fifteen or so miles. I trudged along, mile after mile, pushing the bike, and although at times I risked riding down any sloping stretches, I had poor control of the machine. I thought of Charlie Scarlett and his Rudge Whitworth, a bike I could sail home on happily in an hour. Then I came to a nice patch of quiet moorland near Belmont, left the bike resting beside the stone wall, got over it and lay face downwards on the turfy surface, and let myself have a weep. I felt a sudden relief, and turning over I looked up at the sky, and even began to do some of my favourite exercises, legs up in the air, trunk and abdomen strengthening, to ease my stiffness, got up and did some deep breathing, and resolving to have more courage, and set off wheeling the bike once more.

Going down Belmont Hill, past Wilkinson's Sanatorium, I was feeling very thirsty, and promised myself that at the first temperance bar I came to in Blackburn Road I'd break into my half-crown, and have a nice glass of Vimto. When I was near Waterloo Street, with a good couple of mile to go before I should reach home, I put the old bike up against a lamppost, and began feeling down in my pocket for the coin that I had clung to all along. But even as my fingers began to thrust down into the pocket, I felt a foreboding, and a sudden sinking of the heart as my hands went right down into my pocket, searched and scratched around, but found nothing at all. Then I remembered exercising – that was when it must have happened. It was too far back to go and look for it now, not that I felt I was up to pushing the bike all that way – nor could I be sure of the exact spot. I went back to the kerb, got hold of the bike and set off once more. To think that only this time last week I had all that money in my drawer, money in my pocket, everything going right for me, and now here I was, broke, fagged out, wheeling a useless old bike! And yet I couldn't escape a feeling that it was all my own fault – I had put my trust in money, and it had let me down.

At last I found myself wheeling the bike up Cannon Street, and drawing nearer to home. It was around seven o'clock, and knowing there would be a crowd at the Big Corner, with lots of talk about the ride to Blackpool, I had misgivings as to how I would face up to their fun and leg-pulling, as good-natured as it might be. My nerve failed me when I was still within fifty yards of the Corner but out of sight of it, as I heard the sound of their voices. On impulse I turned into a narrow and deserted stretch called Delph Street, along which there were no actual houses, only the gable-ends, opposite the wall of Emmanuel Infants' School. This would lead me home in a roundabout way, and I felt myself to be safely out of the way when round a corner came Joe Fish, the last lad I wanted to see.

'Bloody 'ell!' he said, '– don't say tha'rt only just comin' whum'!' 'Aye, I am,' I said, facing up to him, 'what about it?' 'What arta comin' this way for?' he said and from the look on his face, knowing well the reason. 'I'm takin' this bloody bike,' I said, 'as tha reckoned were a good bargain, back to Sammy Hart. That's why I'm comin' this way!' Joe's manner changed at my aggressive front: 'Hasta heard about Charlie Scarlett?' he said, just as I was about to make off. I stopped, 'What about Charlie?' I said. 'Hasta not heard,' he said, 'he's gone dead.' The news gave me a shock, for Charlie had been occupying my thoughts – somehow I couldn't believe it. 'He's what?' I said. 'He's *dead*,' said Joe. 'Hasta gone deaf! He got wet through on his bike,' he went on, 'an' they say it were gallopin' consumption or summat on top of that. Anyway, he's dead an' that's the main thing.'

Aye, that's the main thing, I thought, feeling a sense of shame of how I had been envying him and his bike. Happen old Charlie had been too lucky – that was always risky. I must try to remember that, I said to myself, as I stopped at our back-gate, put my finger through the small hole, lifted up the latch, and pulled the bike in after me. My mother was just coming out of the backdoor, the teapot in her hand, about to empty the leaves down the drain, and she looked up with surprise: 'Urra God in heaven save us,' she called out, her face lighting up in a smile, '– is it my lost son home at last from his travels!' Somehow I got the feeling that she hadn't missed me at all.

CHAPTER 33

Mornings at Seven

It was early morning, and I was in my stockinged feet in the back kitchen, trying to adjust my old braces to the new trousers I was wearing. They were my first long pair, but I was not pleased about the change, for compared to the cosy feel of my knickerbockers they felt clumsy and uncomfortable. After running my thumbs along the inside of the braces, to smooth them out on my shoulders – I was a fussy dresser – I took the pair of bib overalls from the back of the chair, and pulled them on over the trousers. The material was stiff and shiny, not like well-washed overalls, and when I got them on I found they were too long, and that they made me feel stifled in some way. It took me some time to get them fastened, as the slit in the metal holder seemed too narrow to get the strips of cloth through. When I had that done I stooped down to put on my new clogs, and felt my face flush from the effort, for I was wearing a collar-and-tie, and trying to suppress a nervous feeling. Our May had explained that in the weaving shed – where I was about to start my first day of work – things were different from the spinning room, where any old muffler would do, since you had to take it off in any case. Now I stood, nervous and dry-tongued, got a peek at myself in the mirror, and it struck me that I looked a real humbug, the first of my breed to have put on the industrial overalls of the skilled man. Mother came into the back kitchen, 'Well, sure don't you look a great man altogether!' she said, and as if sensing my thoughts she slipped a shilling into my hand 'There,' she said, 'for the new trousers!' – the Irish way of treating a youngster who was wearing something new. 'Don't bother, Mam,' I said, feeling that she could hardly have lifted my spirits if she'd have handed me a fistful of Bradburys, but I kept it all the same.

'Will I fry you a nice eggeen, agraw,' she said, 'with the bacon?' 'No, thanks,' I said, '– all I want is a dip' butty, an' some tea, please, Mam.' May came in, 'You'll have to hurry up, our Bill,' she said, but for once she spoke gently to me, 'so's we leave by the half-past seven buzzer – you don't want to be late on your first day.' 'Mam,' I said, 'just give me a nice hot cup of sweet tea, an' mi butty, an' I'll eat whilst I'm movin' around.' I was like my father, who when going to the pit to draw his wages on a Friday was always edgy and would eat his boiled duck egg or two standing up. Then I went into the front kitchen, and my father, who was washed and calm after his night shift, looked up from the *Daily Herald*, and he looked up at me, and said in a quiet voice, 'Well Willyeen, is it off to work you are!' 'Yes, Dad,' May said, 'I've got your mornin' lunch with me – an' a mug for your tea. I'll see you get them when the tea woman comes round.' 'Take care will you now among all them machines,' called my father and Mother came to kiss me farewell, and there were a few Godspeeds, making me feel as though I was going off on a long journey somewhere. Yet despite Mother's humming and cheery manner, as I kissed her I saw a tear in the corner of her eye.

I disliked wearing anything new which might draw attention to me, and clomping along beside May I felt myself to be a walking caricature of what I was – a boy going to his first day in the weaving shed. On our few minutes' walk through the narrow streets and backstreets May began to explain to me who was who and what was what at Kershaw's, so that I shouldn't make too many bloomers; she said that Mr Atkinson, the under-manager, known as Owd Jack, wasn't as bad as was made out once you got used to him, but that he couldn't stand latecomers.

In the week following the June holidays I had gone around supposedly looking for work, but my heart wasn't in it; I disliked asking anyone for some favour, and being shy was only too willing to accept a refusal. I had no idea of what kind of job I did want, except that I had a longing that it be in the open air and not under a roof. I had been eager when I applied for one advertised in the newspaper, that of an apprentice bricklayer, and it seemed the interview went well, until the man explained that there would be the usual ten pounds to be put down by my parents as a binding sum. Such an amount of money, I knew, could not of course be found, about three weeks' of my father's wages, and I avoided telling my mother the reason, not wishing to upset her.

A neighbour, Mr Cheadle, who it was said was a slave to his crippled wife, who ordered him about like a skivvy, came into our house and said that he would speak for me at the loco works, and that if I got taken on there as a grease boy I could work my way up to being an engine-driver. Strange that I was not drawn to the supposed ambition of most boys, for the very idea of being all day in the driver's cabin of a steam locomotive, part of all that noise and movement, with whistles blowing and signals to be watched made no appeal at all to me. The boss in charge may have sensed something of the sort, for before I had got the words out, 'Do you want any lads, sir?' he broke in with 'There's nowt doin'.'

My one longing was to get into the Royal Navy – oh how I envied the young sailors home on leave, looking so fresh and happy in their natty tunics, the girls dashing after them to touch their big collars, said to bring luck. I had got all the information – that boys were taken on between the ages of fifteen-and-a-quarter and sixteen-and-three-quarters; when the second week of unemployment began, and I was feeling ashamed of being seen at the Big Corner, a so-called clever lad who couldn't get himself a job, I made another call at 57 Moncrieffe Street, a tiny recruiting office near the station. The recruiting officer was greyhaired, and wearing his double-breasted blue coat. He seemed to smell of the sea. I asked him was there any chance of getting in the navy at fourteen, and he said he was sorry there wasn't, but went on to say that I should come to see him the very day I turned that age, in fourteen months time, and he would recommend me; meanwhile, if I had a few minutes to spare would I look after the office, as he had an urgent call to make elsewhere, but wasn't allowed to close it. I willingly agreed, and he went off, was away about a half an hour, and returned smelling less of the sea and more of beer.

On the Thursday of the second week, when things were getting desperate, and our May said that if I fancied it she would ask Mr Atkinson, was there any chance of my being taken on at Kershaws, I felt I couldn't refuse. It was arranged I call next morning at ten o'clock to see him at his office, which was the watch-house, set beside the main entrance gate, with a window through which he kept an eye on things. I went there, and met a short, beefy, unsmiling sort of man around the age of sixty – I was to learn that this surly front was part of the job of a boss. He was wearing a working cap, but his under-manager's billycock could be seen hanging on a hook, his brownish suit was on the greasy side, a collar-and-tie, heavy watch-chain curved across the front of his waistcoat, to which was attached a large watch, which he kept pulling out of his pocket, even though there was a clock on the wall. Although he had seen me standing outside, I had to wait a few minutes in silence before he even turned to beckon me in, and when I put on my bright and eager look for him, and told him who I was and why I was there, he responded with a grunt of sorts, that as much as said, Oh aye, well I've seen thy sort before today! I decided he was not a chap to be taken in by a smile, my first hint of smiles not counting for much in the land of hard work. Then he went out of the office without a further word to me, and I stood there waiting; ten minutes later he came back and said in a surly voice: 'Aw reet, tha can start next Monday mornin'. Tha can do a spell of weavin' under Jimmy Bamber, till I can see where to put thee!' And off he went leaving my thanks in the air.

In Derby Street a girl came hurrying across to us, 'May!' she called out, 'Ee, Milly!' exclaimed our May, and she suddenly appeared to come to life, looking excited and happy. 'This is our Bill,' she said, '– it'll be his first day.' 'Ee,' sighed Milly, putting a warm sympathy into it, 'is it really!' 'This is Milly Atkinson,' said May to me, 'you've heard me talk about!' 'Oh hello!' I said. Somehow it didn't seem right to call her 'Milly' at once or to shake hands at that hour of the morning. She was a bonny girl, on the plump side, with a fresh complexion, and a gentle expression. Her appearance, tone of voice, and easy manner marked her at once as coming from a district more posh than our own. When May and Milly began to chat I felt myself to be dumb beside them, so fast did the words bubble out, two minds so keen so early in the day, made me realise how much brighter girls were than boys.

When we came to the wide open gate at Kershaw's May told me I should go and stand beside the watchhouse until Mr Atkinson spoke to me – not speak first. 'It'll feel funny at first, love,' said Milly, but you'll get used to it.' I kept waving to her as they went off, for I had spotted Owd Fred watching us from inside his office, and I felt every bit of influence I could muster was needed. I stood outside his office, alert for any beckon from him, which allowed me to watch without appearing to do so. He was posted at the window of the watch-house, eyeing every worker that came through the gate. Most of the men, overlookers, mechanics and greasers went in ahead of time, and it seemed to me that Owd Fred took mark of each one, but the mass of workers were women, and although there was ten minutes to go before quarter-to-eight, which I could see from the clock, he seemed to be on edge, and kept taking out his big watch to make sure of the time, and then he would give a glance at the clock. I couldn't understand why he seemed to be getting more worked up, since there was so much time to spare before the buzzer would blow, but at twenty minutes to eight he strode out to the gate, unfastened the bolt that kept it open, stood for a few moments, took another look at his watch as a few weavers hurried in, then with the clock fingers a good three minutes to go before a quarter-to, he shut the gate on one woman who was hurrying to get in, but still had a few yards to go. I was not then aware of the rule being that every weaver must be in her own alley the moment the buzzer blew, standing beside her looms, ready to start work.

Owd Fred went back into the watch-house, perched himself on a stool, this time facing the narrow passage through which each latecomer had to enter. The weaver who had had the gates shut on her went past with her head in the air, but this defiant gesture made no impression on him. For the next two or three minutes I watched from outside as he put on a series of frowns, each one darker than the last, aimed at the odd half-dozen weavers that hurried through. If one of them attempted an apologetic smile he scowled in return, and when any women tried to escape his black look by turning her head away, he let out a low growl, like that of a bull terrier, as much as to say, I've spotted you! Next I heard the muffled sound of the mill engine starting up somewhere inside the factory, slowly increasing to full speed for starting time, then at a quarter-to-eight the mill buzzer blew, joined by numerous others. At that signal Owd Fred got off his perch, slipped out of the office and stood square in the path of any further latecomers. One distressed woman came hurrying in, pulling her shawl round her, 'Ee, I'm so sorry, Mister Atkinson –' she began, but he cut her short, 'It's no use bein' sorry,' he said, looking at his watch, 'see as you get here on time in future, or else –!'

I was startled as he suddenly turned to me, 'Hy, thee! – don't thee stand there doin' nowt – t'buzzer's gone! – get thee down to t'Jacquard shed,' he snorted out, 'an tell Jimmy Bamber I sent thee. Tell him I said to find thee a weaver to work wi' fort' time bein' till I see if tha'rt any use or not.' As I made across the yard toward a door on the left of the firehole, through which I had seen weavers going in, I had put on the style of a confident young fellow, but when I got to the door, oily, battered and without a handle, I pushed and shoved but found it wouldn't open for me; then I used two hands and it gave way, but not for long enough to allow me to get through, shutting again violently. I'll look a right fool, I thought, if he's still watching me, and I haven't even the gumption to know how to open a door.

Then a tall man of about forty, wearing blue overalls, the sleeves neatly cut off to the elbow, spotlessly clean and ironed, came along. Apart from his earnest look, I knew at once that he was a decent sort by the way he wore his cap – neither tilted to right nor left, nor on the back of the head or pulled down at the front, but set perfectly straight on him, as though done with care. 'Havin' a little trouble?' he said, in an oddly soft-spoken voice, then half-turned, nimbly pressed his behind against the door and opened it wide enough for both of us to get through. 'Oh ta very much,' I said. 'Could you please tell me how I get to the Jacquard shed – to Mr Bamber?' 'You're a new starter, are you?' he said, and I nodded. 'Well, go through that door you see there,' he pointed to heavy double doors, which had tin strips on each side where they met, 'an' straight along to Jimmy's bench in the corner.' He added, 'You might find it a bit noisy for a start.' And with a smile he went off.

The Weaving Shed

I got myself ready for the encounter with the next door, again a solid one with a rope round a wheel and a heavy weight attached – to ensure it automatically shut itself; I got through without mishap, and found myself in the weaving shed. I gazed in amazement, for I had never seen anything like it – a vast, low-ceilinged place, with countless looms in rows between narrow alleys, every loom vibrating with feverish speed, frames crashing backwards and forwards, picking sticks swinging at each side, masses of pulleys and belts, with women moving eerily about as they tended the looms in the nightmarish light from the glass roof that had been whitewashed, the odd streaks of sunshine showing up the dust in the air.

The real shock, however, was the deafening din, so loud and concentrated that it seemed to be a violent assault on my senses, paralysing my hearing. Had I been suddenly dropped among dancing dervishes, howling and whirling, or found myself in a war dance with tom-toms beating away, it could not have had a more shattering effect. At least they would have been human beings, related in some remote way, but these were all machines, all rattling away with a relentless ear-splitting monotony that kept the flagged floor under me vibrating, and dotted around were women waiting to serve them. I lost all power to think, and stood there in a state of shock.

The next thing I felt something strike me in the back, and startled I turned to see a pimply lad shoving an enormous cane skip on wheels, loaded up with bundles of cloth. He called something out to me, but I could not hear a thing, and he came close up, put a hand to the side of his mouth and yelled into my ear: 'Arta comin' or gooin'!' I tried to speak to him, but it seemed no words came out, for everything I did, even breathing and talking needed effort. 'Mak' up thi bloody mind!' he shouted. I let myself go, and yelled loudly in his ear, 'I'm lookin' for Mester Bamber'. He pointed to the far corner, where I could make out a man stooped over a work bench. 'That's Owd Jimmy,' he said. I made towards him, a short man with a big moustache, and got up beside him, but didn't know how to get his attention. He looked up suddenly, 'What does tha want?' he yelled at me. I was about to answer him when a weaver came up next to me, and I heard her call out, 'Mister Bamber please – mi loom keeps bangin' off.' For some reason this seemed to annoy him, and putting a hand beside his mouth he shouted, 'Then go an' bang t'bloody thing on again!' And with that he stooped over his bench once more, above which hung rows of spanners, pliers and other tools, and began hammering at a piece of belting.

After a time he looked up at me. 'Mr Atkinson sent me,' I shouted. He said something I couldn't hear, but I thought it was, 'He bloody would –' and I went on, 'He said would you please find me a weaver I can work with.' He looked me up and down, muttered something I couldn't make out, and beckoned for me to follow him. He walked swiftly, leading the way between a narrow alley, through rows of looms jerking to and fro on either side, with lines of picking sticks held by leather straps lashing out violently. I would never have dared to venture there were it not that I had no choice but to follow him, pretending I wasn't scared, and I got more than one rap on the elbow from some stick or other. He took me to a corner of the weaving shed where there was a short alley close to the wall, with a woman tending her looms, and he spoke to her without seemingly raising his voice, as she watched his lips. She nodded her head, smiled at me, and he turned and yelled, 'See tha does what Amy tells thee!', and off he went.

Amy gave me a smile of welcome. She was a woman in her late twenties, with a pale face, cherry nose, and sandy hair tied in a bun at the back. A single woman, I was to learn, not even courting – 'I've never been kissed, kicked or run over,' as she put it. She came and took me by the arm and put me beside one of her four looms that was standing idle, waiting for a new beam: 'Just calm yourself down for a bit, love,' she called into my ear, 'until you get used to it all. I expect it seems like a madhouse to you for a start.' It struck me that she could not have been more right.

As I watched her it became clear that she was an exceptionally good weaver, the job appearing to be second nature to her, as the saying went, the way she turned from one loom to another, stroking the newlywoven cloth with her hands as it slowly crept along over the breastplate, much like a mother caressing her child's head, and displaying such a skill when changing shuttles, swiftly and effortlessly, that left me mystified how human hands could be so sure and efficient. She later slowed her action down, to demonstrate to me how to put a cop in a shuttle, pull the spindle out, press the tubular inside down upon it, close the shuttle, then 'kiss' it, when the wisp of weft shot to her lips. I attempted it, but no matter how red-faced I got from kissing, or even sucking-in at the shuttle, it just would not come out for me, yet she had only to put it toward her mouth, and out it popped. At times she would take the shuttle from me and put her arm round me and take hold of my hand to help me grasp the sley – the horizontal wood frame with its wire reeds, which swung backwards and forwards with a driving force, beating each pick of weft into a woven fabric. Weavers were continually doing this throughout the day, when the looms were running and their shuttles were full, but I found myself quite unable to catch it as it was moving. It was a most pleasurable sensation when Amy took hold of my hand and guided it, so that our two hands were swinging in unison on the sley.

There was no clock to be seen, and after a long time had gone by I felt it must be getting toward dinnertime, when I saw there was some side activity going on, and the next thing our May came up to Amy's alley, holding out a sandwich parcel. 'Missis Stewart the tea woman is just comin' round,' she said, 'so here's your mug an' sandwich.' 'May, what time is it?' I asked above the din. 'Just turned nine o'clock,' she said. I could have dropped with disappointment. I seemed to have spent longer in the mill than would occupy a full day at school, and yet it was only nine o'clock! How would I get through a full day until half-past five!

Then she put her lips to my ear, 'Get Amy's mug,' she called into it, 'an' your own, an' come with me, an' we'll get the tea.' Mrs Stewart had a trolley on which were two big urns of tea, and weavers kept one another's looms running whilst one of them went for the tea. That was the strange thing to me, the urgency that attended the job, so that no matter what happened, the tea break or anything, the looms had to be kept running throughout. It was my first experience of the industrial tempo of a weaving shed, where it seemed that amidst all din and vibration, the workers were every one in the grip of some power, compelling them at all cost to answer the demands of the machine. Since I did not feel the urge myself, and was untouched by it, I had an impression of being an idler among a mass of women galvanised by some force of which I was unaware. Yet even so, there were a number of weavers who must have been so dexterous that they could keep their four looms running, yet in between, with hand signs and lip reading, enjoy moments of talking to each other.

It was odd to follow our May along the narrow alley of picking sticks, as she walked swiftly, heedless of them, for I had never imagined she had such a side to her nature. 'D'you think you'll manage to get back to Amy?' she shouted in my ear, 'with the two mugs?' I smiled at her, at the new our May I was slowly seeing, ''Course I will!' I said. But it was trickier than I thought, and after a knock or two there was nothing for it but go the last few yards sideways, as I clutched to the mugs of spilling tea. The tea tasted awful, but somehow that and the bacon butty May had brought seemed to revive me a bit – but I felt I should never in this life get used to the din.

What was to strike me as the minutes crept by was the gulf between school and work, so unrelated that it seemed my nine years of school life had unfitted me for the mill – no wonder the working lads never even mentioned school. I had imagined that everything was accomplished by the mind, and it was a bit of a shock to discover that what mattered in the mill were hands – and hands alone. The more one concentrated, it seemed, the worse one became at the job. Amy pulled me to her, and called into my ear – it was quite nice and ticklish I found to have a woman's lips up beside my face: 'Why don't you go an' stretch your legs a bit, love? If Jimmy or anybody wants to know what you're about tell 'um you're goin' to the whatsit.' I was a bit shy about going, but she called again in my ear, 'The Men's are on t'other side of the firehole,' and with that she gave me a friendly push off. I made my way to May's alley, and seeing her changing a shuttle, her hand dropping lightly on the sley, it was clear that our May was almost as good a weaver as the next. She asked me how was I going on, and I told her that everything was fine, but from the look on her face I sensed she knew just how I felt, for it was only some eighteen months before that she had come to Kershaw's as a learner. Then off I went, smile after smile from the weavers seemed to help me along.

Once the door of the weaving shed had closed behind me the sense of relief was immediate, as though a weight had been lifted from me, and I found myself straightening up and beginning to get a feel of being myself once more. As I was making my way round past the firehole I saw a big broad-built man come walking across the yard, a bit bow-legged, but this seemed to add to the powerful and handsome look, as he gave me a cheery wink – I was to learn it was Jimmy Lloyd, the chief mechanic – and who should come up behind him, carrying the toolbag, and trying to put on a swagger of his own, was none other than Joe Fish. 'Howgo Joe!' I began, all smiles, but all I got from Joe was a curt nod. To think he's only worked here a week, I thought, and he walks around as though it were years. Lucky beggar, his father, a tackler, had got him a job in the mechanics' shop, and now he's putting on that style! I felt myself to be a complete outsider compared even with Joe Fish!

I decided I'd go to the men's lavatory anyway, even if I only stood there pretending to have a pee. There was a line of four W.C.s, all with the doors wide open, yet three of them were occupied, with a loud conversation going on among the men. I hadn't, of course, even thought of glancing in, but as I stood up facing the stall, I heard what was the unmistakable voice of Fred Halliwell, declaring that they could say what they liked about Kruschen Salts – a wellknown laxative advertisement, depicting a man springing over a five-barred gate – or any other salts, but for keeping a chap's bowels open you couldn't beat prunes. Another voice called out, 'He only jumps o'er that gate because he hasn't time to oppen it!' That men of their standing, overlookers, would sit at stool with the door wide open, and chat freely away quite astonished me – and I was not without a touch of envy at their freedom.

Then as I made my way back I stopped by the engine house, where a man stood with a wiper in his hand, the engine-tenter. 'You're a new lad, are you?' he said. 'Yes, sir,' I said – the usual word 'mister' did not come easily to my tongue. I looked in at the engine, and he said, 'Like to see it?' I said I would, and he invited me inside. The place was spotless, with a sweet smell of oil, and to my surprise it was oddly quiet apart from a regular walloping rhythm of the engine with four enormous rope-like belts that sped round a large revolving wheel. I gazed at it in wonder, for I couldn't grasp what it might have to do with the hundreds of looms jerking to and fro, and I ventured to ask, 'How does it all work?' He seemed very proud of his engine, and began to explain: 'Everythin' within there,' he said, pointing to the weaving sheds, 'is driven from here. Not a thing moves in there but gets its drive from my engine, it drives all the shafts in the place.' It baffled me to try and imagine how the multitude of shafts, pulleys and belts that drove the looms could come from this one source.

I had given up hope of the morning ever ending, so slowly did time pass, with nothing to engage my active mind, my fingers frustrated by the demands of every little task to do with cops and shuttles, and I had resigned myself to being there for all eternity, when unexpectedly there came what seemed to be a faltering of the incessant pulley belts above, and at that Amy went to each loom, got hold of the upright iron handle that switched the looms off from drive to free. Then loom after loom around the shed began to go still as big pulleys turned more slowly, and suddenly a strange silence descended on the vast weaving shed.

It was dinnertime at last – oh what a relief to feel a silence! I'm not sure I can stand an afternoon of this lot, I thought – I wish there was some way I could do a bunk. At the same time I put on my false smile, said 'ta ra' to Amy, and knowing our May always enjoyed a dinnertime chat with one of her pals, I went to her alley. 'May, I'll not wait for you,' I said, 'I feel like stretchin' my legs an' getting some fresh air.' She looked closely at me, 'Have you got those funny twirly things jumpin' up an' down around your eyes?' she said. (The word 'migraine' was at the time unknown to us, as also, alas, was aspirin.) 'It'll be all right,' I said. I never cared to admit there was anything wrong with me, and couldn't bear to talk about it, talking seemed to make things worse. She looked at me so concerned and tenderly, 'Don't worry, love,' she said, 'it happened to me like that – it'll go off! God bless –' she called as I went off. Sympathy always brought tears to my eyes, for I was a right softie. I felt that somewhere in the world, miles away from where I was known in Bolton, there must be some kind and understanding person in need of a lad like myself, perhaps with some job for me on a farm, or who needed someone who was good at figures, or a lonely couple who would adopt me. I felt that if only I had a few bob and a good bike in place of the broken-down old boneshaker, I'd be off and the inside of Kershaw's would never see me again.

I dodged anyone I knew until I came to our own streetcorner, and then summoned that jaunty front that was part of my character. I had a feeling that some people could see through it, but as I never admitted it they could think what they liked. Mother was different, of course, for it seemed that she could see through my various guises, but possibly because she was inclined herself never to show the poor mouth, I knew I could rely on her not to pierce them, in a way that might cause me to give way to my feelings. It turned out that way, I glimpsed the look she gave me as I went in home, but nothing was said, the situation saved. What she couldn't quite understand was why I couldn't eat anything for my dinner but a big bowl of broke-down, made with strong, sweet tea.

CHAPTER 34

The Silent World

I felt a bit better after my dinnertime sluice under the cold-water tap, which eased the migraine, and I went back to work in better heart. The afternoon did not seem quite as long as the morning, for time passed more quickly as I tackled the intricacies of weaving with more determination, feeling a bit ashamed that I hadn't done so earlier. I even managed to get a few cops into the shuttles in fairly good order, and literally under Amy's guidance, her gentle hand on top of mine, I learned how to start and stop a loom. The change partly came about, I must tell, from a chance encounter with Jimmy Bamber. Apart from the loom-fettler, Billy Stansfield, I was the only other male around, and I felt that Owd Jimmy didn't somehow care for my presence beside Amy. Around three o'clock I had gone off for another visit to the toilets, and going back I was walking down the alley between the flailing picking-sticks, moving at my normal casual pace, when I felt myself being pushed aside, 'Put a bloody jerk in it can't you!' I heard Owd Jimmy shout. It proved a useful goad, for it took me out of myself, a shift that was needed. It seemed that I had the cast of mind that is more concerned with what it is thinking than what needs doing – no use in a weaving shed and not much use inside any mill or factory. I found I needed to shut my mind off and get moving.

There was no afternoon tea trolley, but what did come as a nice surprise were the pieces of cake, toffee and bars of chocolate slipped across to me from various weavers. Things began to change for the better after that, I sensed that the women rather liked the novelty of a young lad around, and Amy always put her arm around me as our bodies brushed by each other in that narrow space. And at times as I was close up beside her it seemed her face took on a humble Madonna-like glow, the pale and faintly greasy skin I saw as the complexion of some tropical maiden, the flecks of cotton clinging to her hair assumed a kind of halo – Saint Amy of the weaving shed. I realised that I was in love with her, most tenderly so, and envisaged some happy future in which she and I might marry, work together and go home side by side, and have sausages and other nice things for tea, and let our bodies rub nakedly in bed at night.

Finally, when I had almost forgotten that time existed, I was surprised by the slowing-down note in that whirring of belts and pulleys, as though some unseen Power had decreed the workers had done enough for one day and must now rest. Looms began to be shut off all over the place – except for one or two weavers who were behind with their cuts, and kept going to the last pick. Then a deep silence gripped the Jacquard shed once more. But this time it was almost eerie in its density, for not a weaver spoke, not a voice could be heard, not a single clatter of a clog on the stone floor.

Then I felt Amy's hand on my shoulder, and saw her lips moving as she spoke to me, but I heard nothing. She drew me to her, put her mouth close to my ear, and I heard her say, 'Have you gone deaf, love?' So that was it – on top of everything else I'd gone stone deaf. Not that it felt too bad, it was less unpleasant than the din, but it did feel a bit funny, sort of awkward. 'Don't worry, love,' she almost cooed into my ear, 'it happens to all of us on the first day – an' sometimes goes on for a week or two. Same as everythin' else – you'll get over it.' Then she pinched me on the cheek, 'I were just thinkin', love – where's his rosy cheeks?'

Then I saw Jimmy Bamber coming up. He looked at me, and said something to Amy, and went off grinning. Somehow, being deaf meant that nothing anyone said made much difference, which in a way was a bit of a relief – for I felt partly cut off. 'Y'know what he said,' Amy now spoke in weaver fashion, so that I had to watch her lips, 'he says you'll turn out –' and here she made my lip-reading clear, '*Neither use nor ornament.*' I remembered Farmer Akky, and it struck me that Owd Jimmy had taken my measure. But then Amy went on, speaking clearly into my ear, 'But we'll show him – won't we, love! – we'll prove him wrong, for I'll make a weaver of you if it's the last thing I do!' And with that she gave me a lovely big kiss on the side of the chops, and I felt myself going red in the face.

I went out of the gate among a throng of weavers, all gabbling silently away. The strangest sensation, however, was going up Derby Street, folk clattering along in their clogs, lorries and horse-drawn traffic, everything moving in this strange soft silence. Even when two tramcars passed, and one came to what must have been a clanging stop, I heard nothing. It made it that I didn't quite know how to walk, for I felt thrown out of rhythm with the life around me. And yet the feeling of seclusion had its comfort, after all the noise I seemed to have endured that day.

Mother had specially prepared a dish of bacon and cabbage for me, and I found it hard to tell her that I couldn't eat it just then, and would she mind if I had a boiled egg instead, and some tea. 'Arra not at all,' she said, 'for maybe you'd eat a tasteen of it later.' I couldn't hear what was being said to me, but being at home I could somehow make it out. I was glad to get my heavy clogs off, and had a wash and change whilst she was getting the tea ready, and I put on my school knicker-bockers, which though comfortable now felt strange, as though bringing back a memory of the long past. May came home whilst I was eating, and said that Amy had told her I had been a right good learner. It was odd how that single day, which gave me a new understanding of May, was to affect our entire lives, for from then on there was never to be a cross word between us, but only a deep affection.

'Maybe if you was to lie there on the sofa,' Mother said after the meal, 'an' compose yourself for half an hour you'd feel better.' 'All right, Mam,' I said, 'but waken me when you call Dad for pit.' It was only when I laid myself down, and was covered with Mother's shawl, that I realised how weary my legs were after being on them a full day, and it seemed that in a moment I went off into a deep sleep.

It was a surprise to me when I woke up to learn that it was almost nine o'clock and that my father had already gone off to the pit. Although I felt in need of some fresh air I hadn't the heart to go to the Big Corner, but the evening being light I forced myself to do a few exercises with my big duckstones in the backyard to ease my muscles. I found the cotton dust had lodged up my nose, and I tried my old remedy of sniff-ing up salt water to clear it. Although I loved reading, somehow I couldn't settle down to any, but found a new pleasure in resting my limbs. It struck me that I would soon be just like any other lad who worked in the mill – they never read at all.

Mother was preparing the porridge for my father's breakfast, and waiting for our Eddie to come home before raking up the fire with coal dirt, when I kissed her goodnight and went upstairs to bed. I attempted my night exercises but somehow didn't feel up to them, but knelt by the bed to say my prayers. Although I imagined I could still hear an echo of the weaving shed in my head, and now and again was aware of the smell clinging to me, my hearing was slowly returning, the trembling of my hand had ceased, and indeed I began to feel a sense of tranquillity. I got into my place in the bed, turned to the wall, and though unable to go to sleep I felt strangely at peace. When I heard our Eddie come up to bed I pretended I was asleep as I did not feel like talking, and also felt I should not be able to hear him in the dark.

It was as though every minute of the day was stamped on my brain, so keenly that I could not help but live it all over again in mind, but without all the din and upset. I had never imagined working amidst all that noise could be so disagreeable, but if it hadn't killed others, it wouldn't kill me. Although I had done no actual work myself, I had a feeling of having participated in it being done. Not for anything, I felt, would I have changed the lad I was tonight for the half-baked schoolboy I had always been. And I wasn't having Owd Fred and Jimmy Bamber going on about how I wasn't up to the job – one day I'd show the lot of 'em! Nor was I going to let old Amy down – in fact I was rather looking forward to a bit more of our bodies brushing and pressing up against each other in that narrow alley, and she holding my hand. So having got all that nicely in order in my mind, I began to whisper a few comforting Hail Marys and went off to sleep.